More Praise

"Groundbreaking. This is the best . . . . ive porn users and the people who lov . . . . le-structive pattern."
—Barry McCarthy, Ph.D.,
  author of *Men's Sexual Health* and *Rekindling Desire*

"This intelligent book brings a healing voice to an issue that too often divides and devastates partners—it goes way beyond 'just say no,' to offer heart-opening guidance that will help you explore new dimensions of sexual desire and intimacy."
—Gina Ogden, Ph.D.,
  author of *The Heart and Soul of Sex* and *The Return of Desire*

"Larry and Wendy have done a masterful job of defining the problem of porn and giving the reader a marvelous plethora of treatment options. This is a must-read for anyone who cares about someone hurt by porn addiction. For those struggling themselves, this book is a lifesaver!"
—Dr. Ted Roberts,
  pastor, counselor, and author of *Pure Desire*

"With clarity, compassion, and understanding, Wendy and Larry Maltz help readers comprehend the magnitude of the problem and porn's highly addictive nature. Their vast knowledge of healing and regaining a healthy sexuality embedded in a true relationship, provides readers with a wise and helpful guide."
—Charlotte Sophia Kasl, Ph.D.,
  author of *Women, Sex, and Addiction* and *If the Buddha Dated*

"*The Porn Trap* offers much needed insight, direction, and hope to men and women struggling to escape the net of fantasy, sex, and addiction."
—Robert Weiss, L.C.S.W., C.S.A.T.,
  author of *Cruise Control* and *Untangling the Web*

"*The Porn Trap* is a very helpful book for those who find pornography to be destructive in their lives."
—Ralph H. Earle, Ph.D., author of *Lonely All the Time*

"*The Porn Trap* is one of the best resources available for helping people whose porn use has become problematic. Using non-shaming advice, Wendy and Larry present a clear path to re-establishing a positive sense of self, healing an intimate relationship, and reclaiming healthy sexuality. I highly recommend it."
—M. Deborah Corley, Ph.D., The Santé Center for Healing

"Smart and straightforward—without unnecessary politics, finger-pointing, or moralizing—*The Porn Trap* is sure to provide aid and comfort to many men and women."
—Pamela Paul, author of *Pornified*

"Insightful, well-written, and practical, *The Porn Trap* is the authoritative text for understanding and overcoming the negative impact pornography has on self, intimacy, and others."
—David Delmonico, Ph.D., and Elizabeth Griffin, M.A.,
   authors of *In the Shadows of the Net* and *Cybersex Unhooked*

"Porn is like junk food—it provides little in the way of real nutrition for your sexual health. If you or your partner are suffering as a result of consuming these empty calories, this important and timely book shows you how to push away from porn and start experiencing the genuine nourishment of real love."
—Ian Kerner, Ph.D., author of *Sex Detox*

"*The Porn Trap* is an important contribution to understanding porn use and recovering from porn addiction. I highly recommend this book."
—Jennifer Schneider, M.D.,
   author of *Untangling the Web* and *Back from Betrayal*

"Informative and compassionate, *The Porn Trap* shows how porn problems can sneak up and trap you in compulsive sexual behavior before you even realize what's happened. The average reader as well as the seasoned therapist will gain a clear understanding of how to address the problem that now affects millions of people."
—Barbara Levinson, Ph.D., R.N., L.M.F.T.,
   Center for Healthy Sexuality

The Porn Trap

The Essential Guide to Overcoming Problems Caused by Pornography

WENDY MALTZ, LCSW, DST, AND
LARRY MALTZ, LCSW

HARPER

NEW YORK · LONDON · TORONTO · SYDNEY

HARPER

The authors are grateful for permission to reprint portions of the following copyrighted material:

Daniel Ladinsky, "Cast All Your Votes for Dancing" in *I Heard God Laughing: Poems of Hope and Joy/Renderings of Hafiz* translated by Daniel Ladinsky (New York: Penguin Books, 2006, page 8). Copyright © 2006, 1996 by Daniel Ladinsky.

Jack Kornfield, "In the end these things matter most . . ." in *Buddha's Little Instruction Book* by Jack Kornfield (New York: Bantam Books, 1994, page 85). Copyright © 1994 by Jack Kornfield.

HarperCollins books may be purchased for educational, business, or sales promotional use. For information please e-mail the Special Markets Department at SPsales@harpercollins.com

FIRST HARPER PAPERBACK EDITION PUBLISHED 2010.

Designed by Kate Nichols

ISBN 978-0-06-123187-2 (pbk.)

The Library of Congress has catalogued the hardcover edition as follows:

Maltz, Wendy.
The Porn trap : the essential guide to overcoming problems caused by pornography / Wendy Maltz and Larry Maltz.—1st ed.
p.   cm.
ISBN 978-0-06-123186-5
1. Pornography.   2. Sex addiction.   3. Sex addicts—Rehabilitation.
I. Maltz, Larry. II. Title.
HQ471.M335 2008
306.77—dc22

2007038376

14 15 16 17   OV/RRD   20 19 18 17 16 15 14 13

Dedicated to the men and women

who generously shared their stories and

paved the way for others to heal

Contents

Acknowledgments

Behind every book stands a community of people who helped to give it life. We are deeply grateful to the many talented and enthusiastic individuals who joined with us to make this book a reality. Although we can't possibly mention every one of you here by name, we do wish to convey our appreciation and let you know we are truly grateful for your involvement and contribution.

In particular, we wish to acknowledge colleagues: Elizabeth Griffin, Patrick Carnes, Barbara Levinson, Peter Shannon, Pastor Jim Thomas, Diana Clark, Ron Feintech, Jack Johnston, Marnie Ferree, Scot Oja, Michael Castleman, Joe Kort, Jennifer Schneider, Rob Weiss, Steve DeLugach, David Delmonico, Rick Tangeman, Jim Henson, Deborah Corley, David Marcus, Alex Katehakis, Mark Miller, John Miller, David Greenfield, Beverly Whipple, Reverend Debra Haffner, Mike McGee, Rory Reid, Mark Laaser, Mitch Tepper, Annette Owens, Dana Regan, Mary Gossard, Pastor Shannon Kearney, Kay Porter, Ellen Bass, Benoit Denizet-Lewis, Ginger Manley, Karla Baur, Christen McLean, and the late Al Cooper, for your inspiring work, guidance, and active support during different stages of this project. And a special thank you to Steve Hebner, a Eugene polygraph examiner, who gave us a firsthand education in therapeutic lie-detector testing.

We would also like to thank the people involved in the writing and production of this work. Foremost is Leigh Anne Jasheway-Bryant who served as our editorial consultant and writer's helper throughout the active writing phase of the book. Her wisdom, creativity, writing skills, and abundant humor got us through numerous tough spots and ensured a reader-friendly product. We are also deeply grateful to Felicia Eth, our agent and friend, whom we admire for her exceptional competence and steadfast belief in making available resources that address vital psychosocial issues. Similarly, we appreciate Anne Cole, our dedicated editor, and others at the Collins Division of HarperCollins Publishers, including Mary Ellen O'Neill and Joe Tessitore, for immediately recognizing the strong need for this book and skillfully guiding us through the process of getting it published.

In addition we are grateful for the technical help we received from Kim Barker for transcribing interviews; Meagan Shaw, Sylvia Green-Richards, and Mike Wright for research assistance; Jesse Springer for his diagram illustrations on relapse; and Jeff Campbell for his enthusiasm and editorial assistance in developing the preliminary plans for the book.

On a more personal note, we wish to recognize our many family members and friends who provided loving support and a steady cheering section during the four years we were working on this book. In particular, a big thank-you goes to our children, Jules and Cara, for their enduring patience and encouragement, and to our parents, siblings, and other relatives who maintained an active interest and faith in this project. A special thank-you also goes to our dear friend Mariya Masters for her firm optimism and numerous Tootsie Pops that suddenly appeared on our kitchen windowsill. And, if thanks can be made to the soul-stirring inspiration of special places in nature, we are particularly grateful for the wonders of Cannon Beach, Oregon, and the ever-changing beauty of Hendricks Park and the Willamette River here in Eugene.

Introduction

I don't like alcohol. I've never used drugs. I don't like tobacco. That's not my thing. My thing is porn.

—ALEX

Twenty-five years ago, we'd never have written a book on pornography. Back in the 1980s when our practices treating sex, intimacy, and relationship problems were just getting started, we truthfully weren't that concerned about pornography. Like many others in our field, we felt that while porn was often crude and degrading, most of it was essentially harmless. In fact, when we would go to sex therapy trainings and read journals and materials in the field, it was often suggested that X-rated videos and pornographic stories were something we could recommend to our clients to help them become more intimate with their partners.

But our view on pornography began to change in the mid-1990s. It was then that we started seeing a troubling increase in the number of clients coming to us with porn-related problems that were interfering with their ability to maintain healthy relationships. It soon became clear how easily sexual interests and desires could be twisted by pornography, away from real intimacy, and toward technological devices, people, and situations that didn't actually exist. Porn's emphasis had moved from helping couples become more sexually intimate with each other to arousing the user to have a sexual relationship *with it*.

That's an important distinction: unlike many early erotic videos, magazines, and books that were produced to help spice up lovemaking for couples, porn began to offer *itself* as the object of desire. Today's porn teaches users to think only about body parts and specific sexual actions, robbing them of the ability to experience romance, passion, and emotional and physical closeness with a real partner. It *competes* with partners as a sexual outlet.

NOT A HARMLESS FANTASY

In the ten years since we noted growing problems with porn among our own clients, the sheer volume of porn has grown exponentially, as has the ease of getting access to it. As a result, the number of people across the United States and in the world who have developed—and are developing—problems with it has been increasing substantially. Couples and families break up over porn. Single people say their preoccupation with it makes them feel less capable of establishing monogamous, long-term intimate relationships. Self-identified sexual addicts who have spent years in successful recovery relapse with porn, often in more destructive ways than ever before.

Because using porn often involves high levels of dishonesty and secrecy, those who are caught up in it often say they feel isolated, ashamed, depressed, phony, morally compromised, and even in some cases, suicidal. Many are angry, irritable, and unable to sleep. Some tell us porn is leading them on a dangerous path into illegal and risky activities, such as viewing child pornography, having affairs, having anonymous sex at adult bookstores, hiring prostitutes, and viewing porn at work. What we have found really troubling is that many of our clients confide that they are unable to stop using pornography even when they are aware of the negative consequences it is having on their lives. As with alcohol, drugs, or cigarettes, this is one of the signs of a true addiction.

Most porn users we've counseled or spoken with are surprised at how easily porn transformed from an occasional diversion or fantasy to a habitual problem that has the potential to destroy almost every aspect of their *real* lives. What began as fun, escapist sexual entertainment, or a brief but thrilling visit to a taboo world, became a trap. Like quicksand, pornography sucked them in so steadily and quietly that they often didn't even notice they were sinking. For some, porn swallowed up their whole lives, dragging down their relationships, their jobs, their self-esteem, and even their dreams and desires.

But it isn't only those caught in the porn trap whose lives are torn apart by it. The intimate partners of pornography users also seek our counseling. These clients express concern about either being pressured into sexual activities they don't want to be involved in or being sexually ignored. Some feel ridiculed about their bodies, appearance, or sexual performance, which leads them to feel less sexual, both with their partner and in general.

The depth of the problem on the partners of porn users was driven home to us when we learned that two-thirds of the members of the American Academy of Matrimonial Lawyers reported that compulsive Internet use had played a significant role in divorces in 2002 and that well over 50 percent of those cases involved pornography. Eight years earlier, pornography played almost no role in divorce.

Intimate partners not only worry about whether they can continue to live with the porn user, they also often worry about their children being exposed to porn. Their fears are real—it is not uncommon for children to discover a parent's porn stash or mimic a parent's attitudes about sexual behavior and pornography. And if one parent is regularly using porn and the other feels demeaned by it, a child can grow up with a confused sense of what is sexually appropriate and healthy. Partners often feel emotionally abandoned, powerless, and unable to help themselves or their children. Clearly, the porn trap doesn't just trap the user.

WHAT HAS CHANGED?

Nearly all the people who experience porn-related problems say that the ready availability of pornography on the Internet and other electronic devices is at least partially responsible. Porn's promise of easy, commitment-free sexual gratification can be just too hard to resist when pornographic pictures, videos, chats, and games are only a mouse or remote click away, any time, day or night. Our high-tech world allows people to access porn anonymously, without having to face a salesperson knowing they're renting or buying X-rated materials.

Thirty years ago, getting your hands on pornography required time, money, and effort. Today it takes time, money, and effort to *get away from porn*. With unsolicited e-mails, deceptive links, and pop-up windows, porn can make its way into our lives whether we want it to or not. As one man said, "You no longer have to go looking for porn, porn is looking for you!"

Just a generation ago, only a small minority of people would have been considered regular porn users; today porn reaches an unprecedented number of people of all ages and from all walks of life. And it reaches them 365 days a year, 24/7. In the United States alone, forty million people visit Internet porn sites at least once a month. Some visit for only a few minutes at a time, while others stay for hours on a regular basis. A whopping 25 percent of all daily Internet search engine requests and 35 percent of all downloads are for pornography.

As you might expect, most regular porn users are male (75–85 percent), but the number of females using porn has been growing in recent years. You may be shocked to learn—we know we were—that youth under the age of eighteen have become one of the largest consumer groups of porn. With this earlier start, it's no wonder that people are getting hooked faster, more seriously, and in greater numbers than ever before.

Why We Wrote This Book

Seeing the growing impact porn was having on the lives of our clients and listening to their painful and touching stories, we knew we had to do something more to help them than we were able to do in our traditional practice. We began to research the issue and quickly found that the number of people with pornography-related problems was growing rapidly and their problems were becoming increasingly severe. What used to be a small problem for relatively few people had grown to a societal issue that was spilling over and causing problems in the lives of countless everyday people. We asked other therapists, especially sex and relationship therapists, about their experiences, and found that they had seen the same trend—seeing very few clients with pornography problems a decade earlier, but seeing it become a central issue in their practices today.

We began to look for articles and books that could help our clients, but found a lack of information we thought would be helpful. Research on pornography's long-term effects has not been a priority in our society. Our culture tends to avoid discussing sexual issues openly and seriously. Most of the studies that have been done focus narrowly on relatively brief exposures to mild forms of porn, trying to determine whether pornography causes sexual violence. And none of the research included porn use in natural settings, where it is usually accompanied by masturbation. In addition, we found only a handful of studies that dealt with the effect of porn use on an intimate relationship or an intimate partner.

As sex and relationship therapists, we know that pornography use is a relationship issue. Porn affects the user's inner life (the relationship he has with himself), as well as the interactions he has with his partner and other family members. Regular porn use often interferes with a person's ability to maintain good self-esteem and experience mutually fulfilling sexual intimacy with a partner. Dealing with pornography is not solely about stopping a behavior or overcoming an addiction. It also involves reclaiming a sense of personal integrity and manifesting attitudes and behaviors that promote healthy sexual intimacy. Nothing we found in our research discussed pornography use and its repercussions with this type of emphasis.

Since we couldn't find the kind of resource that we felt our own clients and others needed, we decided to write something that would fill in the gap. After many conversations with our colleagues and a thorough study of the professional literature, we began to put together a plan for *The Porn Trap.* We set out to write a book that would plainly and compassionately address pornography issues from a self-esteem and relationship-based perspective—presenting stories, ideas, and insights from real people who have dealt with porn problems, and providing the wisdom of counseling professionals.

In order to protect and honor the confidentiality of our clients, we advertised for interviewees and also talked to volunteers who were referred to us by other therapists. As the interview process got underway, we were impressed by the courage and openness of our contacts. They were willing to share very intimate stories of pain and healing out of a desire to help others escape the trap. Rob, for example, told us he hoped sharing his story would spare others the pain he went through getting caught with child pornography on his computer, and subsequently losing his job, his marriage, and the respect of his family and friends.

"Pornography is not only an individual problem, it's a social and cultural problem. I hope my story helps someone else so that they won't feel so alone and ashamed, and will get the help they need."

We also gathered information from intimate partners of people overcoming porn problems. Karen, a twenty-eight-year-old beautician, spoke of feeling traumatized when she found her new husband's hidden computer file containing sexually provocative pictures of young girls. "The idea of having a child with him suddenly scared me," she said. "What does it mean that he is turned on by this stuff? My trust level fell to zero. It's taken us several years and a lot of counseling for me to feel safe going forward with our plans to start a family together."

Finally, we interviewed therapists, addiction specialists, and pastoral counselors who address pornography problems in both individual and group therapy settings. Their generosity sharing their unique strategies and techniques makes this book an even more valuable tool to those in trouble.

We hope that *The Porn Trap* helps break the silence surrounding pornography for anyone whose life has been damaged by porn. This book can be your lifeline for getting out of the trap, helping you confront your problems honestly, without judgment or shame, and providing you with the information you need to make your own decisions about if, how, and when to quit using porn.

WHAT TO EXPECT

We chose the name *The Porn Trap* because it communicates the danger that pornography use can hold. It also describes how many people feel when they realize pornography is causing them serious problems, but don't want to or can't give it up. What's more, the analogy helps us to organize the stories, research, exercises, and tips into a structure that mirrors the healing journey many people go through—from the first time they see and experiment with porn, to sinking deeper into the trap, to feeling desperate, and eventually discovering how to free themselves.

Throughout the book you will read true stories of people addicted to pornography, or otherwise hurt by it, who decided to change their lives. They often had to endure a lot of suffering before they could see their situations clearly and be ready to make a change. Their stories are dramatic and may at times be difficult to read. They demonstrate how easy and exciting it can be to get sexually involved with porn in spite of having mixed feelings about it. But in the end, these stories are hopeful and uplifting, showing how even the worst porn-related problems can be overcome with the proper knowledge and support.

Most of the stories and quotes in the book come from the interviews we did with porn users and their partners. We have changed names and identifying details to protect confidentiality. In some cases, we have edited material and created composite accounts based on our professional expertise in order to clarify their remarks.

This book addresses a full range of pornography-related problems. It can be helpful to you whether you have just begun using porn, have a well-established habit, or are already involved in a recovery program to quit using it for good. *The Porn Trap* provides an understanding of porn addiction with simple but effective healing strategies. The book is designed to help you:

- identify and evaluate the impact of porn,
- decide whether it's time to quit using porn,
- learn how to stop using porn and deal with cravings,
- rebuild self-esteem and restore personal integrity,
- heal a relationship harmed by porn use, and
- develop a thriving and satisfying sexual life without porn.

In the old Tarzan movies, when someone fell into quicksand, Tarzan would swing in on a rope and rescue them. This book is the closest we can get to offering you a Tarzan-like rescue. Here you'll not only find the tools to pull yourself out of the trap, but you'll also learn how to stay out. We're not going to lie: becoming porn-free, if that's what you decide, can be a really difficult thing to do. Just like an alcoholic drying out, you'll probably experience denial, cravings, and setbacks that will need to be addressed. Even with this book, we recommend seeking the support of a trained therapist or counselor who can help you figure out what course of action to take and navigate it successfully.

You can read this book privately for your own personal needs, or you can use it as a springboard to spark discussion with others. You can read it to understand the gamut of problems caused by pornography, or use it as a guide for making change now or sometime in the future. If you are already involved in counseling, a faith-based program, or a twelve-step addiction recovery program, *The Porn Trap* can be used as an additional tool to strengthen and enhance your healing journey.

If you are not a porn user yourself, but someone you care about is involved with it, *The Porn Trap* will help you feel less alone as you approach your own issues. With this book you'll learn how to engage in constructive dialogue and begin to work together from a place of common and mutual understanding.

We have written this book because we believe you have a right to healthy, love-based sexual expression, and that today's multimedia-driven pornography is interfering with that right. While pornography may promise sexual freedom, it can eventually deliver a form of sexual oppression—robbing people of sexual innocence, sexual self-determination, and the skills to experience healthy relationships based on a loving connection with a real partner. Moving beyond porn's influence can return your personal freedom and give you solid footing to enjoy your life.

I

Becoming Aware

Learn to recognize the counterfeit coins
that may buy you just a moment of pleasure,
but then drag you for days
like a broken man
behind a farting camel.

— Hafiz, 14th Century Sufi poet

1

The Hidden Power of Porn

Tony, a twenty-five-year-old grad student, stared out the window and shook his head in disbelief at how quickly he had sunk into the porn trap. "My live-in girlfriend and I were going through a rough time in our relationship. She left town for a few days and I decided to look at porn on the Internet to satisfy me. Up 'til then I'd never been interested in porn. I began on a Friday afternoon looking at the free peeks. By Saturday I was into the sex chats, and by Sunday I had joined a swinger site. One thing led to another—a domino effect. Two weeks later my girlfriend looked in our computer log and saw what I'd been up to. I lied to her about it, said I had been doing government research of all things. A month later she left me. I never realized that porn had the power to upend my life the way that it did."

Marie, a forty-three-year-old accountant and single mother of two, was surprised by the physical power porn seemed to have over her. "For a long time porn was boring to me. I'd sneak a peek at magazines and videos on rare occasions. Then I discovered masturbating to porn. It was a lot more thrilling than just looking at it. I started craving porn constantly, like a drug. Not wanting my kids to find my porn I switched over to using the Internet. That was a big mistake. On the Internet I could find porn in an instant. The faster I would click the mouse, the more I could see. One night my brain went on overload with the visual stimulation. Next thing I knew, I climaxed. No hands. The computer had control of my mind and body. It was frightening how much power porn had over me."

Dave is a pastor in his fifties, who despite being married to a woman he loves, defines himself as a porn addict. He is still struggling to come to terms with the power porn had over his life, costing him his former job as a school counselor. "Porn was the best sex I ever had. Tremendous rush. I didn't have to emotionally connect. I could pick and choose. I chased the golden-haired Eve. It was all very attractive, very mysterious, very cool. But it wasn't cool when I got caught. Porn has a destructive side. I lost my job and nearly my wife. If you keep doing porn long enough it will ruin your life. I don't think the power of porn is really understood by most people."

For many years, using porn has been the shameful secret many of us have shared in common but no one has talked about. Most women are terrified to admit to using porn. Most men assume that other men do it at least occasionally. After all, "it's a guy thing," since at least three out of four porn users are men. But porn still has a sleaziness about it. It's not something you tell someone on a first or even a fifteenth date. Definitely no one talks about it in a job interview. You certainly can't tell your mother, although if you are a male your father might expect it. You may bring it up with your friends, but probably only in a joking manner.

Most of us would be loathe to think of ourselves as porn addicts or even porn users. After all, we all have a picture in our minds of the typical porn user, and he (or she) doesn't look or act like us. On the other hand, chances are we probably wouldn't picture a grad student, an accountant, or a pastor as a porn user either. But that's who uses porn. Regular people. People like you and me and the person sitting next to you on the plane and your doctor and your mechanic.

Despite their differences, what Tony, Marie, and Dave share, as do most of the people we have interviewed for this book, is their shock at the destructive power of pornography, something they originally got involved in because it seemed simply to promise a harmless good time. "How," they wonder, "can something that isn't a drug, isn't an extramarital affair, isn't actually sex with someone else, cause such devastating problems as divorce, getting fired, and not being able to get sexually aroused by a real live partner?"

The truth is, using pornography can make you go blind—blind to the power and control it can eventually have over your life. Though we might stare intensely at it, we don't see, often can't see, *how and why* it is so powerful. Did you know that porn can actually rewire your brain? That's one reason why some people who use porn become preoccupied with sex, develop problematic sexual desires, and experience sexual functioning problems. And if your brain has been changed, it can be difficult to see clearly exactly what is happening and how it's affecting your life.

Porn is an extremely alluring and compelling "product," capable of delivering sexual pleasure while at the same time setting one up for great pain. Porn is like other controlled substances, such as alcohol and cigarettes, that promise good times, sometimes deliver them, but can end up causing much more damage than pleasure. And unlike booze and tobacco, no one warns us of the potential side effects.

Most of us come to porn unprepared. In school, they teach us about the dangers of alcohol, drugs, cigarettes, even overeating. But chances are, you've never heard a teacher discuss the problems associated with using porn. Porn magazines, books, videos, and Web sites do not come with a list of ingredients educating us about their production standards or potency. When's the last time you saw a Surgeon General's warning on a porn product?

Our goal is to help you learn more about porn and the kind of power it can exert over you physiologically, emotionally, and socially. As we explore porn with you, it is our hope that whether you are currently using porn or not, or are the intimate partner of a user, you will begin to understand why porn can end up playing such a significant role in a person's life. We also believe that the information we share and guidance we provide later in the book will empower you to succeed, if and when you decide to cut porn out of your life for good. Perhaps most important, we hope that what you learn here will help you become more forgiving, both toward yourself and others whose lives have been hurt by porn problems.

Pornography is a difficult and complex issue. It takes time, and a lot of discussion and self-reflection, to gain an accurate understanding of what it means to you. The more you know about it, the more likely it is that you will be able to talk about porn concerns with others and avoid being stuck in its trap. Free of porn, you can create a life filled with healthy sexuality, satisfying intimate relationships, and a better sense of self-value.

Porn Defies Clear Definition

In the 1950s *Superman* television series, the townspeople regularly gathered on the street, pointed up at the sky, and exclaimed, "It's a bird. It's a plane. It's *Superman!*" If only it were that easy to clearly identify what pornography is. It's hard to think of anything more difficult to classify.

Our general sense of what porn is can differ dramatically depending on whether we like it and use it, or fear it and think it should be banned. Porn advocates are quick to call it "harmless visual stimuli," "free speech," and "eye candy," while porn critics call it an "insult to sex," a "cultural pollution," and a "sex-crime manual."

Depending on circumstances and perspectives, porn can function as lots of things: a product, a fantasy, a sexual stimulant, a sin, free speech, a game, a drug, a sexual competitor, a guide, a show, a sexual predator, a perversion, art, a crime, or a joke. We can experience porn as one thing at one time in our lives and another thing later on. Or we can relate to it as several things at once. Our confusion about what to call porn contributes to its hidden power and ability to influence our lives. Without a clear consensus on what it is, as a society we are constantly debating its nature instead of studying its impact and agreeing upon the smartest and healthiest way to deal with it.

In addition, each one of us has our own sense of whether a specific drawing, photo, book, or film is pornography. Whether we see something as pornographic depends on a number of factors, such as our age, sex, upbringing, and cultural background, as well as on how porn impacts us physiologically, emotionally, and morally. This is why couples fight, for example, over whether the *Sports Illustrated* magazine's annual swimsuit edition is pornography.

More than forty years ago, Supreme Court Justice Potter Stewart made the now famous comment about pornography, "I can't define it, but I know it when I see it." While his comment generated a few chuckles given Justice Stewart's notoriously poor eyesight, it brought home the point that porn is in the eye of the beholder. What this means is that when something looks and feels like pornography to you, for you in that moment, it is.

We describe pornography as *any sexually explicit material that is intended to be or is used as a sexual outlet.* Our definition doesn't rest on how sexually graphic porn is or on the nature of its subject matter, but rather on the *type of relationship* a person develops with the sexual material. Unlike sex education materials, which provide accurate information about sex, and erotic art and literature, which are produced to celebrate the human body and sexuality, the goal of porn is to sexually arouse and, ultimately, involve the consumer in a sexual relationship *with it.*

Porn's power comes from its ability to provide an experience of sexual stimulation coupled with immediate gratification. Porn asks the potential user, "Why bother with setting the mood, meeting the needs of another person, or even taking off your clothes, when sex can be just a mouse or remote control click away?"

The Superhighway to Porn

The word "pornography" comes from the Greek words "porno" and "graphie," which literally translate into "the writings of or about prostitutes." Since its emergence as a product for public consumption several hundred years ago, pornography has continually evolved in form and potency based on new inventions. It got its first big push from the printing press, and then continued to expand its offerings and range with the availability of each new device from still and moving cameras to television, video players, computers, and other digital technologies, such as iPods and cell phones. The Internet has brought porn to your laptop in more ways than one.

As the road to porn has evolved into a superhighway, with multiple routes taking you to all kinds of new places at ever-increasing speeds, porn has remained true to its original association with prostitution. It consistently delivers whatever sexual activity the consumer wants, no matter how extreme, without having to take into consideration the feelings and sexual needs of anyone else. Like prostitution, porn avoids important aspects of human sexuality, such as displays of genuine affection, communication between partners, foreplay, afterplay, and concerns about safety and the consequences of sexual activity. In his 1989 book, *Pornography*, University of Alabama media researcher Dolf Zillman wrote, "Pornographic scripts dwell on sexual engagements of parties who have just met, who are in no way attached or committed to one another, and who will part shortly, never to meet again."

Over time, porn has dramatically increased in power and effectiveness as a sexual stimulant. For example, sexual drawings were like a dirt road on which a horse-drawn buggy carried sexually explicit images. Then photographs provided the asphalt, allowing users to get to sexual arousal more quickly and with fewer potholes. As pornographic films and videos emerged on the scene, the highway of porn really started rolling, finally reaching concrete superhighway status by merging with interactive chats, live feeds, Web cams, and specialized electronically coordinated sex toys. These new changes have taken porn to new levels of realism and immediacy. Pornography has evolved beyond sexual fantasy into a world of electronically facilitated sexual experience. No matter what on-ramp you take, you can get off almost anywhere these days. And with these new powers porn can easily compete with a real life partner for sexual attention.

One of the reasons so many men and women have "porn problems" these days is that there's so much of it everywhere, and it is easy to access and afford. It has more of an opportunity to become something of significance. There are more than 400 million pages of pornography on the Internet. As Ned, a sixty-five-year-old single man who looks more like someone's grandfather than a guy struggling to overcome a porn habit, told us, "I've seen pornography go from scarcity to abundance in the last fifty years. I used to have to go out of my way, to special stores and theaters, to get it. Nowadays you'd have to be a clam shell on the moon to avoid coming into contact with pornography."

Ned's comment reflects the reality that in recent years pornography has become big business. It is not only produced and distributed by small operations, several major U.S. media corporations have gotten in on the action, and profit. Commercial porn Web sites, magazines, books, videos, DVDs, cable television, etc., generate more than $97 billion dollars annually worldwide (an increase of 70 percent from 2003 to 2007). In the United States alone, porn revenue is larger than all combined revenues of all professional football, baseball, and basketball franchises. And you thought athletes were bringing in the big bucks.

Today's pornography has the added advantage of easily presenting almost anything that might appeal to you. From tasteful nudes wearing lingerie to sex with a goat, it's all there. There is definitely something for everyone these days. With so much variety, porn can offer something we haven't seen or done before, something we often can't get in real life. Rob, a forty-three-year-old advertising executive and former porn user explained, "I loved having access to an unlimited amount of free pornography over the Internet. Click, click, click. Wow, there it is. I wonder if this is out there? Click, click, click. Wow, there it is!"

Given that porn presents a peephole into a taboo and forbidden world of sex, to remain effective and exciting in a time when people are being inundated with explicit sexual imagery, porn has to continually push the outside limits of what it reveals. Kirk, a forty-eight–year-old postal clerk who gave porn up last year, shared, "Over the last thirty years I've seen porn become more explicit and edgier. The first girlie magazine I saw as a kid didn't even show pubic hair. When I first saw porn films, soft core was in. It featured a lot of simulated sex, with few or no erections, not many close-ups, and dumb plots. Then came hard core, showing close-ups, intercourse, oral sex, and ejaculation, and no plots. Before I quit, what had become 'standard porn' was starting to bother me. Rough blow jobs, facial ejaculation, anal sex, coercion, sex with kids, crude talk, and kinky stuff were commonplace. I couldn't believe what was turning me on."

PORN DELIVERS

Porn's hidden power is not limited to its elusive nature, availability, and compelling styles and formats, but is also based on its ability to produce extremely pleasurable experiences. Let's look closer at these experiences and find out how porn is able to deliver them.

Instant Sexual Turn-On

One of the turn-ons of porn is that it does just that—turns you on. It is engineered to turn us on and then get us off. In this respect, porn has traits in common with sex toys, aphrodisiacs, and medications like Viagra. Porn stimulates the sexual organs of the user, increasing blood flow and in turn, sensations. However, unlike other sexual stimulant products, porn gets stored in your mind, making it possible to recall it for some sexual stimulation at a later time. The mental nature of porn makes it possible to be "using" it without anyone knowing but you.

Most types of pornography come at sex "genitals first," focusing directly and repetitively on images of sexual body parts and sexual activities. Porn's single-minded focus on sex is accomplished by avoiding anything that might in real life get in the way of arousal, such as an argument with a partner, a ringing cell phone, concern about work, or even a tender feeling. As Brian, a nineteen-year-old man who had traded a childhood skateboarding hobby for a porn hobby, told us, "When it comes to sexual arousal, porn doesn't beat around the bush—it gives you the bush!"

Porn is not swallowed or rubbed on the skin. It enters the body directly through your senses, such as your eyes and ears. This gives it a direct link to your central nervous system, specifically, the pleasure centers in your brain. Porn provides instant arousal, a real enticement in these days of "give it to me *now!*" The physiological changes that happen when using porn happen almost immediately: your heart beats faster, your breathing gets shallower, and you start to feel a throbbing in your genitals.

Studies have found that just by being exposed to graphic sexual material, males get erections and females lubricate. The reactions are instinctual. Porn is so powerful as a sexual stimulant that the physiological changes can happen automatically even when the viewer doesn't like the idea of porn or feels uncomfortable with some of its content. In terms of triggering a sexual response, our eyes see no difference between sex on the screen and sex in real life. So as far as your sexual arousal system goes, when you are watching porn, *you are there.*

Pornography's effectiveness as a sexual turn-on also appears to relate to its ability to stimulate the production of testosterone, the hormone of sexual desire. We know that male monkeys produce dramatically more testosterone when they watch other monkeys copulate. Testosterone is not only directly associated with sexual desire and libido, it also relates to sexual motivation and aggressiveness. Even though both men and women produce it, the average adult male body produces about ten to fifteen times the amount the adult female body does. So even though you're not ingesting porn directly into your body, simply seeing and hearing the sexual images and sounds most likely changes your hormone level, leading you to feel hornier and more assertive in meeting your sexual needs.

James, a twenty-three-year-old college student who spends more time looking at porn than socializing and meeting new people, told us, "Pornography is pure excitement—what a turn on! You don't have to have a girlfriend. It's great for getting your rocks off." And Kyle, another college student, adds, "It's everywhere, it works, and it breaks the boredom of regular masturbation."

Drug-like Euphoria

"Oh come on," you're probably thinking. "How can porn be like a drug? I can't smoke it, drink it, or shoot it up." But the fact is that porn can have as powerful an effect on your body and brain as cocaine, methamphetamine, alcohol, and other drugs. It actually changes your brain chemistry. Porn stimulates an area of the brain known as the "hedonic highway," or median forebrain, which is filled with receptors for the neurotransmitter dopamine.

Dopamine is released when you get sexually aroused. It is also released by other pleasurable activities, such as kissing, intercourse, smoking a cigarette, or taking other drugs. Porn causes the dopamine production in your system to spike. This dramatic increase in dopamine produces a drug-like high some researchers believe is most similar to the high caused by crack cocaine. Sam, a shy young man in real life, explained the effect like this, "Doing porn felt like an incredible rush of life blowing through my veins and the good part was I could always go back for more."

Using porn also increases production of other "feel-good" chemicals in our brain, such as adrenaline, endorphins, and serotonin. Unfortunately, by overloading your brain with pleasure chemicals, porn reduces your body's own ability to produce and effectively release them under normal life circumstances. This is one of the reasons a porn user may find himself needing higher levels of sexual stimulation and excitement to become aroused and satisfied. Ted, a thirty-year-old stockbroker, shared, "No matter how much porn I looked at, my mind was always ready for more."

Sedative and opiate drug-like changes can also occur. When porn use is combined with masturbation, the end result is orgasm. And we all know the power of orgasm to create pleasure, numb pain, and generate a state of deep relaxation.

Porn's power to produce experiences of excitement, relaxation, and escape from pain make it *highly addictive*. Over time you can come to depend on it to feel good and require it so you don't feel bad. Cravings, preoccupations, and out-of-control behavior with using it can become commonplace. Porn sex can become your greatest need. If you have been using porn regularly to "get high," withdrawal from porn can be as filled with agitation, depression, and sleeplessness as detoxing from alcohol, cocaine, and other hard drugs. In fact, people in porn recovery take an average of eighteen months to heal from the damage to their dopamine receptors alone.

Power Trip

Nothing beats a feeling of being powerful and in control, especially in something as instinctive and primal as sex. And porn delivers. Using porn as a source of entertainment can give you *the illusion* of being powerful and in control of what is happening. Tim, a reference librarian in his late forties, really got off on the power of porn. He says, "Porn makes me feel like a pasha enjoying his harem. I just show up and sit there. All these women perform for me—dancing, gyrating, and showing their bodies. They're under my control, performing *for me.*"

Steven, a twenty-nine-year-old mental-health worker, agrees. "The part I liked best about pornography was that I had control over the sexual action. I didn't have to beg for sex. I could have sex when I wanted, with the kind of person I wanted, in exactly the way that I wanted. I didn't have to adjust my behavior in any way. It was time for me."

The sense of power experienced in sports like hunting can be similar to how you feel when searching for arousing pornography on the Internet, on cable TV, or in adult stores. As with capturing prey, you can look for it, circle around it, target it, and then go in for the "kill" by purchasing or downloading the porn. Some porn users tell us that the hunt and conquest feeling that blends with sexual arousal is even more satisfying than having an orgasm. Porn users can also feel quite powerful in being able to acquire free porn, secretly access it, and cover up their porn use so they won't get caught.

One of the things many people like best about porn is that it allows them to be a voyeur, which may be a power trip of its own, since it involves something that is illegal in real life. Voyeurism is the act of achieving sexual arousal by observing an unsuspecting and nonconsenting person who is undressed, unclothed, and/or engaged in sexual activity. In the role of voyeur you get to look at things you're not supposed to be seeing. You're able to watch other people while they can't see (or stop) you in return. Voyeurs have the upper hand in a relationship because, while they have the prerogative of critiquing, judging, and—with the simple click of a mouse—rejecting someone else, they don't have to suffer being similarly scrutinized or sexually snubbed.

Of course, intellectually, we all understand that the power pornography gives us isn't real. The sexy, willing partners portrayed on the screen or in magazines aren't actually available to us. We are not really in control of the sexual situations and fantasies. Someone else is creating the scenes, calling the shots. Unfortunately, believing for a few moments (or hours) that we do have that kind of power can mislead us into believing that power over someone else is more important than caring about and being responsive to a sexual partner. Porn's focus on power teaches a self-centered approach to sex that causes all kinds of problems in real life.

Slot-Machine Excitement

Using porn has a lot in common with gambling, especially now that pornography is delivered through devices that allow you to rapidly click through a never-ending stream of stimulating material. Hoping to find just the right porn site, the exact sexual activity you want, or the ultimate fantasy partner, can make you feel just like you do when hoping for a jackpot at a slot machine in Vegas. As businessman Nigel explains, "I know exactly what I am looking for in terms of a specific look and a specific type of sex. I know it's there somewhere. I love the hunt, looking and searching for the best and most exciting, my ideal. And there's always the chance I will be able to find something better than I had before."

However, when searching for porn you only get your ideal content—a picture of the "perfect" woman or man, or the sexual act of your dreams—every now and then. This type of setup is called an "intermittent reward system," and it is designed to hook the user just like casino gaming machines. That's why it can be so easy to be at your computer and look up at the clock and find that several hours have passed in what seems like just minutes.

Online pornography has an intermittent reward system that rewards on a *variable ratio schedule*, meaning you never know just how many photos you will need to look at before you find one you want. The number keeps changing. This is the most potent method for shaping behavior. In scientific experiments, pigeons put on this type of random reinforcement schedule almost starve to death pecking at a single dot that *might* produce just *one* pellet of food.

The brief delay that occurs, that moment of erotic anticipation, just before you download a picture or click on a site, can trigger additional release of the pleasure chemical dopamine in the brain. Thus, the gambling-like nature of online pornography combined with its sexual turn-on doubles its potential for creating an addiction to porn. With online porn, and porn that is accessed *on demand* through any device, you can be influenced not only by the *content* of what you see, but also by the *delivery system* with which it is presented. The gambling nature of porn was a lot less potent in the past, when porn magazines came in the mail, one issue a month.

Love Affair

Do people fall in love, or at least in lust, with porn? You bet. Many of the people we interviewed were attracted to porn because it provided them with a temporary or alternative sexual outlet. While they weren't writing love poems or songs to porn, they often spoke of their relationship with porn in terms often reserved for love affairs. "It's sexually thrilling," "I was with it for hours," "I can't wait to see it again," and "Porn gave me the best orgasms ever."

While porn may seem like a way to have sex with another partner without *actually* having sex with another partner, it is more real than it seems. Although the women (and men) in porn magazines and videos are two-dimensional and made out of paper or digital dots on a screen, focusing on them through fantasy while masturbating can generate feelings similar to relating to a real human in real life.

As we mentioned earlier, watching porn stimulates the release of powerful chemicals, such as dopamine and testosterone. These chemicals not only relate to sexual arousal and pleasure, but also are released in real life when someone is sexually attracted to and falls in love with someone else. In addition, powerful human bonding hormones, such as oxytocin and vasopressin, are released with orgasm. They contribute to establishing a lasting emotional attachment with whomever, *or whatever*, you happen to be with or thinking about at the time. The more orgasms you have with porn, the more sexually and emotionally attached to it you'll become.

A relationship with porn can act like an affair. It can take time and energy away from an existing intimate relationship. People who use porn often operate with the same kind of secrecy and deception as someone having a sexual affair. When a porn user is confronted by a partner, there is often denial, lying, and attempts to cover up the wrongdoing. Without realizing it, maintaining a "love affair" with porn can become more important than staying connected to someone in real life. Also, if you use porn regularly, the mental images and scenarios of porn can keep playing in your mind during sex, making it hard to feel connected and intimate with the real person in your life.

THE BAD OUTWEIGHS THE GOOD

There is no doubt that porn has many attractive and powerful properties—from sexually arousing and fulfilling you, to giving you an easy escape from your real life, to helping you feel powerful and desirable. But using porn also creates problems, many of which evolve so slowly that you don't see them coming or feel them happening until they are quite serious. As we'll discuss more in upcoming chapters, porn can:

- conflict with your values, beliefs, and life goals,
- compromise your ability to be honest and open in a relationship,
- upset and compete with an intimate partner,

- harm your mental and physical health,
- make you less attractive as a sexual partner,
- cause sexual desire and functioning difficulties,
- shape your sexual interests in destructive ways, and
- cause a variety of family, work, legal, and spiritual problems.

We believe that the risks of porn use far outweigh any short-term benefits. In our practice and with the people we've interviewed, we have seen enough to know that porn use today compromises almost everyone's ability to relate in intimate, meaningful ways to a real partner. Max, who is only in his early twenties, already recognizes these problems in himself: "Porn distorts sex. There's no real consent, equality, or mutual respect. It teaches you to take but never give love. Porn doesn't truly reflect what's best for us sexually. It's unreal. You can't find any joy or lasting sexual happiness there."

As powerful as porn is, it can't compete with the many life-affirming pleasures that can come from approaching sex in ways that strengthen self-esteem and emotional intimacy. Nothing beats experiencing genuine love, caring, and sensual pleasures with another living, breathing human being. Sex is infinite in terms of how it can be learned and expressed. If you have developed an attachment to porn, or adopted some of the attitudes and behaviors it promotes, you can, if you want, undo and unlearn them. It will be well worth the effort.

Many people who give up porn report that they are more satisfied, not only sexually, but morally, socially, and psychologically as well. Corey, thirty-four years old, who ended up in jail because of where porn led him, told us, "I have enough experience now to know that porn wasn't really satisfying. I experience better sex in real relationships without porn than I ever did with it. Sex with a real partner is more work in a way, but the rewards are better. A healthy sex life improves the quality of your life, unlike the quick fix you get with porn. Porn doesn't have any long-term benefits, just long-term costs. My life is much better now without porn. I could have saved myself and other people a lot of grief if I'd never gotten involved with it in the first place."

2

First Encounters

When we think about porn, we think about adults. After all, stores that sell pornographic magazines and videos are often called "Adult Stores" and pornographic shows on cable warn of "Adult Content." But the fact is that most people have their first experience of viewing porn when they are, on average, eleven years old, and almost everyone who has ever been exposed to porn (and that's the majority of us) first gets an eyeful well before the age of eighteen.

If you have issues with porn today, chances are they can be traced back to your early encounters with pornography. Childhood is a formative and vulnerable period in a person's life, a time when our attitudes are shaped and many of our behaviors take root. And as we move from childhood to adolescence we develop our sexual appetites and preferences.

Brad is a good example of someone who, like many other children, first saw porn when he was young. He developed a strong habit of using it well before he left home. His story shows how easy it is to be introduced to porn in childhood. Brad is a twenty-seven-year-old salesman, married, with one child. He's been in porn addiction recovery for the last four years.

BRAD'S STORY

My first exposure to pornography happened when I was six years old. My older brother and I were down at the local elementary school riding our bikes around the parking lot and messing around. It was on a weekend during summer break. There was no one else around except for these two hippies who were hanging out on the jungle gym. We didn't pay much attention to them until they called us over to show us something.

One guy opened up a Penthouse *and showed us some very explicit pictures of nude women, which I can still recall. It wasn't a traumatic experience. But it was very sharp. It left a rock solid imprint on my mind. Crystal clear. It was strange and somewhat pleasurable, but I wouldn't call it erotic. I was too young to even know what that was or have any of those kinds of feelings.*

We went home and told my mom what had happened. Well, she just flipped. She went down to the school grounds looking for these two guys. They had disappeared by this time, but left this material scattered all over the playground like they were disseminating this stuff everywhere. She went around collecting the stuff and throwing it away. I didn't understand why she was so upset because it was just, you know, naked boobies or whatever. To me it wasn't even a real huge deal. But my mom's intense reaction, and the fact that we never talked about it, left a strong imprint on me.

After a while my curiosity about porn just kind of died off. Sexual thoughts took a back seat to other things, like being part of a little club with some of the neighborhood boys, riding bikes, having BB gun wars, getting involved with sports and school, and that sort of thing. It wasn't until one summer, seven years later when I was thirteen years old, that I saw some more porn.

It was a hot summer. My parents would go off to work and leave my brother and me at home with enormous tasks to do on our ranch. We hated it. The way that we rebelled and killed time was to watch a porn video my brother had recorded off a decoded XXX channel and a Playboy channel at my cousin's house.

We knew pornography was taboo because of my mom's reaction to it after the playground incident. We also knew that we had to hide what we did, because if we got caught watching this stuff, there would be hell to pay. I watched it anyway, partly because my brother said it was great, and also because I was now old enough to get a good sexual rush when doing it. At first I couldn't

masturbate, didn't know how. But it didn't take long to move into it. My first
orgasm came from looking at that videotape.

Soon, instead of being upset and dreading all the chores they were making
us do, we were enjoying it when my parents left. The desire for the hunt and
the fantasy kicked in at that point. Even when my parents were home I'd be
replaying the videos in my mind. I began masturbating daily, multiple times a
day. I know now that my behavior was compulsive. At the time, of course, I had
no clue what I was doing. All I knew is that it felt good and it was something
I wanted to do as often as possible.

That was the starting point and my interest in porn continued from then
on pretty much unrelenting. Every opportunity that I had to get more material,
whether X-rated magazines or videos, I would take. If I was over at a friend's
house and his parents were gone I'd suggest we find his dad's porn. By the time
my parents realized I had an issue with porn, the root was already there, very
strong. Their lectures were like water off a duck's back. I'd put on the face, the
façade that I was sorry and wouldn't ever do it again—blah, blah, blah. The
next day, of course, I couldn't wait to get my hands on some more porn.

The morning Brad pedaled his bike to the school playground with his brother, he had no way of knowing he would have his first exposure to a substance that would become the focus of his sexual energy as an adolescent and that would later result in compromising his sense of integrity and almost costing him his marriage.

It's Easy for Us to Come in Contact with Porn as Kids

One of the things that surprised us most in our interviews and with our clients is just how often porn use starts in childhood or adolescence. Our first exposure may happen in many different ways, but most of us are exposed when we're much too young.

Thirty-two-year-old Tyler, for example, remembers seeing his first pornographic magazine when he was just *five* years old and playing at a friend's house. "The magazine belonged to my friend's dad and it was just sitting around their living room. The father didn't seem to care. I remember seeing lots of pictures of women with big breasts and some of naked men and women having intercourse," says Tyler. "I found it fascinating. Obviously, I didn't understand anything about the mechanics of sex, but I was drawn to it because it was so new and mysterious. It's something you don't see every day when you're five."

Gil, a thirty-four-year-old millworker, stumbled across a *Penthouse* in his father's desk drawer one day. He was *nine* years old and home from school with the flu. Gil says, "I wasn't consciously looking for anything. I just came across it. I thumbed through it. I was curious and it confused me a little. And somehow it got me thinking differently about my dad. I put the magazine back in a different place from where I found it. I think I was trying to let him know I'd seen it. But I never heard from him about it."

Finding a parent's porn stash is a common way kids are exposed to porn. To a child, discovering porn can feel like finding buried treasure. After all, the porn stash must be very special and precious, or else the parent wouldn't have gone to such lengths to hoard and secretly hide it. The value of the stash is further increased by the fact that it is very eye-catching and stirs up strong, visceral feelings for the viewer. Most children intuitively know they can't share their discovery with their parents, because they will either be punished or, at the very least, no longer have ready access to their newfound treasure. But the mere existence of the stash teaches the child about being secretive and hiding things from others. When it comes to porn use, this pattern is often one that is continued through a lifetime.

Another common way kids have their first exposure to porn is by having it introduced to them by a relative or friend. Being shown porn enthusiastically by someone who is older or perceived as more worldly can make an experience of looking at porn by a child feel particularly exhilarating. In fact, a kind of "contagious excitement" can take place. When we're young we often take our cues for how to feel about something from those we look up to and want to emulate. We imitate them. We register and adopt their reactions.

Justin's story is a good example of being exposed to porn by a relative. When he was *nine*, his uncle showed him porn for the first time while babysitting him. "He sat me and my two younger brothers down on the couch next to him. We thought he was going to read us a story, but instead he pulled out a *Playboy* magazine and showed us the pictures. I couldn't believe my eyes. Uncle Fred got very excited flipping through the pages, and so did we. I got a great rush from it, like an alcoholic's first drink. He showed them to us again, numerous times after that, whenever he babysat."

In another example, Rob, forty-three years old, was shown his first porn photo at home by his older brother. "I was *seven* years old and just sitting on my bed," says Rob. "My brother trumpeted it as a big thing. He held the magazine behind his back and announced: 'I'm just about ready to show you something amazing. Get ready for this. It is gonna really blow your mind.' Then he pulled it out and opened it up. It was a picture of a half-naked woman. She was incredibly beautiful. I can still see her clearly in my mind's eye to this day. Her image got burned on my brain and put in the vault."

Among those we interviewed, looking at porn with friends, being shown porn by relatives, and finding a parent's porn stash were the most common types of first encounters with porn. Today, however, more kids are stumbling across porn on the Internet. In fact, one in four kids who have Internet access experience accidental exposure to porn in any given year. Nine out of ten children between the ages of eight and sixteen years old report they have viewed porn online. And according to another study, nearly half of the children who viewed porn by accident say they cannot forget that first image. As a result, premature exposure to sexual material that is meant for adults is a problem that is rapidly becoming a pandemic.

WE ALL REACT DIFFERENTLY
THAT FIRST TIME

For some of us, porn is "nothing to get all excited about," while for others, it is "everything to get all excited about!" Gil, the millworker, said, "Looking at the pictures of the beautiful, seductive women was like, 'Wow, there's this whole world I had no idea existed.'"

Most of the people we interviewed for this book described their first encounter with porn as exciting and stimulating. Only a few people characterized their first experience with porn as traumatic. Some of the people we spoke with did, however, refer to their initial porn experience as "shocking" and "confusing." Betsy, a nineteen-year-old college sophomore, who saw her first pornographic movie when she had just started high school, said, "It shocked and bothered me. I became a little sad and depressed. Seeing firsthand the subtle and overt violence against women was a big turn-off. Porn is so degrading to women. My parents said that sex was really beautiful. Porn wasn't. I want to *make love* with a man, not have him expect me to be like the women are in porn. I couldn't stand to be with a man who wants to treat me like the men treat women in porn."

Our reactions to porn can have a lot to do with how old we are when we encounter it the first time, whether we're by ourselves or with friends, whether we seek it out or have it thrust upon us by someone else who wants to show off or shock us with it, and just exactly what images we see that first time. You can imagine that a six-year-old seeing a bondage video would have a much different reaction than a twelve-year-old finding his dad's fairly tame girlie magazine collection. And gender can also play a role. For instance, young girls are generally more upset and more likely to cry when exposed to porn than boys.

Other factors that play a role in how we respond to porn that first time (and subsequent times as well) include our religious values, family expectations, and social environment. A thirteen-year-old who is in a family that promotes open discussion about sexual issues and concerns will likely have a different reaction to coming across porn than a thirteen-year-old who is in a family where there is underlying shame about sex and discomfort talking about it.

Thirty-three-year-old Alex is a good example of how religion and family values can affect one's response to porn. Alex was attracted to the excitement and taboo aspects of porn because it transcended the religious restrictions he'd grown up with. "I was raised in a very religious Mennonite family. You know the big Mennonite joke: *Why don't Mennonites believe in premarital sex? Because it might lead to dancing!* Well, pornography was never mentioned on the lists of 'don'ts.' At nine years old I bought a stash of about twenty mainline pornographic magazines— *Playboys*, *Penthouses*, and some *Hustlers*—from my best friend's older brother. I read them when I was supposed to be doing homework. It was pure excitement and arousal."

Our Parents' Reactions Can Make Matters Worse

Remember how Brad and his brother rushed home to tell their mom about being shown the *Penthouse* magazine by the two hippies at the playground? Brad had many questions for her about what he had just seen, but instead of remaining calm and providing information, she "just flipped" and ran down to the playground in search of the hippies. As a child, Brad never had the opportunity to ask any questions or receive any answers regarding pornography.

As an adult and father himself today, Brad can understand his mother's reaction: she was angry that anyone would show that kind of thing to her young boys, and perhaps also scared that the hippies might have been using the porn as a "grooming technique" to later sexually abuse her children. But her reaction at the time scared Brad and confused him even more about the incident.

Like most six-year-olds Brad had a natural curiosity about human bodies and the biological differences between boys and girls. Unfortunately, Brad's mother's reaction made him feel bad about his curiosity, guilty and ashamed for what had happened, and afraid to ever mention anything about pornography to her again. By the time Brad was a teenager and his parents became concerned about his use of porn, it was too late. The communication lanes were closed. Brad had already learned to keep his porn use secret and, when confronted, to lie.

Most of the people we talked with about their early porn experiences told us they got similar reactions from their parents. When they try to talk about porn with their parents, kids learn quickly that the subject is off limits. This may be in part because like Brad's mom, many parents lack the knowledge and skills to know exactly what to do or say. Instead they may ignore the questions, dismiss possible porn problems, and avoid discussion altogether. Some parents may not want to talk about porn because they fear discussing it will bring up issues about their own porn use. Or it may be part of a bigger "don't ask, don't tell" policy that many families have about sex in general.

Unfortunately, when parents are unable to be there for their children to discuss porn issues when they first arise, many dominoes begin to fall: emotional honesty and closeness between children and their parents begins to crumble, kids learn to feel unnecessary shame about their sexuality, and in fact, compulsive porn use may actually be fueled.

This might be a good place for you to stop and think about your initial experiences with porn. We've designed the exercise below to help guide your understanding of how you first came in contact with pornography and what impact it had on you at the time.

When Did *You* First Encounter Pornography?

1. How old were you when you first saw pornography?

2. What were the circumstances you were in? Were you alone or with someone else?

3. What type of porn did you encounter? What type of sexual behavior and experiences were portrayed in the porn?

4. What was your immediate reaction? How did you feel? Were you excited, confused, anxious, ashamed, intrigued, scared, sexually aroused, disgusted, angry, delighted, sad, etc.?

5. Did you talk with others about your experience? If so, what do you recall about their reaction? If not, how did it feel to be carrying this "secret knowledge"?

6. Did your first encounter with porn make you want to see or search out more of it? If so, how?

7. Is there anything that bothers you about your first exposure to porn, such as how young you were, the type of porn you saw, or the situation you were in, that you wish would have been different? Why?

Kids Continue to Use Porn
for Different Reasons

While some people told us that they became "hooked" on porn from the moment they first saw it, no matter how young they were, most described moving in and out of an involvement with porn depending on their needs at the time and the circumstances of their lives. No matter whether you grew up in the era of bobby socks, drive-in movies, and rock 'n' roll or in the world of low-rider pants, computers, and rap music, if you used porn on a regular basis, it was most likely because you discovered that porn could in some way satisfy one (or more) of the following normal childhood needs:

1. Learning about sex
2. Belonging to a group
3. Sexual permission and pleasure
4. Coping with emotional stress

Let's look at each of these needs and how they affect people who experiment with porn as children.

1. "This Is Unbelievable!" (Learning About Sex)

Kids are naturally curious about how sex works, what a naked body looks like, and what goes where. By the time we become teenagers, our raging hormones kick in and we don't just want to know, we *need* to know, and we need to know *now*!

Unfortunately, the level of sex education in most schools and the "birds and bees talk" provided at home almost never satisfy our need for very specific knowledge about how real live people have sex and how they *enjoy* sex. It's not enough to learn solely about abstinence, pregnancy prevention, and all the potentially harmful sexually transmitted infections that exist. As kids, we may be curious about things such as what people look like having sex, what different sexual positions are possible, and what kinds of sexual expressions and sounds occur.

Kevin, a thirty-four-year-old investment banker who attended seminary at age fourteen in order to train to become a priest, found that whenever sexual information was withheld, it just made him more determined to get it. "During movie night, the priest in charge would hold a handkerchief over the parts of the film where there was kissing or sexual interest between partners. His making such a big deal about it only fueled my drive to want to look at porn. I developed a strong craving to see what it was we weren't supposed to see."

Because porn can be so easy to obtain—and displays so much more graphic sexual behavior with real life descriptions, sights, and sounds than traditional sex education materials—many of the people we interviewed turned to porn when they were young as their primary source of information about sex. Hector, a doctoral student, explains, "I first started looking at porn when I was about ten. I went with my older brother to his friend's house to look at magazines and videos. It was mostly an informational kind of thing. I was looking at porn to try and figure out what sex was all about—how things are done, different positions—to learn about things that I might like to implement one day."

Zane, another college student, had a unique approach to "homework." "Early on in high school I discovered that there were naked chicks on the Internet. I became endlessly fascinated with them. Part of the fascination was being a horny teenager and just being insanely curious about sex, but I was also drawn to the porn because of the endless amount of new things I could see. Following that first exposure, I would look at porn for several hours a day, mostly when I should have been doing my homework."

Patty, now fifty-five years old, told us how porn provided her information about sex she wasn't getting anywhere else. "One night after putting the children I was babysitting to bed, I saw a stack of *Playboy* magazines in a cupboard behind the sofa in their television room. I was twelve. No one in my family would have ever dared to subscribe to this kind of magazine. The sex stories made me realize there was a whole world of sexual possibilities. Unlike with the other families on the block, I was always available to babysit for those neighbors whenever they needed me."

Without us realizing it, the information porn provides us about sex when we're young is often misleading, and in some cases, ludicrously wrong. While it can teach us what certain body parts look like, things are often, well, let's just say, out of proportion. What guy hasn't looked at a male porn star and wondered if he has somehow been shortchanged? Or looked at his wife and wondered why her breasts weren't huge *and* perky?

Believe It or Not!

The average size of a man's erect penis is 5.8 inches long.
The average size of a male porn star's erect penis is 8 inches long.
85% of female porn stars have breast implants.
100% of the pictures of porn centerfolds have been enhanced.
Porn stars frequently undergo hair removal, genital cosmetic surgery, and liposuction procedures.

Source: *Men's Health* magazine, March 2004, and *The Smart Girl's Guide to Porn*.

Probably the most misleading "educational" aspects of porn are the "facts" many kids end up believing, such as: porn sex is the ideal sex one should strive for; casual and anonymous encounters make for great sex; no one ever feels exploited or bad after sex; and any type of sexual activity will be tolerated and satisfying to any partner. As adults, we eventually learn that none of this is true.

2. "I'm One of the Guys" (Belonging to a Group)

For many of us, porn provided a way to bond with other kids or members of our family. In our research, we heard numerous stories from people who shared, traded, stole, and watched pornography with their friends or siblings. As you might guess, usually the groups were either all boys or all girls. Like Brad, who spent a summer watching porn with his older brother and later searching for porn with his middle school friends, many people told us they looked at porn videos and magazines with others. With today's technology porn continues to be easy to share with friends: kids can include a porn Web site in an instant message or pass around a jump drive loaded with their favorite sexual images.

Sharing something forbidden and taboo is one way we strengthen social connections and support each other when we're young. We feel more like part of a group when we have something in common with others, and if that thing is something we're keeping secret from the adults, it can create an even stronger bond. Passing around porn is like passing around beer, cigarettes, or marijuana to your friends—it's a way of upping your "cool factor," especially for boys.

Ivan, a twenty-two-year-old auto mechanic, liked how porn helped him feel part of a small group of loyal friends. "In seventh grade a classmate stole a *Penthouse* from the market near our school. A group of us boys looked through it together. By the time we were in high school, we passed around hard-core videos. We would make jokes and comments about what we were seeing. But we never really talked about what we thought or how we felt about it. We went for the humor and shock value—stuff that was outlandish, ludicrous, and borderline disgusting. It wasn't about getting jacked up sexually. It was about doing something together. I had my reservations about some of the things I saw, but I kept quiet to stay part of the group. Looking back on it I think obsessing about women's bodies gave us a safe way to emotionally connect with each other."

Thirty-eight-year-old Don also talked about bonding with his friends through porn. When he was twelve, he would often look through his father's collection of *Playboys* with a friend. "We looked through each magazine, one at a time, commenting on them, what we saw, and giving our own personal evaluations: 'Gee, she looks great' and 'Boy, aren't those nice,' or saying things like, 'This is what I would do with this.' Throughout my youth, looking at porn with my friends reinforced my fascination with pornography and also made me feel closer to my dad."

A lot of the men we interviewed, as well as many of our male clients, reported this porn-bonding experience. They were attracted to porn because they felt it was "a guy thing" and thought that doing it would somehow initiate them into manhood. Corey, who at thirty-four years old is in recovery from a lifetime of porn use, told a similar story. "My friend and I used to stay up all night, drink, and watch as many movies as we could that had nudity and sex. It was our version of all-night sports. I felt somewhat guilty, but it was reassuring to me knowing the porn was out there and that everyone else is secretly looking at it too."

For Ralph, a thirty-six-year-old mechanic, porn bonded him to his brothers and dad. "I grew up in a large family with five older brothers. My dad and brothers were all into pornography. We had *Penthouse*s, *Playboy*s, and other soft-core 'weenie magazines' lying around the bathroom all the time. We had a common pot from which we all shared. When I was fifteen, my brothers let me share their collection of hard-core videos."

Women are a lot less likely to sit around with their friends watching porn as a way to bond and socialize. Even when it does happen, their responses are often different. Lacy, a twenty-seven-year-old hairdresser, recalls her experience. "One time in boarding school, a group of us girls watched a pornographic video just for the fun of it. We sat there and laughed at it at first. Then it got pretty gross. After a while, we began complaining that the men in it were ugly, the sex in it was weird, and the dialogue was a joke."

In this case, porn's power to strengthen the closeness of the group came about because of the way the girls unified and bonded in their *dislike* of the product. It's interesting to note that these girls felt free to openly discuss and criticize the porn. The boys, on the other hand, seemed to abide by an unspoken rule forbidding them from expressing anything negative about porn to each other, even if that's how they felt.

3. *"I'm Okay for Feeling This Way"* (*Sexual Permission and Pleasure*)

When you're between the ages of eight and eighteen, one of the worst things in your own mind is to be considered "weird" or "different." We all want to fit in and feel "normal." When puberty kicks in, many of us think something is very wrong with us, especially if we don't have the guidance of a parent or other adult to help us understand that the sexual urges, feelings, and fantasies we are having are natural and normal.

With its explicit views of sex and its "no holds barred" approach to expressing sexual desires and activities, pornography gives kids a playground in which they can privately explore sex and create sexual experiences for themselves. According to erotic art photographer and writer David Steinberg, "Pornography is still the medium that most vociferously advocates free and diverse sexual expressiveness, a radical stance in a culture which is still essentially puritanical and sex-negative."

Porn gives the message that it is okay to have sexual feelings and for our bodies to do sexual things, such as become aroused and enjoy orgasm. Porn not only validates our budding sexuality, it encourages us to pursue the pleasure that comes with it. It tells us feeling sexual is normal and good.

Porn can be especially liberating for anyone who grew up feeling sexually ashamed or repressed. Rory, who at sixty years old was one of our oldest interviewees, said this was part of the big draw of pornography for him. "Growing up, I was filled with sexual shame and self-loathing because of my sexuality. I had a tremendous visual hunger to look at naked women. I wanted to stare at them and feel the way my body could light up. *Playboy* showed me this was fine to do—something that sophisticated, cultured men value. It made me feel less of a cockroach because I had genitals. I could stare at centerfolds all I wanted without offending any one. I like to joke that I was twenty before I realized women didn't have staples in their navels!"

The homosexual men we spoke with said gay porn had a similar effect of helping them feel comfortable with their sexual feelings and desires. Unlike straight boys and teens, gays have extremely few opportunities to learn about homosexual relationships, so porn fills a huge gap for them. Alan, a thirty-eight-year-old chef, told us he felt alone and deviant about his emerging sexual feelings until he saw his first gay porn video. "Pornography gave me my first depictions of male-to-male sex. Being raised in a conservative community, I had no other way of finding out who I was sexually and how I could be with a partner."

Regardless of sexual orientation, pornography can help validate a young person's budding sexual thoughts and sensations, and natural desires to pleasure themselves sexually. Masturbation is a common form of sexual expression during childhood. It usually increases, with a focus on achieving orgasm, during adolescence. Porn approves of and even encourages masturbation. The actors in porn fondle themselves frequently, and the people around them don't condemn them for it. Ed, a forty-seven-year-old former porn user, explained, "Pornography served a very important purpose for me that helped break the bonds of my sexual repression—it justified my self-pleasuring and sexual release."

While we may be attracted to porn when we are young because of its pro-masturbation stance, it doesn't take long to discover that it offers more than a message. Porn not only encourages masturbation, it provides a *focus* for it and *facilitates* it. Porn provides an abundance of ready-made sexual fantasies as well as images of people we might find sexually attractive.

Martha, an artist in her late forties, enjoyed *Playgirl* when she was in her teens. "I have always been a very visual person. I remember seeing my first *Playgirl* magazine when I was in high school in the mid-1970s. It featured naked men in lots of poses. One guy, who I can still remember today, just struck me as beautiful, exceptionally erotic. He was laying back in a casual pose as innocent as could be. His hair was dark, his eyes were smiling, and his skin was golden and smooth. But best of all he had this large erection that just lay against his hip. I used to fantasize about him a lot."

Helping us feel that we are not alone when we are being sexual is one of porn's most compelling attributes. It may also be one of the strongest reasons it is popular among boys, especially given that most boys grow up in a culture where they are often pressured to assert their masculinity and "prove" they are not gay. For heterosexual boys, porn offers a way to "heterosexualize" masturbation. Rather than focus on the fact they are stimulating male genitals (their own), they can focus on the reassuring presence of a female. Pornography allows the experience of masturbation to shift from "self-loving" to "doing to" someone else. It doesn't matter that the someone else is only an image on a piece of paper or a screen.

George, a fifty-six-year-old grandfather, says that his youthful interest in porn had its roots in searching out sexually explicit materials to help him masturbate. "Like many a young lad in my teens, I started out masturbating using sexual pictures. It was the 1960s. I used the only thing that was available: images of bare-breasted women in *National Geographic* and the pictures of scantily clad women in the underwear sections of the Sears and Roebuck catalogs. I progressed to pornographic magazines when I was old enough to buy them. Masturbating to pornography was entertaining and offered me a pleasurable escape."

Though twenty-two-year-old Max grew up in an era inundated with graphic images of sex, like George, he also turned to porn as a teen when he masturbated. He shares, "I don't like how the women are treated in porn, so I wouldn't watch it just to watch it. I'd only look at porn when I needed to get off sexually. It was right there on the Internet when I wanted it. It gave easy and instant gratification. But, once I climaxed, I was done."

Max also says that having porn as his sexual outlet in his teens made sense because he didn't feel ready to be in a sexual relationship back then. "Looking at porn and masturbating helped me to keep my sexual drive in check. If I hadn't used pornography, I would have felt more compelled to have sex with a girl. That would have taken a lot of courage that I didn't have. It didn't feel appropriate for me when I was that young. I wasn't ready to invest the time, energy, and emotional commitment it would have taken to have a meaningful sexual relationship."

4. *"Make the Pain Go Away" (Coping with Emotional Stress)*

Another reason many young people develop an ongoing involvement with porn is that they discover it can help them escape from the stress of their daily lives. Like reading, television, and video games, pornography can beam us out of our own life and into one where we don't have boring homework, a mom nagging us to clean up our room, friends who spread rumors about us, and someone we have a crush on who doesn't seem to know we're alive.

But porn is not limited to just serving as a handy distraction, a ready-made form of entertainment and amusement like television. Because it has powerful drug-like properties and the ability to facilitate a mind- and body-altering sexual response, kids in situations in which they feel powerless, neglected, afraid, abandoned, humiliated, attacked, or betrayed on a regular basis and for extended periods of time can easily find themselves becoming mesmerized or obsessed with pornography. If you grew up in a family with alcohol, drug, sexual abuse, or anger issues, for example, you may have found an even stronger reason to lose yourself in porn.

Remember Brad's experience the summer he and his brother got heavily involved with porn? To some extent Brad's behavior was triggered by feeling upset about having to spend his summer break stuck at home working in the yard and garden. Brad resented being left alone and not being able to have the freedom to do other things, such as hang out with friends, play baseball, and even spend time with his parents on a vacation. Watching porn videos provided a way to deal with his anger and resentment toward his parents. Porn was his ticket to turning an uncomfortable, boring summer experience into something exciting that he looked forward to. Quite a transformation, given that Brad and his brother watched the same video recording all summer long.

No matter how their childhood challenges varied, we kept hearing the comment that porn was a form of childhood stress management. For example, Kirk Franklin, a Grammy award–winning gospel singer, shared on television that he developed a childhood obsession with porn in large part due to having been abandoned by both of his parents at an early age. As a young boy, Kirk felt rejected and insecure and turned to pornographic magazines and videos for "company."

For Ethan, a forty-year-old architect, looking at and masturbating to pornography became a way he coped with the chronic anxiety and fear he felt living with an alcoholic father who frequently flew into angry rages. "I was a very anxious and insecure child. My dad was a bully who frightened me. I discovered early that I could find escape and comfort in pornography. It was exciting and it calmed me. Starting when I was seven years old I'd steal porn magazines from my parents' room and then read them in my room lying across my bed. I had my first orgasm while doing that when I was nine. I'd go through the magazines repeatedly to soothe myself when the stress in the family was high."

Justin used porn to deal with his own anger as a child growing up in a family that lacked emotional closeness. He told us how he used pornography like a drug to help him deal with his problems. "I was a very unhappy and angry kid. I used to pound on my brothers all the time. Once I actually tried to strangle one of my brothers and was stopped by an uncle who ran into the house and pulled me off him. Pornography was like a drug. I had a hard time with impulse control. The magazines gave me something to obsess over. The fantasies I'd weave about the women in the pictures gave me a sense of artificial intimacy that helped me to control my anger. By the time I was a teenager, I was masturbating to pornography two to four times a day."

Laura, a thirty-five-year-old businesswoman, began using pornography regularly when she was eleven years old to deal with the stress of having been sexually abused. "My two older brothers got into my dad's pornography. They showed me the pictures and read me the stories, and then did to me what they had seen and heard. I became their learning tool. It may sound strange but later on I would sneak into their rooms and look through the magazines by myself. I developed a fascination with stories of women who felt threatened in sex. I had a nightly routine of masturbating to the porn. It gave me an escape from the reality of what my brothers were doing to me and enabled me to get to sleep. I used pornography this way even after they stopped abusing me."

It is clear from the stories in this chapter that there are many compelling reasons we can get involved with pornography when we are young. Porn can start out as something novel we are curious about and end up as something we use to connect with others, or feel we *need* regularly to medicate our stresses and help us cope with upsetting experiences and feelings. Although some kids leave behind their early involvement with porn as they grow up and form real relationships, as we shall see in the next chapter, too often early childhood experiences with porn contaminate their lives for decades to come.

Like most kids who get involved with porn, your initial exposure to porn probably wasn't motivated as a way to get sexual needs met, although it has probably ended up there. Sadly, when children are exposed to porn early in life, it tends to make them prematurely interested and active in sex. In fact, many of the people we interviewed told us that porn became their first ongoing sexual relationship. And our first sexual relationship usually has a powerful, long-lasting effect on our psyche and our sexuality.

3

The Porn Relationship

Most of us don't think of having a "relationship" with porn, but if we use it regularly, that is what it becomes. We may not place a personal ad that reads, "*In search of someone unreal who can meet my every sexual desire whenever and wherever without asking for anything in return*," but that's because with porn we don't have to. Like the suitor who won't take "No" for an answer, porn is always there, seducing and enticing us to start or continue a relationship. And as with most relationships, breaking up is hard to do.

When asked to think back on what led them to their current "serious relationship" with porn, most of the people we spoke with said they didn't see it coming. Using porn was all about having a good time, escaping worries and pressures, and getting a chance to do things they couldn't do in real life. They didn't stop to think that while they were enjoying porn they were also developing an emotional and sexual relationship with it that could—or should we say, would?—lead to a whole host of other problems.

Whenever we don't pay attention to how we relate to porn—what it means to us and where we are going with it—it's easy for porn to silently slip into the role of our "Significant Other." This is not surprising. We are likely to become both emotionally and physically attached to *anything* we regularly turn to for emotional comfort and sexual satisfaction.

As we've seen in the last chapter, when we are young and are first introduced to porn we are often clueless as to what it is and how it might impact us. We can easily develop a serious involvement with porn well before we are old enough to know better. But when we are adults, we are in the driver's seat in terms of where we go with our own lives. Now we are responsible for whether we continue our relationship with porn or move on and create relationships that are sexually, emotionally, and socially healthier for us.

While many of us may flirt with pornography from time to time during our adult lives, some of us become more deeply engaged. Studies show that about half the men and one-tenth of the women who are exposed to pornography in childhood go on to use it regularly as adults. Something obviously acts upon us, leading some people to continue their involvement with porn, while others leave it behind and move on with their lives.

Porn habits often change and shift over time depending on varying life circumstances and personal experiences. A man may be more drawn to using porn when he is a young and single college student than when he is a husband and father of three children. And similarly, when a woman shifts from being a soccer player to a soccer mom she may be far less inclined to fool around with pornographic materials. In general, however, use encourages more use because we learn to associate pleasure with each interaction. And by staying involved with porn we may forfeit time and energy we might otherwise spend improving our ability to create satisfying real-life relationships.

In this chapter you will get an opportunity to take a good look at what kind of relationship you have developed with porn throughout your lifetime. Did you drift away from porn as a young adult or did you get more heavily involved with it? Are you in a process of leaving porn or are you "going steady" with it?

We will identify important factors that influence if, why, and how you relate with porn. This information gives you the understanding necessary to take responsibility for the type of relationship you create with it. Once you are informed, you can then choose which attitudes and behaviors concerning porn you'd like to develop.

The factors that influence the type of relationship we have with porn fall into two main categories. There are *inhibiting* factors that discourage our involvement in porn. They cool off and diminish passion for porn. Then there are *accelerating* factors that encourage use and pull us deeper into the porn trap. Accelerating factors heat up and expand our interest in it.

At any given time both accelerators and inhibitors are influencing us, pulling us toward and pushing us away from a porn relationship at the same time. The critical issue is identifying the factors that are strongest in your own life and exert the *most* influence over you. When your inhibitors are strong and plentiful they can tip the scale so that you have the strength to move away from porn over time. When your accelerators outweigh your inhibitors, on the other hand, you are more prone to stay involved with porn and get sucked in deeper.

DRIFTING AWAY FROM PORN

Let's begin by meeting Jack. He is twenty-seven years old and manages a sporting goods store. Jack experimented with pornography when he was a teenager growing up in a small, rural community. Jack used porn pretty regularly for a year or two, but his relationship with it cooled when he went to college and became involved in sexual relationships with women. Jack is a good example of someone whose *inhibitors* increased as he got older, eventually overtaking his *accelerators* and effectively ending his relationship with porn. As you read his story, see if you can identify parts of his history, lifestyle, attitudes, and experiences that might have contributed to his putting the brakes on his use of porn.

JACK'S STORY

I didn't have much contact with pornography when I was growing up. We lived in the mountains and didn't even own a television or a video player. I saw my first Penthouse *when I was ten, looking through my father's closet for a fishing pole. It was a turn-on, for sure, but it also bothered me a little that dad had bought it and kept it hidden.*

The women in the magazines seemed strange. It wasn't their nudity—I had seen plenty of naked people. Nearly everyone in our local community would sunbathe and swim nude down at the river on real hot days. The women in the pornographic pictures just seemed unreal. They gave off a sassy energy and made fierce, intense stares. I found them attractive and sexy, but also scary. They didn't seem happy or content with themselves like the real women I knew—my mom, my aunts, my older sister, and teachers.

In my late teens when I was still a virgin, I started looking through soft-core porn magazines as a way to practice and prepare myself for having sex with a woman for the first time. Using the magazines was like using training wheels to learn to bike. I started out looking at naked women, but soon found that I could practice better with models dressed in some clothes. I am naturally attracted to women who are healthy and like the outdoors, so I looked at Lands' End–type models instead of Victoria's Secret.

The few times I've seen pornography flicks, I've found them disgusting. The focus on penetration and orgasm is so unsexy. Hard-core is purely animalistic and doesn't even make me want to have sex. It doesn't fit with my personality or my values. Friends of mine talk boldly about masturbating to hard-core pornography. I just can't relate. If I'm going to look at porn, I prefer looking through soft-core magazines than really explicit hard-core stuff.

For a while I experimented with masturbating to hard-core porn and didn't like it. My orgasms came relatively fast and were unsatisfying. It left me feeling empty. When I work at it and come up with my own sexual fantasies, the satisfaction I get lasts longer because it's both physical and emotional.

I discovered that the less graphic the porn, the more it enabled my own fantasies to take flight. If you're watching direct penetration with shaved cunts, what is there to fantasize about? So back then I would look at hard-copy images, and then once I had the images in my mind, I would project the images of real girls I had crushes on onto the pornography and masturbate to those superimposed images. In this way I personalized the pornography and made it more real to me by fantasizing about a possible future girlfriend. My porn use disappeared on its own when I entered an ongoing sexual relationship, and even though that relationship has been over for several years, I rarely look at porn now.

After reading his story, if you had to bet on whether Jack will go on to develop a problem with pornography down the road or stay away, what would you bet? Based on our clinical experience, we'd put our money on him staying away. His reactions to porn, the way he used it when he was involved with it, the type of porn he was turned on by, his sexual experiences, and his relationship goals just don't seem to support his developing the need or motivation to go any further with porn than he has. Jack is probably going to settle into a long-term relationship with a woman and his relationship with pornography will most likely go by the wayside.

As Jack's story illustrates, there are primary inhibiting factors that often contribute to a person losing interest in porn as an adult. These include:

1. Personally disliking porn
2. Having limited contact with porn
3. Feeling sexually secure and satisfied
4. Wanting to experience emotional intimacy

As we delve deeper into each of these inhibiting factors, you may want to think about how significant they are in your life and how they might be influencing your current porn relationship. Many people find that by strengthening their inhibiting factors they can significantly reduce their interest and involvement in porn.

1. A Personal Dislike

No matter what the product or activity, we all have our own personal preferences at any given time. Yankees or Red Sox? Plasma TV or LCD? Hybrid or Hummer? Ice cream or apple? The same goes for graphic sexual imagery. Some of us see it and automatically love it, while others of us find it weird, too intense, or just plain disgusting. It's not unusual, however, for our knee-jerk reactions to porn to change over time, but those first gut feelings about porn are the ones we often return to over and over again.

Some people tell us that their negative reactions to porn feel visceral, much like a reaction you might have to being faced with the prospect of eating something you don't like. Others object from a more philosophical, spiritual, values, or political level.

Like many teenagers, Jack found his first *Penthouse* magazine sexy and exciting. But he also had a number of negative personal reactions to it that muffled porn's ability to completely "wow" him. Besides finding them attractive, Jack experienced the women in the pictures as strange, otherworldly, unhappy, and intimidating. The porn triggered some anxiety as he wondered what it meant that his father had one hidden in his fishing tackle closet. Even as a ten-year-old, Jack seemed to have already formed some pretty clear values regarding what is acceptable behavior for a man when it comes to sex.

Other people we talked to were turned off by the fact that porn seemed one-dimensional and boring. No matter how diverse, the plots and stories are usually shallow, and it is clear that the actors and actresses are picked primarily for one thing they do well on screen—and it's not their ability to further a storyline. Sam, a twenty-year-old lifeguard, shared, "I was really turned on to porn at first. But after a few months I lost interest. The women in porn are unreal. They don't look like regular people I come in contact with in my everyday life. I stopped being able to fantasize about them because they are so fake-looking. Why get used to thinking about someone sexually I would never meet in real life?"

Similarly, Bonnie, a twenty-one-year-old coed, found the people in porn off-putting. "I thought it would be really exciting, but porn is really boring. A guy in porn looks like he loves his body more than I ever could. Porn shows things I'd never want to do, like have sex with a stranger or with another couple. The infidelity and mental nonpresence in porn is a big turn-off to me."

For Jerry, a rehab counselor in his mid-twenties, it wasn't so much the look of the porn stars or promiscuity that bothered him, it was that he didn't like the way women are portrayed and treated in porn. "I used to watch porn in high school with a group of guys, but it always felt awkward to me. I didn't really enjoy it. One friend and I would sometimes talk about how a girl displaying herself in the porn was somebody's sister or daughter. It didn't feel right."

Chad, a single twenty-four-year-old, dislikes porn because of how it affects his emotions as well as the emotional energy of other males when they watch it. "I find porn arousing, but I don't like the predatory energy it brings up in me and other men. Last month I was with a bunch of guys from my basketball team and we were drinking and eating roast beef sandwiches at this one guy's apartment after a game. The guy started playing a porn DVD. A group of the players began hooting and hollering out derogatory comments at the women on the screen. 'Do it baby,' 'Hey big tits'—that sort of thing. They were scoring the women's bodies by attractiveness and shouting out orders for what they wanted the girls to do next. I didn't like the energy. I felt like I was witnessing a gang rape. I moved to the back of the room and left that scene as soon as I could." Chad's negative feelings were so strong they overrode what must have been tremendous peer pressure to stay.

There are people who stay away from porn because they are low risk takers, fear getting caught, and do not want to suffer the embarrassment or shame of being found out by someone else. Others avoid porn because they feel it has a contaminating influence, much like encountering a harmful chemical in the environment.

Our personal feelings about porn often differ vastly according to gender. More women than men have a personal dislike of porn. Porn is a product geared to portray male sexual fantasies, help men masturbate, and serve as a sexual outlet for men. It often ignores the sexual needs and interests of females. For instance, women's sexual fantasies often involve sensuality and relationships that are based on caring, affection, and commitment. Porn focuses on body parts, acts, and anonymous sex. Regardless of the physiological arousal porn is likely to stimulate in a woman, she may come to dislike porn because it is demeaning and degrading to women. In a 1975 *Playboy* interview, writer Erica Jong said this regarding her reaction to porn films: "After the first ten minutes I want to go home and screw. After the first twenty minutes I never want to screw again as long as I live."

2. Limited Contact

As easy as porn is to access, it still requires contact with the devices that store and deliver it, money if it is not free, time to peruse it, and privacy from the potentially critical and judging eyes of others. When these conditions are lacking, it is more difficult, and thus less likely, for someone to have an encounter with porn. Lifestyle choices in which porn is not a high priority and in which contact with porn requires an extraordinary effort, tend to inhibit a person's use of it.

Jack, for example, loves his job working as a manager in a sporting goods store. He lives with several other male roommates who are more into cooking organic food meals, practicing yoga, reading books, and hanging out with lovers and friends than being alone in their rooms. They have an old television and video player they use so infrequently Jack isn't sure it still works. Jack uses a computer at work for keeping track of inventory and communicating with other stores and suppliers, but he doesn't like being in front of it for very long, preferring instead to be out on the floor talking with customers. In his free time he likes to be outdoors as much as possible, interacting with nature and not plugged into an artificial world of sights and sounds.

For Jack, getting involved with porn again now would require him to go out of his way to get it and find the time to do it. He told us he barely has time to do the many other things he enjoys doing. Porn is not his first, second, or even fifth priority among the many things he wants to surround himself with and spend his time on.

Even in these days of "free" porn over the Internet, financial concerns can limit the contact some people have with porn. Buying videos, DVDs, and devices to play them on costs money, as does paying to enter many porn Web sites and download materials. Frank, for example, told us he refrains from buying porn because he doesn't like the idea of spending his hard-earned money on a sexual fantasy product. "I've never ever been interested in paying for any kind of pornography. That seems ridiculous. I'd feel like I was being duped and exploited."

No matter what the reason for limiting contact with porn—time, money, or priorities—when your exposure to porn is reduced, it has an inhibiting effect on your present or future involvement with porn. It's a lot like getting over an ex-lover—the less contact you have, the easier it is to move on with your life.

3. Sexually Secure and Satisfied

Many people who watch porn experience feelings of sexual arousal that flood their bodies with intense sensations and stimulate a desire for sexual release. But this type of fantasy-oriented, product-driven sexual experience does not appeal to everyone. People who thoroughly enjoy sex with their current partner, or those who feel good about their non-porn masturbation practices are less likely to feel a need or desire for pornography. In our counseling work we've noticed that one of the things many people who *do not* cultivate an ongoing relationship with porn have in common is that they feel secure and confident about themselves sexually.

Take Jeff, for example, a forty-five-year-old small business owner who has been married for twenty years. He shared, "When I was in my twenties, I was curious about pornography, because I wanted to know what different types of women looked like naked, and how different women behaved when sexually aroused. I also wanted to discover the different types of sex acts that I could explore with my wife. As time went by, however, my curiosity about pornography dissipated. I think that happened because I was so completely fulfilled in my sex life with my wife. I experienced her accepting me and enjoying me sexually. We have really good communication, and I can explore my curiosity about sex with her without feeling bad or ashamed. And, I can experience things sexually with her that I could never get through pornography: the smell of her, the feel of her, and the body-to-body contact. It turns me on to experience her sexual arousal and enjoyment. Also, when I masturbate, I prefer to fantasize about a great sexual experience I've had with my wife in the past, or something I'd like to experience with her in the future. Looking at porn puts images in my head that get in the way of what I already enjoy and am satisfied with. I just don't want that!"

Like Jeff, we heard from a number of people that their porn use disappeared on its own as soon as they became more sexually experienced and secure. This is what is happening for Jack, the sporting goods manager, as he gains real-life experience in a sexual relationship. His porn "training wheels" are no longer necessary. He now prefers sexual self-pleasuring that doesn't involve pornography. His real sexual experiences have replaced porn as fodder for his erotic imagination. He has his own past experiences and more realistic future imaginings to draw upon for sexual stimulation.

Thirty-three-year-old Phil told us how his desire to be present in his own experience clashed with the fantasy world of porn that didn't involve him. "I dislike how porn takes me *outside* of myself. For me the most pleasurable sex happens when I'm *inside* myself—aware of my sensations and my own sexual thoughts. I avoid porn for selfish reasons. I want control over my own sexual experience."

The feeling that porn offers an inferior version of sex is central to why some people give up porn when they move beyond adolescence and their early twenties. For some, experiencing the sensual and immediate pleasures of sexuality with another person immediately makes porn an unsatisfying substitute for the real thing.

4. Wanting Emotional Intimacy

The desire to be in a close, meaningful sexual relationship can work as a strong deterrent to getting regularly or heavily involved with porn. It doesn't take viewing much porn as an adult to realize that it doesn't place value on or portray intimate and committed sexual relationships. As a writer for the group *Men Against Pornography* wrote, "Pornography, many men find, actually prevents intimacy between people. Even though it seems to 'turn you on,' it actually encourages you to 'shut off' those feelings that help you feel really close to someone."

Phil's interest in sex with a real life partner contributed to his moving away from porn. "Sex is always best when I'm with a lover. For me sex has always been something sacred. It's private. When I'm with a partner I want to be fully present and relating well *with her*."

Richard, a twenty-eight-year-old waiter, also values intimacy with a partner. He became aware of how porn can work against emotional closeness one evening when he and his girlfriend watched some porn together. He told us, "It was a real hot movie. We got very aroused and started making love about halfway through. The images from the movie kept replaying in my head even as I was touching my girlfriend. The sex was intense, but mentally we were each off in this other world. As arousing as it was, we felt we had just *used* each other for physical release. I missed the kind of closeness we share when we are making love and it is just the two of us in the bed, *and* in my mental awareness." Richard said that the memory of this event helps squelch any desire he might have to rent another porn movie.

Max, still in his twenties, was influenced by his parents' close marriage and eventually wants to experience a relationship like they had. This goal of a long-term, happy, committed relationship with someone has contributed to his waning interest in porn. "I knew from interacting with the opposite sex and from having good role models in my life that pornography is a fantasy realm," he said. "It's never been anything I'd want to replicate in real life. It shows no real sexual intimacy or partnership. Why bother with it?"

In addition, Max respects the fact that a close, intimate relationship requires honesty and openness—a tall order for anyone who is maintaining a relationship with porn on the side. He explains, "I never felt completely comfortable looking at porn by myself because of the secretiveness of it. It wasn't that I worried I'd get caught—my parents completely respected my privacy. I just felt bad about doing something I had to keep secret and hidden behind closed doors. I don't like the idea of anything keeping me emotionally separate from people I care about."

When people value and desire emotional closeness in a relationship they may also choose to stay away from porn to honor their partner's desires. Duncan, a twenty-two-year-old college senior, said, "My girlfriend doesn't appreciate porn. And, she's told me in more ways than one that she doesn't appreciate me appreciating it. Porn makes her feel that she is not enough and that I have to seek sources outside our relationship to feel sexually satisfied. That's the total opposite of my reality. She is much more exciting than porn. I understand her feelings, though, and don't want her to be unhappy, so I stay away from porn."

As you can tell from these examples, the factors that inhibit forming a relationship with porn vary widely and often interrelate to one another. If you are turned off to porn because of how it can interfere with emotional closeness with a partner, you will be less likely to surround yourself with it, and thus come in contact with it less often. Similarly, if using porn goes against your religious or spiritual values and you have matured enough to feel more confident about your sexuality, these two inhibitors may work together to encourage you to become less involved with it. The stronger the inhibitors you have in your life, the more likely you will move away (and stay away) from having a relationship with porn.

The inhibiting factors working in your life will be as unique as those of the people whose stories we have told here. We encourage you to do the following exercise, "What Moves Me Away from Porn?" to understand the factors that are working to prevent or limit your porn use right now. Keep in mind, however, that your score may vary over time, depending on new experiences and insights, and the future choices you make regarding porn.

"What Moves Me Away from Porn?"

Identifying My Inhibitors

The checklist below can help you determine what factors reduce the likelihood of your either developing or maintaining a serious involvement with porn.

Put a check (✓) next to each item with which you agree:

____ I lack easy access to porn and want to keep it that way.

____ I find porn boring and uninteresting.

____ I dislike the way people and sex are portrayed in porn.

____ I prefer getting information about sex from non-porn resources.

____ I feel good about myself as a sexual partner.

____ I don't like the idea of getting turned on by strangers.

____ I don't want to risk becoming reliant on porn.

____ I feel embarrassed and uncomfortable using porn.

____ My life is too busy to include doing porn.

____ I would not want to offend or emotionally hurt an intimate partner by using porn.

____ It is important to me to be honest with others.

____ Porn is contrary to how I think about sex.

____ I enjoy creating sexual fantasies on my own.

____ I enjoy masturbation more when it does not involve porn.

____ Porn leaves me feeling sexually dissatisfied.

____ My best sexual experiences have been with someone I cared about.

____ I enjoy being fully present during sex.

____ I don't want to risk getting caught using porn.

____ I dislike the porn industry and do not want to support it.

____ I do not like how I feel when I use porn.

____ I have effective ways of dealing with life stresses that don't involve porn.

____ I do not like having an orgasm while watching or reading porn.

____ I prefer using porn with a partner rather than alone.

____ I value being truthful and open with people I love.

____ Porn does not belong in homes or workplaces.

____ I think children should be protected from exposure to porn.

____ I think of porn as an "adolescent" sexual activity.

____ I find porn overstimulating.

____ I have better things to do than look at porn.

____ The older I get, the less interested in porn I have become.

____ *Total score*

You may want to repeat this exercise every six months to reevaluate the factors that help prevent you from becoming overly attached to porn.

GETTING DEEPER INTO PORN

Now that we've discussed the factors that can slow down or break up a relationship with porn, let's turn and look at those that could *increase* our involvement with porn.

Corey, a thirty-four-year-old computer analyst whom we heard from in the previous chapters, became increasingly involved with pornography after his early childhood use. Like Jack, Corey grew up in a small, rural community and didn't get into porn heavily until after he left home. But, as you will see, that's where the similarity ends. Corey's upbringing and involvements with porn were quite different than Jack's, and as a result of the many *accelerating factors* Corey had present in his life, he ended up with a much more involved relationship with porn that caused serious problems in his life.

COREY'S STORY

In my family, porn and anything sexual, was regarded as dirty and wrong. I didn't dare ask my parents about sex. The community we lived in was so conservative that any type of reality-based sex education was banned in the schools. I grew up shy, sexually ignorant, and extremely guilty about masturbating. Like other boys, I saw porn on occasion, mostly pictures of naked women in magazines that were passed around by my friends. It really turned me on. Still, I didn't usually look at porn when I was young. It was there and I wanted to do it, but I worried there must be something weird about me for wanting it. I did use images from porn when I masturbated though. During college, I occasionally rented porn videos and bought magazines, but still I was too ashamed and afraid to use porn regularly.

After college I began dating Alice, a cute woman I didn't know very well. I figured if a girl shows interest in me, seems to like me, and I find her attractive, then I should marry her. She said yes, but we agreed to abstain from sex for religious reasons until we got married. Alice and I were engaged for four years. We didn't even kiss. As you can imagine, being in my early twenties, it was incredibly sexually frustrating.

About this same time I went to work at a computer firm. I was paid to research and catalog Usenet groups. These are virtual communities where anyone can post anything anonymously. A large percentage of the Usenet groups are devoted to porn. If you are into an unusual type of sex, you can find porn about it easily. In the Usenet group you know that the other people posting to the newsgroup are also into it. I became fascinated with these anonymous porn worlds and the sexual content they contained. For example, I had a little bit of a foot fetish. One of my favorite groups featured the barefoot category. I'd go there and look. I also became interested in sexual photos of underage girls and visited a lot of those sites.

I didn't hide from my fiancée the fact that I used Internet porn. Alice seemed jealous and hurt, but tolerated it. I felt a lot of guilt about the porn and the masturbation, but my bad feelings only seemed to intensify my orgasms. And I justified it by thinking, It's better than being sexually frustrated all the time, or sexual with someone else. *As time went on, though, I turned my sexual attention more to the pornography and less to the relationship with my fiancée. I developed a pattern of masturbating to porn whenever I was feeling lonely, frustrated, or bored. Our decision to hold off on sex, coupled with how easy it was to access Internet porn at my job, turned my porn use into an addiction.*

Corey's relationship with porn took on an urgency and intensity when the circumstances in his life changed: he was involved in a sexless, committed relationship for a long period of time, and he took a job that put him in regular contact with porn, a product that had always intrigued and sexually excited him. These changes were accelerating factors that escalated his involvement with porn and set him up for serious problems later on.

Corey's story provides a helpful framework for identifying and understanding the primary accelerating factors that can seduce a person into a deeper relationship with porn. These include:

1. Associating porn with pleasure
2. Having frequent and easy access to porn
3. Using porn to medicate distress
4. Having difficulty being intimate in relationships

We'll look more closely at each of these accelerators to help you get a better understanding of how they may be affecting your relationship with porn.

1. A Strong Pleasure Bond with Porn

Even though Corey had misgivings about porn when he was young because of its association with masturbation, his automatic reaction to it was consistently one of sexual excitement and pleasure. As a product, there wasn't much about porn's content that upset him or turned him off. Like many other porn users, Corey was drawn to it because of its ability to satisfy his curiosity and produce a pleasurable feeling in his body. Starting with his earliest experiences with porn, he developed a strong association with it as something that would quickly bring him intense pleasure.

Positive feelings about porn are often reinforced by how effective and convenient it can be as tool for masturbation. Marie, a forty-three-year-old accountant, said, "When I discovered masturbating to pornography there was no going back. Plain masturbation was boring. With porn it was just a lot better. I could really get into the moment with the sex I was watching on cable TV. It was a big high."

Porn's ability to deliver appealing sexual fantasies is another reason some people associate it with pleasure. Dan, a man in his twenties, likes that porn instantly envelops him in a fantasy of abundant sexual possibilities. He said, "Pornography gives me the feeling that I'm with a continuous, willing sexual partner who is always available whenever I want or need sex."

In the sexual fantasy arena, porn caters particularly to the sexual interests and needs of men. In porn you just have to show up and the woman will give herself sexually without any questions asked. The fantasy of a woman who wants *him* can be pleasurable to even the most macho guy. Men often experience having to "knock on doors" and ask if they are welcome and can come in when it comes to sex. Men can feel an intense pleasure bond with porn because when they are using it they don't run the risk of sexual rejection or critique.

Individuals who are highly visually stimulated when it comes to sex may be more likely to develop a strong connection to porn. The fact that many males are sexually aroused by visual stimulation may help explain why men prefer viewing pornography, which is highly graphic, to any other type of online sexual activity including chats, dating, and sex education sites. Studies show that men are twice as likely as women to report feeling attracted to visual erotica. However, some experts believe that these male/female differences are likely to decrease as more young females are exposed to the visual world of sex on the Internet.

There are also other aspects of the pornography experience that can increase the pleasure bond. As we discussed in chapter 1, porn has many attributes that make it a powerfully engaging and pleasure-producing product, from the high-tech systems that deliver it to the drug-like euphoria it can induce. People can connect porn with intense pleasure because they have become particularly intrigued with the adventure of the hunt for new materials, the thrill of the slot-machine–like experience it offers, not to mention the ecstasy of the orgasm it can stimulate.

We know that orgasm stimulates the release of some of the most pleasurable chemical highs our bodies can produce. And whatever becomes associated with stimulating orgasm can get powerfully reinforced. Not surprisingly then, people who have their peak sexual experiences with porn, or need porn in order to enjoy masturbation and climax, build a strong emotional and physical connection with it. In fact, one of the reasons some people who use porn when they are single have difficulty giving it up when they get married is because they have developed such a strong pleasurable attachment to it.

If you have come to associate your most pleasurable orgasms with porn, your memories of those experiences, conscious or not, will influence your wanting to use porn more. It's natural to want to repeat something that feels good. And the more we do something that is pleasurable, the more accustomed to it we become, and the less we question whether it is good to continue doing it. Your enjoyment of porn can increase your tolerance and acceptance of it and override other concerns you may have about using it.

2. Frequent and Unrestricted Access

Given how much porn exists in our environment, it is not surprising that ease of access, especially to things that often seem to have little or no financial cost and can be looked at privately, is one of the most significant factors in whether or not someone develops an adult porn relationship. Not that long ago, in order to use porn you had to go out, pay for it, come home, and hope to get lucky enough to find something that would turn you on. With the Internet, you can sit in your office or home and easily access categories of porn that you find exciting. In addition, whether you go looking for it or not, chances are you'll be exposed to porn through teasers, pop-ups, and ads on other sites. You may find yourself in this situation almost every time you turn on your computer, constantly having to choose whether to tune porn in or tune it out.

The cultural shift into high-tech porn appears to be changing porn use patterns for many people. According to a recent survey in *Men's Health* magazine, 71 percent of men say they looked at porn more since the advent of the Internet, and one in two men wonder if they interact with porn too frequently or for too long.

Easy access is one of the major factors that led to Corey's porn relationship. He said, "Cybersex pulled me in. The convenience and ease of narrowing a search to the kind of image I wanted to see were powerful attractions. I could indulge my interest in pictures of feet and young girls. Knowing there were other people on the Internet looking at the same things made me feel more 'normal' about what I liked. The difficulty of finding the kinds of porn I wanted in a store, the amount of time it took, and the cost of buying magazines and videos had served to limit me in the past."

Victor, a fifty-one-year-old social worker now into his fourth year of abstinence from porn, noticed a dramatic increase in his porn involvement when he discovered what he could get over the Internet. "From time to time during my marriage I would get a hold of some printed pornography," he told us. "Although I found it compelling, I was uncomfortable keeping it around, so I would destroy it. This happened several times over twenty years. Then in 1998 I became exposed to pornography on the Internet and my fascination with porn very rapidly progressed to a full-blown pornography addiction. Until then, I had been able to keep my porn use under control. I never used cocaine, but I identify with the observation that Internet pornography is the 'crack cocaine of sexual addiction.' It certainly was for me."

For Todd, a thirty-five-year-old deliveryman, the inexpensive nature of Internet porn is what opened the floodgates on his use of porn. Prior to the Internet, cost issues with porn had kept his use in check. "I've never had a lot of disposable income. I could justify spending $16 on porn magazines on one visit or $20 in a strip club now and again, but I didn't have the money to be able to do that every day. Well, I could have got the money, but my wife would have cut me off pretty quickly. That kind of compulsive behavior was not sustainable. But it is sustainable with the Internet. I used to do those activities maybe ten times a year at the most. Now, I can be looking at pornography over the Internet for two to three hours a day. So that barrier of 'I better not or I'm gonna have to explain where this money went,' has disappeared."

For Brad, the ease of accessing pay-per-view porn movies on the road is what recharged his sexual involvement with porn. "Before my wife and I were married, fantasies of having sex with her took the place of porn," he says. "But about six months into the marriage I took a job in sales that involved a lot of travel. I was out of town, driving around the state. Every hotel I stayed in had pay-per-view movies. And of course, pornography is the number-one-selling cable movie channel on pay-per-view. I started accessing porn as often as possible when I was out of town. My porn habit cropped up again, even worse than it had been before."

Pastor Jim Thomas, who directs a program to help men with porn problems at the Faith Center in Eugene, Oregon, believes accessibility to both the Internet and cable porn stations has been one of the biggest contributors to relationship problems for members of his congregation. "It's one thing to drive to an adult bookstore or porn shop and risk somebody seeing your car parked there. But if you can click on and off of an adult Web site, it's easy to get involved. Some guys are on the edge, and if they had not been faced with the temptation of porn, may not have succumbed. In private where nobody knows and it's secret, that is the hook. That is where these guys are vulnerable."

Ben, a twenty-two-year-old college student, developed a serious problem with porn during one weekend of marathon surfing on the Internet when his dorm roommate was out of town. "I didn't even set out to look for pornography. But I got on the Net and it was everywhere. Something tweaked my curiosity and wham—I just clicked it open. I never had to think what I was doing because it all happened so fast. Internet porn just sucked me in."

Exposure to porn can increase desire for it in much the same way seeing the candy bars at the checkout stand at the grocery store can make us want to buy one even if we're not hungry. Easy, unrestricted access feeds into our desire for immediate gratification and cuts down the opportunity for critical decision-making. When porn becomes easier to get to in our environment, it is harder for us to "just say no" to it. Like the candy bar you didn't really need or want, porn can slip into your life before you even realize what has happened. In his booklet, *A Male Grief: Notes on Pornography and Addiction*, writer David Mura writes, "The greater the frequency of [sexual] images, the greater the likelihood they will overwhelm people's resistance."

3. Medicating Problems with Porn

People who use porn as a tool for coping with sexual and other kinds of problems can easily get caught up in a deeper relationship with it. Porn, and its accompanying sexual experience, can appear to be a cure-all for whatever ails us. If you learned to use porn as a coping mechanism when you were young, you may automatically turn to it for comfort when you feel overstressed or when you feel lonely, needy, frustrated, or desperate. Financial, professional, and marital stress can increase a desire to click your mouse on a porn site or turn on a cable porn movie if you learned early on that it can provide quick and powerful (although temporary) relief.

Even though Don, a thirty-eight-year-old musician, enjoys an active sex life with his wife, he feels he still needs porn to help him to cope with the stresses of daily living. He tells us, "My wife provides a form of sexual release, but that isn't enough. I have to have fantasy too. It's my escape. My wife exists in real life, which is the source of my emotional pain, whereas in my porn fantasies, there is no pain. It's all pleasure. Not only that, but I'm in control of it."

Albert, a middle-aged divorced father of three, still uses porn to escape from daily life. "Porn gives me momentary relief from the pains of life. I don't care about the future. What matters is I have escaped for now." When it comes to unwinding from stress, porn can be like television. We tune into an alternative reality so we don't have to deal with our own problems. As Albert sums up, "Porn is my in-hand, ready-made escape mechanism." The relief porn brings comes not only because the user is transported into an alternative world of pleasurable fantasies, but also because sexual arousal triggers a significant increase in blood flow and, following orgasm, a decrease in muscle tension.

It's not uncommon for the porn relationship to deepen when porn is used as a way to treat unpleasant emotions such as anxiety, sadness, anger, and resentment. Porn became a steady companion for Kevin when he and his ex-wife were having serious marital problems. "As my relationship with my wife worsened, I started going to an adult bookstore," he shared. "Using pornography helped numb the pain of my struggling marriage."

People suffering from certain psychological conditions, such as depression, obsessive-compulsive disorder, attention deficit disorder, and addictive personality are especially vulnerable to developing serious problems with pornography. Todd, for example, told us, "I struggle with attention deficit problems and depression. Pornography is a constant emergency escape. Any time the pressure gets very high at all, boom, porn is there and I don't have to deal with the real issues going on in my life."

Sexual dissatisfaction with a partner can also trigger a new or deeper relationship with porn. Rather than address sexual concerns directly with a partner, a person turns to porn. This was true for Corey, who entered into a four-year engagement that was not only sexless, but kiss-less as well. Remember how he attributed his sexual frustration with his getting deeper into porn? Some people who are sexually active in a relationship like to keep porn on the back burner, as "plan B" for those times when their partner is absent or otherwise unavailable. A twenty-three-year-old man summed it up well: "Pornography supplements my sexuality. I use it as a reserve backup plan." And unlike a real-life partner, porn can become the alternative that never says "No" or gets upset about particular sexual needs and interests.

Jim, a forty-year-old electrician, found that his porn use increased when he and his wife were undergoing treatment for infertility. At the time he felt pressured to be "sexual on demand." Jim said, "My wife and I had marked days on the calendar for sex, several days in a row, to be performed at particular times. It created a lot of tension for me. I had to have sex whether I felt like it or not, or the doctor and my wife would be disappointed. I got into porn then because it gave me a feeling of open-ended sexual freedom where I could choose by myself whether to have an orgasm or not."

Sexual difficulties are some of the most common stressors the people we talked with said increased their involvement with porn. Porn can seem like a solution for people suffering from problems such as low sex desire, erectile and orgasmic dysfunction, and reproductive difficulty. Reflecting back on his porn use, Carson, a fifty-five-year-old former professional athlete, told us, "I think I got into porn heavily a few years ago because I didn't like feeling a lack of sexual drive. I wanted to feel the same genital excitement and urgency I felt when I was young. Having a lack of sex drive made me feel old, weak, and inadequate."

Not having a real sexual partner is another situation that can stimulate interest in and heavy involvement with porn. Len is a typical example. He clearly sees porn as a substitute for a real relationship. He said, "I live alone. I don't have a girlfriend. Porn provides me with sexual excitement and release. I use it as a sexual outlet, pretty much on a daily basis. I expect I'll continue along about the same unless I should enter a relationship."

When porn is used as a way to cope with relationship, sexual, and other life stresses, other coping techniques that would be healthier and less likely to result in serious problems don't have a chance to be fully explored and developed. Porn use *seems* like an easy fix to our problems because it can work quickly and well in the moment. But just like with mood-altering drugs, porn can eventually lead us to dependence and addiction. And if we learn to depend on porn instead of using our own coping skills, we end up falling deeper and deeper into a relationship with it.

4. Difficulty with Intimacy

Another factor that accelerates porn use is having difficulty with intimate relationships. Many of the people we counsel and talk with who have developed serious problems with porn will say things like, "Intimate relationships are too much work," "I'm not comfortable sharing how I feel," "Sex is about having a good time, not about love," and "There is no way I could be fully truthful in an intimate relationship."

Porn can be an attractive sexual outlet for anyone who dislikes or is uncomfortable opening up to another human being, being vulnerable with others, or caring for someone else's needs and desires. Real relationships are work. Porn comes easy, so to speak. As Pastor Jim Thomas shared, "In porn, the sexual response occurs outside the context of a relationship. This feels preferable to some boys and men who don't know how or are afraid to get close to a female. Sexually, males are hardwired to be able to go right from their eyes to their reproductive organs. With porn, they get the message that it's okay to react like that on their own. Porn use becomes a way they can experience sex without the complexities of a relationship."

A primary reason Jackson, a twenty-six-year-old law clerk, increased his involvement with porn was because it shielded him from possible criticism and rejection. He said, "When I'm doing porn I don't have to perform sexually or worry about pleasing my partner. My celluloid girlfriends and the women on the other end of the telephone in phone sex feel safe. The stakes are lower. And, I don't have to worry about being a failure if I climax quickly or before they do. In real life relationships I don't have this sense of absolute freedom to focus on me."

Peter, another man in his mid-twenties, shared similar feelings about how porn gave him the pleasure of a self-centered sexual experience. Reflecting back on his involvement with porn, he told us, "There was no need for foreplay. No sense of anybody else's sexual needs other than my own. Porn gave me what I wanted and I was like a kid who wanted sex now."

Anyone who is unsure about their sexual attractiveness or skills as a lover (and most of us are at some time in our lives) is also vulnerable to porn's lure. Using porn is a sexual activity that allows us to avoid scrutiny by others. No one sees you. No actual human touch or connection takes place. Porn also can feel like the perfect experience for the person who believes the sexual ideal is to maintain power and control at all times. Unlike having to negotiate sexual times and activities with a partner, the porn user always gets to make the choices about what, who, when, and how the sexual interaction will occur.

Ron Feintech, a Portland, Maine, sex therapist, says, "Pornography is a free ticket to an imitation of ecstasy without the risks involved in obtaining ecstasy in bed with a real woman with whom you have a real relationship." Men can be drawn deeper into porn because with it, they don't have to suffer the possibility of sexual rejection.

It's not just that there is less pressure with porn—some people just don't place as high a value on being emotionally honest and intimate with a partner as do others. Being regularly involved with porn often requires that people are able to tolerate engaging in deceptive practices such as lying about how they spend their time and hiding what they've been looking at. Studies show that about 70 percent of people keep their porn use secret. And even when people are up front about their porn use, as Corey was with his fiancée, they often hold back sharing *detailed* information in order to prevent upsetting their partner. They may consciously omit sensitive information such as exactly what types of porn they looked at or the fact that they needed it to masturbate.

Corey never told Alice that he regularly masturbated to images of underage girls. Looking back on his experience, Corey sees how his inability to resolve his sexual needs within the relationship and his lack of complete honesty with Alice contributed to their eventual estrangement. He said, "The intimacy that I needed from our relationship never really materialized. During the course of our engagement and marriage my porn use escalated and I continued leading a double life that set me firmly on a course toward messing up my life, and other peoples' lives, big time."

At different points in our lives, we may have some, or even many, accelerators spurring us toward a deeper relationship with porn. We may be dissatisfied with our sexual relationship, find porn readily at hand, need something to help us mellow out from the stresses of our life, or want to feel more sexual like we used to in the past. When these factors are not equally counter-balanced by the inhibitors we discussed earlier, the chance of a porn entanglement intensifying and perhaps getting out of control is very high.

Once again, we've provided a checklist, this time for the accelerators that may be driving you deeper into a relationship with porn. Now that you've heard other people's stories, you may want to take a few minutes to identify which factors are present for you.

"What Takes Me Deeper into Porn?"

Identifying My Accelerators

This checklist can help you determine what factors you have in your life right now that may be leading you into a stronger relationship with porn.

Put a check (✓) next to each item with which you agree:

____ I hide my porn from others.

____ I lie to maintain my contact with porn.

____ I daydream about times when I can use porn.

____ I am entitled to use as much porn as I want.

____ I have an addictive nature.

____ I am related to someone who has a porn problem.

____ I maintain a stash of pornography.

____ I turn to porn when I am bored.

____ I would like to experience the sex I see in porn.

____ My friends and contacts are also into pornography.

____ I'm excited by the new high-tech devices that deliver porn.

____ My greatest sexual satisfaction occurs when I am using porn.

____ I use porn when I am feeling distressed and want to feel better.

____ I turn to porn instead of real people for comfort.

____ I continue using porn even though it is inconsistent with my values and beliefs.

____ I need to use porn or think about it in order to become sexually aroused.

____ I use porn as my model for how to have sex.

____ My best orgasms have been with porn.

____ I think about porn images during sex with a real-life partner.

____ I like porn that features illegal or abusive sexual activities.

____ I arrange my life to make sure I have regular time to be with porn.

____ I make sure I always have access to porn whenever I might want it.

____ I am most attracted to people who look like porn stars.

____ I need porn as a sexual outlet if I am not in a relationship.

____ I am uncomfortable with masturbation unless I am using porn or thinking about it.

____ I prefer using porn alone rather than with a partner.

____ My sexual interests have become more extreme since using porn.

____ The possibility I could get caught makes porn use more exciting.

____ I become upset at the thought of giving up porn.

____ I have become more involved with porn as time goes by.

____ *Total score*

You may want to repeat this exercise every six months to reevaluate the factors that may be pushing you toward becoming more attached to porn.

Whether or not we get pulled deeper into a relationship with porn depends on which set of factors—the ones that floor the accelerator or those that slam on the brakes—are informing the choices we make in our lives. Take a moment to compare your total scores on the "Identifying My Inhibitors" and the "Identifying My Accelerators" checklists. Which total score is higher? Which inhibitors and accelerators do you think impact you the most? This information can help you evaluate your present relationship with porn and what direction it's moving.

E very day we are either moving further into porn or away from it. If we move away from porn, like Jack, the sporting goods manager, did, the likelihood of developing serious problems decreases each time it is rejected. But, as we'll see in the next chapter, if someone moves deeper into the porn trap and hasn't stopped to look at what is happening to them and why, the results can be serious and devastating. It's like getting in your car and driving, and suddenly realizing you're lost and in trouble, and you have no idea how you got there. This is what happened to Corey. His porn use led him down a dangerous road and took him over a cliff: he acted out sexually on his stepdaughter, his wife left him, and he wound up in jail.

In your relationship with porn, you need to be aware of what is going on and where you are headed. As one man we interviewed said, "This is not a game we are playing. Porn is a fantasy world that spills over into real life."

4

To See or Not to See—The Consequences of Porn

"When I was in law school, I invited a really smart, good-looking woman from one of my classes up to my apartment to listen to some music," Brent, a twenty-seven-year-old attorney, recalled. "As she made her way into the living room to have a seat, I slipped into the kitchen to get us some drinks. Less than a minute later, she showed up at the kitchen door with a sour expression on her face and started making excuses about why she needed to go home. After I called her a cab and walked her out, I went back into my apartment. There, spread out on the coffee table in my living room next to a box of tissues, were some porn magazines and DVDs I'd forgotten about and left out from the night before. This nice woman hasn't even looked at me since that night even though we sit near each other in class every day."

It took only that one incident to open Brent's eyes to one of the consequences of his porn use: that a real woman with whom he might want to start a relationship had become turned off to him, not just sexually, but with who he was as a person. Even knowing this, Brent didn't give up porn right away—he simply decided to hide it better when there was a chance he'd be bringing someone home.

Brent's response is completely understandable because when anything brings us pleasure, we don't want to give it up. No one wants to stop doing something that is fun and exciting, that makes them feel better. Unfortunately, many of the things we do in life that promise or deliver instant pleasure also cause pain, or will eventually. All too often, however, because of our desire not to give up our quick pleasure fixes, we don't see their dangerous side effects, or if we do, we are likely to look the other way when they stare us in the face.

Alcohol is a good example of something pleasurable that may end up causing some people serious consequences. Many of us enjoy a glass of wine, a beer, or a mixed drink now and then. It tastes good, helps us unwind, and can take the chill out of a cold evening or a cold conversation. Like porn, alcohol is easy to obtain, comes in various flavors and strengths, and may be consumed privately or in more social settings. We also have a hard time avoiding it. Alcohol ads are everywhere encouraging us to drink, and alcoholic beverages are available in many venues.

But if we start imbibing regularly, we may start to notice that drinking alcohol produces some unpleasant side effects. One too many and our speech may start to slur or we may say something stupid in a conversation. Our judgment may become impaired and we may lose motor control, causing us to forget things, stumble when we try to walk, and be unable to drive our own car. Chronic alcohol abuse can negatively affect our ability to follow through on family, job, or social responsibilities, and it can tear apart an intimate relationship. In extreme cases, when someone becomes a hardened drinker, they may find themselves with serious physical problems such as liver disease, sexual problems, or addiction-related chemical dependency. They may also find themselves in jail for driving while under the influence.

But that cold bottle of beer or glass of wine can be hard to give up when we've become accustomed to it. Many people have built drinking into their daily routines and menu choices—a cocktail every day after work, and a beer with a slice of pizza or a hot dog. When we are faced with the realization that alcohol is causing problems, it's easy and natural to rationalize our use and deny the problem. Eventually, however, if we continue to ignore what's really going on, the problems compound and become increasingly difficult to tune out.

When you're a porn user, you're likely to have similar experiences of ignoring the problem and then rationalizing your use and denying the consequences. At first all you may see are the positive things porn brings to your life. Subconsciously, you may have an inkling that your behavior might cause trouble down the road, but when you're having fun right here right now, it's hard to consider what could be waiting for you around the bend.

But as with alcohol, eventually porn use can cause problems and get out of hand. At that point, it becomes more difficult to hide our problems from ourselves or anyone close to us, no matter how hard we try. For most porn users we've talked to, eventually things get out of control. Unfortunately, most porn users are unaware of how destructive their behavior really is until they're already deep into the porn trap. By then the damage is done.

Rob, forty-three years old, had masturbated to porn every day since he was fourteen. He provides a good example of how oblivious we can be about the consequences of our porn actions. He told us, "Porn didn't appear dangerous like other 'bad habits.' With gambling, you eventually run out of money. With drug use you eventually degenerate, can't function, and become physically ill. Porn didn't impair my driving or do things like that. I didn't see it as consequential. There were limited physical side effects. So porn didn't concern me. I wasn't worried about it. When my life began to fall apart because of my porn habit, no one saw it coming—least of all me."

In this chapter, we will identify the most common problems caused by adult porn use, explain why these problems can be so difficult to see, and discuss the ways porn users rationalize their behavior even after they realize porn is causing them trouble. Through the stories of porn users and those who have stopped using porn because of its negative consequences, we hope to help you get a better understanding of how porn use can cause serious physical, emotional, relationship, sexual, and career problems.

THE NEGATIVE CONSEQUENCES OF USING PORNOGRAPHY

People who are involved with pornography may be basking in the sunshine of instant pleasure, but like storm clouds, problems are brewing just over the horizon. In the words of people who have struggled to move beyond the porn trap, the nine most common serious negative consequences of using porn are:

1. "I'm easily irritated and depressed."
2. "I've become isolated from other people."
3. "I'm sexually objectifying people."
4. "I'm neglecting important areas of my life."
5. "I'm having problems with sex."
6. "I'm making my partner unhappy."
7. "I'm feeling bad about myself."
8. "I'm engaging in risky and dangerous behavior."
9. "I've become addicted to porn."

Any one of these nine consequences can indicate a significant problem with porn, but the more consequences you experience, the more deeply entrenched and challenging your porn problems are likely to be. As you can see from the list above, the consequences of porn occur on both personal and interpersonal levels. Porn can affect how we think and feel inside as well as how we interact and behave with others. And we can encounter serious problems with porn without being "addicted" to it.

Let's look closer at each of these consequences.

1. "I'm Easily Irritated and Depressed"

Whenever we do something privately that we feel bad about, it has an impact on our emotions, even if we're not aware of why we're feeling what we're feeling. Becoming easily irritated at even little things and eventually becoming depressed are common occurrences for regular porn users. No matter how much pleasure they may be getting from their porn use, most users understand—at least subconsciously—that many people disapprove of their behavior. Most porn users keep their activities a secret, because they know that society as a whole labels people who use porn regularly as sexually "perverted" or "predatory."

Even when we can "get away with it" and no one is the wiser, using porn as a sexual outlet often creates conflicting feelings that can start to take a toll on the user on an unconscious, internal level. We may experience a strong desire for it, but also be ashamed of doing it. When this happens, we are pulled in two different directions and our physiological and emotional systems get stressed. We can only endure this tug-of-war of emotions for so long before the consequences of our porn use spill out into other parts of our lives. Because we don't usually feel comfortable talking to loved ones, friends, coworkers, or even health-care professionals about these conflicting feelings we're having, many of us suffer in silence—getting angrier, more anxious, and more deeply depressed.

Many former porn users tell us that as their porn use continued, they began feeling easily irritated and annoyed with things that in the past had been easy to ignore or be patient with. The driver behind us becomes an "asshole," our significant other is "stupid" for forgetting to pick up an item at the store, our children are "annoying." Without realizing it, we project our upset and negative feelings about our porn behavior onto situations and people in our lives.

Bill, who is in his mid-thirties, said, "When I was using pornography heavily, I was angry a lot. I was not together professionally and I was not together personally. I'd compare myself to my wife and felt very inferior. She seemed so productive in her life. I was frustrated with my shortcomings, always defensive about things, and afraid of being caught. My feelings manifested as anger. I had a short fuse, a hair-trigger reaction to almost anything that bothered me. It was a huge side effect and I really wasn't aware of its connection to porn at the time."

As unpleasant as negative emotions such as anger and anxiety are, they can also lead to increased porn use. Negative emotional outbursts create distance between a porn user and whomever he fears might discover his porn use. Many porn users take the old cliché "the best defense is a good offense" to heart. They strike out at others as a way to deflect attention away from themselves and their secret activities with porn. In addition, they may pick fights, harbor resentments, or hold grudges in order to justify acting out with more porn. Rudy, a former porn user, said, "While I was still using pornography, I was a very angry person— verbally abusive, mean, and controlling. My wife and I fought all the time. Then I'd go comfort myself by using porn and telling myself *she* drove me to it."

Porn users also often feel angry when they discover just how hooked they have become on porn. Anger can unconsciously be used to mask their underlying feelings of shame and embarrassment at not being able to get the porn images out of their minds or stay away from using it. Keith, a father in his early thirties, told us, "I thought when I got married the porn would stop. Well, it stopped for a few months. Then I figured it would stop when I had my first child. Again, it stopped but only for a few more months. And when we had our second child, same thing. With each failure my anger only increased. I snapped at everything that moved."

While some people like Keith show their anger externally, others internalize it and their anger turns into depression. Rather than get upset with others, a porn user may turn his feelings of disappointment and hopelessness against himself. Depression is also very common whenever we feel trapped in a situation that is causing us stress but can't see a way out or can't manage to do what it takes to get ourselves out. For some people, when depression and hopelessness persist for long periods of time, they may begin to entertain thoughts of suicide as well.

Unfortunately, porn doesn't come with warning labels and it can take a long time to make the connection between porn use and these negative emotional responses. Corey told us, "In the past, I didn't associate the long-term effects I was experiencing to the behavior of out-of-control porn viewing. For example, I felt fatigued a lot. Lack of energy for me is a major indicator of depression. Instead of seeing it as related to my compulsive use of porn, I attributed it to not eating right and having other health problems. I don't think I even thought about my lack of energy and depression as possibly being related to porn use until I went to prison and actually experienced relief of some of my symptoms."

Ideally, when negative emotions such as depression, anger, and anxiety surface, we can become motivated to get help and make important life changes. Sometimes, however, people respond to their unpleasant feelings by turning even more to porn, their "drug of choice" for soothing emotional distress. Porn works, but only temporarily. In the long run it just fuels more feelings of anger and depression, and it sucks the porn user further down into their emotional suffering.

2. *"I've Become Isolated from Other People"*

While regular porn use doesn't require you to live your life in a cave, away from other people, on some level it can feel a lot like that. Many porn users tell us that one of the worst side effects of porn is how lonely and isolated from the important people in their lives they have become. This consequence of porn is ironic given that our early curiosities about it often involve a desire to vicariously reach out and touch someone. Porn users are often shocked to discover that what they thought were fun visits to a fantasy world could actually in time make it difficult, if not impossible, for them to maintain close and genuine loving connections with real people.

Regular porn use is isolating because it involves tuning out and turning away from other people. Porn users often talk about how they have taught themselves to "compartmentalize" their porn use—separate it off from their real life and access it at times when they are alone. As one man said, "My porn use is not part of my real life. It's just a little something I do on the side for entertainment and sexual relief. It doesn't have anything to do with the rest of my life or my relationships." Problems arise because maintaining a secret "compartment" for porn means you have to be secretive and dishonest with others. Habitual porn users automatically and instinctively pull away from others in order to hide and maintain their behavior. Given this dynamic, it is easy for porn users to start choosing porn over people.

Finding time alone with porn and searching out porn that "does the trick" drains time, attention, and energy that might otherwise be spent in social activities or with an intimate partner. Simon, a college foreign exchange student, told us that he'd often spend his Saturday nights alone in his dorm room in front of his computer looking at the "coed porn" sites instead of going out with friends to events and parties on campus.

Anyone who spends a lot of time online eventually feels lonelier and more isolated from the real world. Technology may be one of the major reasons that Americans have on average only two close friends, down from three in 1985, before the Internet influenced so many of our lives. Being hooked on Internet porn interferes with developing close, meaningful relationships, including relationships that are physically intimate and mutually sexually satisfying. This is an important issue because genuine, personal, face-to-face connection is a basic need for all humans.

Porn users may be fearful and anxious about building new relationships. What if that new friend or lover judges them for their porn use? What if they reach out to someone only to be rejected? What if they can only have an intimate relationship if they agree to stop using porn? Worries about socializing with others can lead to an isolating nervousness. One former porn user explains, "As long as I was doing pornography I was unable to have an intimate relationship, either a sexual relationship or even a friendship. I felt guilty about using pornography and masturbating all the time. My relationships only went so deep. I didn't want to make good friends or get involved with anyone who might expect me to be totally honest with them about what I was really doing in my life. I had too many guilty secrets."

For Len, a thirty-three-year-old man, porn has become a roadblock that is stopping him from meeting someone and getting sexually involved with a partner. "Porn actually makes it more difficult for me to find a relationship. It gives me a ready source of release and gratification. I don't have to deal with the fear and difficulty of meeting new people and trying to connect."

Another way porn use can isolate a person is by teaching an approach to relationships that turns other people off. Using porn regularly can cause you to become increasingly self-centered. After all, when you're in a relationship with porn, it's all about you. Porn also plants and reinforces the idea that when it comes to sex and relationships, power and control are more important than empathy and caring. If you regularly use porn, especially during the years in which you could be learning the crucial skills that enable you to be empathetic, caring, sensitive, and loving, you can become emotionally stunted when it comes to interpersonal intimacy. Sex with your partner can become "porn sex" rather than an intimate, loving connection.

As a sexual "partner," porn can be very possessive. It seduces you to be alone with it, and limits your ability to experience intimacy in a loving relationship with a real sexual partner.

3. "I'm Sexually Objectifying People"

"I am looking at you right now in a sexual way whether you like it or not. Never mind the fact that I don't know your name, care to know your name, or have any idea who you are. I don't really care about you. You serve as an object for my sexual pleasure. I only care about how sexually aroused you can make me feel." This is how a former porn user describes the way he used to look at people when he was heavily into porn.

We refer to this process as "pornifying" someone. It involves looking at people in a sexual way and essentially turning them into a character in a live ongoing porn production. Pornifying is a form of sexual objectification that tries to turn real life and real people into the same kind of fantasy that is portrayed in pornography. The more we look at porn and get sexually aroused by it, the more likely we are to experience the consequence of pornifying people in real life.

Martha, a middle-aged artist, told us that she became concerned with how her porn use was affecting her when she realized how much she was pornifying the people in her life. "It's more than merely noticing attractive people," she said. "I'd go for a run in the park and reflexively scrutinize everyone I saw as to how sexually stimulating they were to me. I felt like an alcoholic who couldn't go to a sports game, enter a restaurant, or a grocery store without sampling the booze. A guy might be praying in church, and I'd wonder how exciting he would be without his clothes on. I'd do it even when I didn't want to be thinking of someone this way."

Not only can pornifying distract you from your real life, it can also turn you off to potential intimate partners. The dating pool becomes really limited when you're only willing to relate with someone who looks and acts like a porn star. Zane, a college senior, said, "The girls on the computer are so hot. Their bodies are perfect. I've spent many hours fantasizing about being with them. But lately, it seems like I can't accept imperfection in the women I meet. I'll start talking with a really nice girl at a bar. She's cute and has a great sense of humor, but my interest only goes so far. She's not a 'ten.' She has flaws. Her boobs are too small, her waist too thick, or her thighs too wide. I know it's wrong to be rejecting women because they don't look like the image of the supermodel girls I find sexy. Porn has created a huge gap between the kind of woman I enjoy being with and the kind of woman I actually desire sexually."

Randy, a twenty-six-year-old man, explained how years of pornifying women stymied his efforts at developing a relationship with a real woman. Porn use left him lacking in skills necessary for making friends with women and showing them respect. He said, "I treated women as sex things. If she turned me on I'd talk with her; if she didn't, I would ignore her. Most girls were turned off by my porn-inspired advances. I couldn't appreciate a girl for being cute without seeing her as a possible sexual conquest. I didn't realize there is a big difference between *using* someone for sex and *sharing* a sexual experience with them. Porn made it impossible for me to see women as people and treat them well. I am very sad about that."

The more time you spend in the world of porn, the more your views and values become about using people or being used, and not about sharing and connecting with others. Too much porn can blur the line between sexual fantasy and reality and impair your ability to respond to yourself and others with empathy and compassion.

4. *"I'm Neglecting Important Areas of My Life"*

Consuming porn may start out as an exciting form of entertainment or a way to facilitate and enhance masturbation, but over time it can shift from being something extra you do on the side, to an activity that significantly interferes with other pursuits in your life. Many porn users tell us that they have become so involved with porn that it is compromising their career goals, family responsibilities, health, and spiritual life.

Anything that provides a lot of pleasure can create a level of obsession—whether it's fixing up a vintage car, playing online poker, or watching sports on television. Because so much of today's porn is delivered via high-tech devices that are always right at hand, it's easy to shift over from other interests to engaging with porn. And even when you're not actually doing porn, you can lose a lot of time thinking about images you recently saw, imagining what you might see next, setting up circumstances in which you can be alone with porn, and covering your tracks so you don't get caught. Numerous studies show that as the number of hours spent doing porn increase, the more likely porn users report that they are having a serious problem with it.

When it comes to your health, a time- and energy-consuming porn habit can really interfere with important self-care activities such as exercising, eating well, getting enough sleep, and even bathing and grooming. Sleep problems, such as exhaustion, inability to fall asleep, and sleep deprivation are a particular problem for porn users, given that many people access porn before going to bed or in the middle of the night. Porn users can literally stay up night after night jeopardizing their health, family relationships, and work. Having a busy schedule to begin with can only make matters worse for people who are preoccupied with getting their daily dose of porn. Rob explains, "I was working full-time to support my family, going to college in the evenings, maintaining the house, trying to be a good husband and father, and getting by on four to five hours of sleep at night. I'd work on my homework from nine until eleven or twelve, then I would search the Web for porn until one or two a.m. It got out of hand with the time I was spending. I'd often have a hard time functioning the next day."

Besides taking up time that could have been spent sleeping, porn can also make it difficult to fall asleep. The visual centers in the brain can have a hard time calming down after all that stimulation. Long hours on the computer doing Internet porn can also result in eye problems, back, neck, wrist, and shoulder pain, which make it difficult to sleep and make life more difficult during the day as well.

Spending significant amounts of time doing porn also wreaks havoc on work and school pursuits. When your mind is frequently focused on porn, even when you're not actually using it, you have difficulty paying attention to your own educational or career goals. One man told us that when he was into porn he became 75 percent less productive at work and it cost him his job.

Corey describes how his porn use stifled his developing career in the computer field. He said, "As my porn addiction got stronger, I started to ignore other parts of my life, particularly my job. I'd procrastinate and fall behind in my work. I was spending three to four hours a day on something that had no benefit to me whatsoever as far as becoming a better person, gaining skills, understanding the world better, or enhancing my relationships with other people. It was pretty sad. I wasted huge tracks of time, and time is most precious."

For Bill, it wasn't so much the time he lost that bothers him about his past porn habit, it was the lost chances. He said, "I'm an ambitious person in a lot of ways, and the pornography provided a very easy diversion from that ambition. Instead of pushing myself, I would just look at pictures for several hours a day. There were milestones that I should have been hitting as a stockbroker and I wasn't hitting them. I kept diverting myself. That's what bothers me—the lost ambition, the squandered opportunities."

Regular porn use can compromise a person's ability to fulfill family and relationship responsibilities as well. As we noted before, porn users often pull back from their partners and children in order to have more time for themselves and to keep their porn activities secret. Doing porn can become more important than spending time with your children, relaxing with your partner, or attending to useful household chores. One man said, "I've become invested in my own pleasure at the expense of everyone else in the family." Another man described how his fascination with porn changed the way he related with his family. "I got into a habit of sneaking porn videos into the house and masturbating to them whenever my wife and daughter went shopping. Sometimes they'd ask me to go with them and I'd refuse. There were days when I couldn't wait for them to pull out of the driveway."

It's not only time that is drained away from the family when porn is the center of attention. Some porn users spend a lot of money on porn, obtaining access to specialty Web sites, magazines, books, videos, DVDs, electronic equipment, and subscription services. These choices can drain money important to the family welfare. There are also drastic financial consequences that can occur if a porn user loses a job because of logging on to porn sites at work, or gets arrested for illegal porn behavior, such as child pornography.

Simply having porn stashes in the home, including those on computer files, can jeopardize the welfare of children by increasing their risk of exposure to porn and the likelihood that they will be upset or emotionally harmed by what they uncover. As we've seen, serious problems with porn often have their roots in early exposure to porn in childhood. And a child's view of their parent can be negatively impacted if that parent's porn use is discovered or revealed.

The spiritual part of a person's life can also suffer when porn is a priority. When asked what area of their lives was most likely to improve if they went cold turkey from using porn, respondents in a *Men's Health* magazine survey listed their spirituality. Not only does porn use take time away that might otherwise be spent in church or reaching out to others in need in the community, it can also compromise a person's core values and create feelings of shame and hypocrisy. In fact, if you think about it, the things we ordinarily associate with worshiping in one's faith, such as commitment, contemplation, and fascination, become directed at "worshiping" porn. Some porn users tell us they feel too ashamed to go to church or express their spirituality in the ways that were once meaningful to them.

5. *"I'm Having Problems with Sex"*

It is disconcerting when porn users discover that a product promoted as an effective and harmless way to enhance sexuality ends up causing serious sexual problems. A fifty-seven-year-old man recently e-mailed our HealthySex.com Web site: "I have this sex problem," he wrote. "I have been masturbating to porn for so long that when I am with my loving girlfriend I'm unable to naturally get turned on. This is causing terrible problems for us. I want to have a normal sexual relationship with her like I used to have before I got into porn. I have no physical problems in maintaining an erection. Sorry for being so blunt. I do not want to lose this woman. I just want my natural self back."

Unfortunately, this man's experience is not unique. Habitual porn use can cause a wide variety of sexual difficulties. Here is a checklist of some of the most common sexual problems we see in our clinical work with porn users. You may want to consider whether any of these apply to you or your partner.

Top Ten Sexual Problems from Using Porn

_____ 1. Avoiding or lacking interest in sex with a real partner

_____ 2. Experiencing difficulty becoming sexually aroused with a real partner

_____ 3. Experiencing difficulty getting or maintaining erections with a real partner

_____ 4. Having trouble reaching orgasm with a real partner

_____ 5. Experiencing intrusive thoughts and images of porn during sex

_____ 6. Being demanding or rough with a sexual partner

_____ 7. Feeling emotionally distant and not present during sex

_____ 8. Feeling dissatisfied following an encounter with a real partner

_____ 9. Having difficulty establishing or maintaining an intimate relationship

_____10. Engaging in out-of-control or risky sexual behaviors

As humans we are born with the body parts needed to feel sexual sensations and enjoy sexual relationships. But for the most part our sexual appetites and behaviors are learned behaviors. Porn provides powerful sexual training. It can shape our sexual interests and the way we experience sexual pleasure. For instance, porn teaches us to associate our orgasms with being alone and lusting after strangers rather than being with an actual living, breathing, and loving partner.

With porn as a model, it's easy to wind up with unrealistic expectations of what sex is like with a real-life partner. Instead of being exciting and fun, our sexual experiences with a partner can prove disappointing. Real sex can feel like an inferior substitute for what is portrayed in porn. As one man told us, "I've spent so many countless hours engaged in solo sex with centerfolds, burning my eyes on countless visions of the unreal, that normal sex with one, regular-looking person feels unnatural and boring."

For Len, his years of masturbating to porn left him cold about the idea of even being in the same room with someone else when he has an orgasm. He said, "I'm uncomfortable being sexual with a real woman. I've always done porn in isolation, privately, with no one else around. The few times I've been with an actual woman, sex felt strange and unacceptable."

Porn also creates unrealistic expectations about the amount and frequency of sex in a relationship. When Alex got married in his early twenties he expected his young bride to be as sexually accessible as his porn had been and as the people in porn were to each other. He said, "I assumed I'd be able to have sex as much as I wanted it inside a marriage. Porn primed me for availability and frequency at fairly high levels. It set me up for frustration and caused a lot of stress in my marriage, because no person on earth can perform continually like pornography."

Steven, a man in his late twenties, was disappointed with his early experiences of partnered sex because no woman he dated wanted to do the things porn had trained him to find most sexually stimulating. He said, "When I began having sex with girls in college, I had to face the fact that real girls don't want to do a lot of what is in porn. Things I found incredibly exciting from watching porn—such as ejaculating on a woman's face and anal sex—just don't fly. I thought certain acts were the norm. Now, it's a letdown that they're not."

Forty-year-old Ethan also ran into problems when he attempted to re-create in real life what he had become accustomed to in porn. "Because of my excessive contact with porn, I had an expectation, a fantasy of what a partner should look like and how she should act sexually. She had to be blond with large breasts and a tiny waist. I only wanted to be with women who could arouse the envy of other guys. It was also very important to me that she saw me as powerful and desirable. Instead of questioning the fantasy, I got angry with my sexual partner, and tried to push her into having sex with me in certain ways. I couldn't appreciate the unique beauty and sensuality in every woman and I had no clue how a healthy sexual relationship works."

Many of the sexual problems that porn causes come about because porn creates an overdependence on visual imagery for arousal. Other factors, such as the sensations going on in one's own body or the emotional and sensual presence of a partner during sexual relations, fade into the background. As Jack Johnston, MA, an online adult sexuality educator, told us, "Pornography use interferes with your ability to be aware of how you are actually feeling in the moment of sexual arousal. The extent to which you tune into an external image reflects the extent to which you are not tuning into your own internal experience. Watching something like a video has a hypnotic effect. And habitually training yourself to be in this kind of trance makes it less likely that you will be able to tune in to a real-life partner's experience in the moment during sexual relating."

John Stoltenberg, author of *Refusing to Be a Man*, bluntly shares his opinion of porn's role as a sexual trainer when he writes, "Once man's ideal of sexual experience has been mediated by photographic technology, he may become unable to experience sex other than as a machine-like voyeur who spasms now and then."

One man we interviewed said, "In order to stay hard during sex I have to keep thinking about the porn I've seen. Sometimes I'll use porn like a 'visual Viagra.' I'll watch it before a date so the images will be fresh in my mind. I have to superimpose the porn on a girlfriend so I can climax."

Besides a need for greater visual stimulation, some habitual porn users also unknowingly condition themselves to need more intense physical stimulation to reach orgasm. Frequent and compulsive masturbation can desensitize a person to common types of touch and stroking. It may become difficult to feel adequately aroused without vigorous or rough handling of their genitals. Normal vaginal stimulation may not do it. This can create problems for a couple if a porn user tries to re-create the same level of intense stimulation to his penis—that he has gotten used to during masturbation—when he is inside a female partner. As one man said, "My wife complains that I'm banging her, instead of loving her."

The sexual training porn users acquire can make it difficult for them to maintain high levels of sexual interest and arousal during sex with a real life partner. One man said, "When I'm with porn I can turn the page, click onto another Web site, and encounter many different women to keep me excited. But in sex with my girlfriend, I get anxious and can easily become bored or distracted. After all, while she is a nice woman, she is only *one* girl. I start to lose my sexual charge when I just focus on her."

Habitual porn users tell us that even when they are able to adequately function during sex, they feel sad, disappointed, or unsatisfied afterward. Real sexual experiences can be a lot of "work"—trying to achieve and maintain arousal, battling intrusive thoughts of porn, and getting enough mental or physical stimulation to have a satisfying orgasm. One thirty-year-old woman who learned to masturbate by watching her father's porn told us, "In order to climax I have to imagine myself as one of the women in the porn scenes I used to watch. I don't know how to be myself, in my own body. Although I can make myself orgasm, I'm unable to be mentally and sensually present with my partner. He's a wonderful guy and I don't think it's fair to him when I'm essentially using his body to get off while I fantasize. I'm worried I'm becoming an observer in life, unable to really feel and be close with someone who cares about me."

6. *"I'm Making My Partner Unhappy"*

When thirty-five-year-old Chuck was single, he estimates he spent one to two hours a day looking at pornography in magazines and on the Internet. His favorite sites were the amateur porn sites that featured pictures of normal-looking naked women. Chuck says, "I wanted women a little bit older, a little bit heavier—more real—like ones on the street or in a grocery store." After Chuck got involved with his girlfriend, he cut back on his porn use for a while. But he soon took it up again, secretly, because masturbating to porn had become "a long-standing habit."

Like many long-term porn users who enter relationships, Chuck didn't see his porn use as anything to be concerned about. To him, his involvement with porn was normal for a man. What he hadn't considered was how likely it was to upset his girlfriend if she found out. On the day she stumbled upon the porn files on his computer, "she was pissed" and threatened to leave him if he didn't stop. This reaction put Chuck in a bind. He was concerned about his girlfriend's reactions and unhappiness, and yet, he also didn't want to give up his involvement with porn. Like many porn users who find themselves in similar situations, Chuck sought a solution that would make both of them happy. He promised her he would stop using porn to put her at ease, and then took measures to better hide his future porn use from her.

But still, even though Chuck had temporarily "solved" the problem of his porn use, he couldn't help but notice that something had changed in their relationship. His girlfriend acted distrustful and suspicious of his behavior. He worried that she was checking up on him behind his back—going into his computer when he wasn't home or digging through his closets in search of magazines.

Partners may not be able to put a finger on the real problem, but they invariably sense something is wrong with the level of honesty and emotional closeness in their intimate relationships. One man told us, "My wife sensed that something had changed in our relationship. She confronted me and asked whether I was having an affair. I told her no, of course, because I wasn't. Then she caught me looking at porn on the computer late one night and asked if I was into it. I made up some story about reading the news and the porn just having popped up on the screen as she entered the room. She bought it for the moment, but pulled back from me emotionally and physically after that night. I felt a lot of confusion about whether I should lie or be honest with her about my need for porn. I think probably the biggest fear for most men, if they are married, is that their wife will find out how weak they are. It was for me."

Sexual intimacy almost always suffers when one partner has a longstanding porn habit. Porn is, after all, a competitor for sexual energy and attention. Partners of porn users frequently complain of being sexually neglected. Fighting can erupt over the lack of sexual intimacy in the relationship. Dr. Jennifer Schneider, an expert on sexual addiction, found that 70 percent of couples in which cybersex addiction is a problem report that one or both partners lose interest in relational sex. Contrary to popular belief, it is most often the porn user, not the partner of the porn user, who is not interested in having sexual relations.

And even when the porn user and his or her partner do have sex, there are often problems. The lack of skills for tuning into a partner's needs and integrating loving feelings with sex can result in a porn user being sexually demanding, distant, and insensitive during sex. Justin told us his inability to be close to his lover upset her greatly. "I approached sex as a very mechanical thing. I had no conception of sex as making love or being intimate in a sacred way. My wife felt hurt when I'd leave her alone, but then when I'd approach her for sex she felt I was trying to force her. Sex with my wife became fairly nonexistent and a major bone of contention."

7. *"I'm Feeling Bad About Myself"*

Perhaps the most difficult negative consequence of porn to "see" is the toll that it can take on our self-esteem. Your self-esteem has to do with your self-respect and integrity, and how good you feel about your actions and relationships with others. If you find yourself thinking "I don't know who I am anymore," "I hate myself," or "I've become a hypocrite," your self-esteem is in jeopardy. As one man said, "I just don't like who I've become. I'm a liar and a cheat. And my relationship with porn has become the vortex of my self-hatred."

Whenever we experience a difficult life problem as a result of porn use, such as an upset partner, a sexual problem, or poor job performance, it's normal for our self-esteem to plummet. Injuries to self-esteem are like football injuries. We shake them off the first several times, but eventually they add up and we can't even get up off the field.

It's hard to feel good about yourself when you're plagued by shame, fear, and a constant need to hide part of your life from those around you. Nick explained it like this: "I felt very guilty on the one hand but also very justified in using porn on the other. And, I figured 'I'm a piece of shit anyway—I might as well prove it.' I was caught in a never-ending cycle of shame, and I couldn't find the strength to pull myself out of it."

For Brad, his low self-esteem catalyzed many angry fights with his wife, Paula. "I had lots of shame and anger in my heart," he said. "I'd project it on to her and she'd get mad. I felt guilty all the time because I was doing something I knew I shouldn't do and didn't want to be doing. The character I had was not the character I wanted, and I was mad at myself for not living up to the expectations I had for myself and the person I wanted to be."

One significant way porn damages self-image is that it is contrary to the moral and religious values of many users. For example, more than 50 percent of Promise Keepers, a Christian evangelical group dedicated to uniting men to become "godly influences" in their families and in the world, report having a problem with pornography. It doesn't feel good to present yourself as a moral authority when you are engaged in activities that go against your values and moral code. As one man said, "Pornography relegated me to being a spectator in the church. The secret life I kept and the shame I felt neutralized my power as a role model and took me out."

Rob spoke of how demoralized he felt when he was faced with the incongruity between who he thought he was and the reality of his behavior. In a remorseful voice he said, "My wife went out shopping with our kids. I said I had work to do, but instead I spent the afternoon online looking at some pretty intense hard-core. I heard her pull up in the driveway and I got up to go help her unload the groceries. Well, I forgot to disconnect the computer.

"Our daughter walked in there and saw this image on the screen and yelled, *'Mom!'* My wife went down there and said, *'What the hell is this?'* I felt so ashamed and humiliated. But I lied to my wife and said it was some stuff that popped up when I was on the Internet. I didn't want her to believe that I would be out there searching for that stuff. I didn't want her to think of me as that person, somebody who would do that. It was devastating—devastating to her, devastating to my daughter, devastating to me. I thought of myself as rigorously honest about so many things in my life, and then I had this porn thing going on over here, in this other world.

"At that moment, a door had opened up into my secret life. My wife was going, 'Okay, who is this guy? Who is he?' Ironically, just a few days before this happened, I remember my wife telling her mother that I was the most honest person she knew. I thought, *Oh my God, I am actually the biggest piece of shit you know.*

Feelings of low self-esteem can also be fueled by the fact that on some level most porn users realize that porn is exploitive and degrading to others, especially women, children, and people of color. One man said, "I know that people are exploited in the making of porn films. Sometimes I can actually see and feel the exploitation in the movies. I see it in the women's eyes and faces. Boy is that a killer—watching a movie and knowing something wasn't right there."

Porn users who are into particular types of pornography, such as porn depicting molestation, rape, bodily injury, sex with children, and sex with animals, often suffer from tremendous feelings of guilt and shame. These feelings make it difficult to be genuine with others, have inner peace, and a good sense of self-worth. Len was drawn to reading stories of parents who sexually abused their own children. He told us, "Sometimes I feel morally deficient and not up to the same standards as the average person. What kind of person am I, given that I find pleasure from things that most people find unacceptable?"

When porn leads someone to develop an interest in abusive and criminal sexual behavior, the damage to self-esteem and self-worth can be severe. One man shook with tears telling us porn had turned him into a "pervert" and "a visual rapist."

8. *"I'm Engaging in Risky and Dangerous Behavior"*

"Porn gives you what you want, but also makes you want things you didn't start out wanting." These are words we hear often in our counseling with porn users. Sometimes people are referring to the extreme types of pornography they became interested in, and other times they are talking about sexual interests they act out in real life.

By watching porn that features activities such as sex between strangers, violent sex, and unprotected sex, we run a risk of inadvertently training ourselves to feel more comfortable with the idea of engaging in these behaviors ourselves. It's common to want to imitate some of the behaviors we see others do, especially if they look like they are enjoying themselves and "getting away with it." But if we masturbate to images of certain risky and dangerous activities, we may train ourselves to focus on how exciting and pleasurable they seem and ignore how disruptive and hurtful they really are. As one man said, "As my porn habit progressed, I gravitated to more and more twisted and violent pornographic images. Material that once nauseated me became my favorite sexual fantasy."

The sexual arousal high that goes on when doing porn can contribute to impairing judgments and lowering inhibitions in real life. As another man said, "My ability to reason took a vacation whenever I had an opportunity to get high on porn." Being engaged in any type of risky sexually arousing behavior increases chemicals in the body such as dopamine and adrenaline that further enhance sexual arousal, as well as create a powerful feeling of invulnerability. And porn users who combine porn with ingesting mood-altering substances such as alcohol, methamphetamine, or cocaine can also increase the likelihood of acting in sexually abusive and destructive ways.

The slide into becoming interested in risky sexual practices can begin without a strong conscious intention to get into the more extreme varieties of porn. As Len explains, it can be just a matter of following your natural curiosities about sex. He told us, "Out of curiosity and for a change of pace I'd read most anything—stories of bondage, incest, gang rape, torture, and all of those sorts of bizarre things that you don't normally find in standard suck-and-screw porn. It's a matter of becoming accustomed. I'll find anything new and interesting at first. Then it becomes familiar and isn't as exciting. If you have free chocolate cookies all day, they're still chocolate cookies and they're pretty good, but you start to feel that something else would be nice. So I look for some other type of sex that's new and interesting, and on I go."

After a while, seeing one type of porn loses its effectiveness as a sexual stimulant and is replaced by a desire to explore more extreme types of porn. The porn user realizes that in order to get the same "high" off the porn, he or she has to raise the shock and shame factor of the porn. James, a college student, said, "I need things that are a little more perverse, a little more dangerous to get the good feeling I'm after. Even just thinking: *This is bad* or *This is really bad,* can pump me up. And nowadays it's not hard to find hard-core with people slapping, choking, cutting, urinating, and even vomiting on someone. I know it's not a good idea to watch that stuff, but I keep getting pulled in for the high."

Looking at a lot of extreme porn can fool us into thinking that degrading, dangerous, and violent kinds of sexual behaviors are more common and tolerated than they really are. Some porn users feel they will be missing out on something exciting if they don't try acting out the behaviors that they see in porn. And because the potential problems and painful outcomes of certain sexual behaviors are not shown in porn, porn users may get a false impression of risk and conclude that some of the extreme behaviors would not be that bad to actually do in real life.

Using porn as a regular sexual outlet can desensitize a person to violence. It teaches us to regard people as objects, not as human beings with feelings, needs, and essential rights. Studies show that people with histories of violence and impulse-control problems who regularly masturbate to porn demonstrate an increased potential for being sexually violent in real life.

Having certain types of porn in your house or on your computer can be very risky, as we all know from newspaper headlines. We spoke with a number of men who ended up in jail for having child pornography on their computers. Some of them were "pedophiles": they desired to engage, or had at some time in their lives engaged in, sex with minors. Pedophiles use images of children as a source of sexual arousal. But some people who are caught and prosecuted for child pornography were accessing it out of curiosity or because other porn had become boring. A few received child porn accidentally. Though it's rare, child porn can sometimes enter a computer without the owner's knowledge. E-mails, Web sites, newsgroups, Web chats, peer-to-peer networks, and file-sharing programs are all potential sources of child pornography showing up on one's personal computer.

Experts say that as much as 20–25 percent of the pornography on Internet Web sites contains child pornography. Pictures of nude children, sexualized children, and children engaged in sex (under the age of eighteen) are photographic records of children being sexually abused. If you have child porn in your possession or on your computer, it is a serious crime regardless of whether or not you consider yourself to be a pedophile. Law enforcement officials do not interpret the meaning of a person's sexual fantasies. Rather, they make their decisions according to the evidence they find.

The location where a person accesses porn is also of importance. Regardless of the nature of the content, it is risky and dangerous to look at porn on a computer at work. The sense of online anonymity and privacy is actually an illusion. Much of what occurs online is traceable and recordable through corporate network systems. Nancy Flynn, author of *The ePolicy Handbook*, writes, "If you work in an office, you should assume you are being monitored." A number of people we talked with lost their jobs because they were watching porn at work, thinking it was "safer" than watching it at home. They became so caught up in it they lost track of the fact that accessing porn at work could cost them their jobs.

9. *"I've Become Addicted to Porn"*

Most of us think of addiction as a possible consequence of using drugs or drinking alcohol. We may not realize that it's also possible to become addicted to engaging in a behavior, such as watching and getting sexually aroused with porn. Anyone can become addicted to any behavior that both produces pleasure and relieves painful feelings and emotions. Gambling, shopping, and using pornography are potentially addictive because all of them can function in this way.

As we discussed in chapter 1, using pornography can change your body and brain chemistry. It stimulates the pleasure centers of your brain and can trigger the release of a cascade of pleasurable hormones and chemicals—such as dopamine, endorphins, adrenaline, and oxytocin—that alter the way you feel. Some scientists have likened the changes in brain chemistry that occur when using pornography to those that occur when using cocaine. We also now know there are significant differences in the brain scans of people addicted to sex and porn compared to those who are not. There is compelling evidence that porn enters our bodies (through our eyes) and alters important biological systems just like drugs do.

Due to these neurobiological and body chemistry changes, addictive use of porn can change a person's primary reasons for using it. You don't just use porn to feel good, you use it because on some level your body has become accustomed to using it and now needs it. Addictions to any substance or behavior can be difficult to recognize because they often develop slowly over time and on a biological level. Just as we're not aware of our cells building and dying, we're not aware of the biological transformations that happen each time we are involved with porn. And for those of us who are more biologically prone to developing addictions, the problem is even more severe. Unfortunately, we don't often discover whether we have a predisposition to addiction until we are solidly under the spell of one.

A good way to answer the question "Could I be addicted to porn?" is by evaluating your relationship with it. There are three key features that are present in people who engage in porn use addictively. Porn addicts:

1. Crave porn intensely and persistently,
2. Can't control it and ultimately fail when they try to stop using, and
3. Continue to use it despite being aware of significant harmful consequences.

*C*raving—*C*an't *C*ontrol it—*C*ontinuing despite *C*onsequences.

Thinking about the letter "C" can help you to remember these key features of porn addiction.

Being addicted to porn causes us to lose the ability to decide for ourselves whether, when, what, how, and how much of it we will consume. The substance dominates and calls the shots. Without realizing it, we can come to need it in order to feel good. As a teenager Rob developed the habit of masturbating daily to porn. He didn't think of it as anything strange or compulsive, it was just something he liked to do and was used to doing every day.

What surprised Rob was how much he continued to crave porn even after he got married and had an active and exciting sex life with his wife. In his words: "Even though we were having sex nearly every day, I still needed my porn fix. Instead of buying magazines, I switched over to going to adult bookstores. They had these little booths with porn films, so I'd pop my quarters in there. No matter how much sex my wife and I had, I still needed the vicarious thrill and stimulation of watching porn to satisfy me."

Marie began using porn regularly after her husband died. It started out as a way to distract herself from her grief, but soon became something she couldn't do without every night after putting her kids to sleep. "Watching Internet porn began as a natural thing but quickly turned into a compulsion. It became a craving, like a drug. It felt unnatural if I didn't look at porn in the evening."

As part of their craving, porn users often develop their own rituals for obtaining, storing, and spending time looking at porn. Checking favorite Web sites for new pictures every day, stopping off after work to visit an adult bookstore, or getting up in the middle of the night to watch porn, can become routine behaviors that people develop and feel they need. Satisfying cravings for porn can become so important that it takes priority over meeting work, relationship, and family responsibilities, or taking good care of one's health. One man said, "Not only did I create opportunities to use porn, I used it whenever I had the opportunity."

People who are addicted to porn often experience that they've lost control over their behavior with porn when they try to manage the amount of time they spend with it. For example, another man told us he became worried when he tried to go a week without using porn, but he could only make it for three or four days.

Len is just recently becoming aware of how little control he has over his porn use. He told us, "Every now and then when I'm on the computer looking at porn I'll think, *I've gotten carried away. I'm spending too much time on this.* I clear off the bookmarks and clear the addresses of the various sites from my computer. I clean it all up, all the pictures I had saved off the computer. But then shortly thereafter, maybe just a few days later I'll think, *I shouldn't have done that.* Then I go and put everything back on. I start over and download everything again from the Internet."

Hector, a doctoral student, feels frustrated that he keeps turning to porn to deal with stress instead of focusing on handling the stress in a healthier way. He said, "I'll have lots of work to do on my thesis, but instead I'll go jerk off to porn. Afterward, I'll notice how much time went by and wonder, *Why the hell did I do that?*"

Sometimes the failure to control porn use shows up as difficulty controlling the amount and types of porn being consumed. As we've discussed earlier, habitual porn users often become accustomed to one type of porn and then need to watch something more extreme to get the same effect. This happens when your brain becomes less sensitive to the type of visual and chemical stimulation porn provides. Increasingly unusual and shocking material may be necessary for porn to "work." Rob explains, "I developed an increasing desensitivity to what was stimulating. I still found the women in *Penthouse*s and *Playboy*s attractive, but over time I needed more and more graphic and intense representations. Like with drugs, I needed more of it and in a stronger dose. My addiction progressed from looking at nudity to simulated sex, to actual sex, to group sex, to lesbian sex, to anal sex, to teen sex. It was just like more and more and more. I lost control over where it went."

One reason people who are addictively involved with porn have difficulty controlling their porn use is because of the uncomfortable withdrawal process. Many people tell us they experience symptoms such as restlessness, depression, insomnia, and irritability when they try to go without porn. As one man shared, "I tried to quit it, but I couldn't. I couldn't sleep and my body would shake. I'd think about how the girls in porn were being exploited, but I still couldn't give it up. I felt miserable. I was trapped and unable to do anything about it."

Justin realized he was addicted to porn when he kept using porn despite the fact that it had created serious sex problems in his marriage, caused his wife to divorce him, and was keeping him isolated from other people. Regardless of how much pain it brought, he found himself unable to stop. He said, "It was almost like a panic in some ways. Porn felt like my drug, and I needed my drug *now*. I tried to kick it, but I couldn't. My urge to masturbate with porn just took over. It scared the hell out of me."

Taking Porn Problems Seriously—Or Not

When the negative consequences of porn start knocking louder and louder on the porn user's consciousness, they can be enough to convince and motivate him to make permanent changes. He recognizes the problems and takes steps to get porn out of his life forever. But this reaction isn't typical for most of the habitual porn users and former porn users we know. They tell us that their initial response when problems started surfacing was to ignore them and pretend nothing was wrong.

It's common to react to porn problems the same way smokers might react when they realize cigarettes are causing breathing and sleeping problems, or creating barriers with friends and lovers. No matter what it is, we don't want to believe that something we've relied on for personal pleasure and to energize us is in fact harming us in a significant way.

For example, Rob felt miserable the day his young daughter and wife came home from shopping in the middle of the day and discovered his hard-core porn on the computer. But he didn't blame his porn use for the problem. Instead he got upset with himself for having been careless.

Rob said, "That incident should have made it crystal clear to me that I had a serious porn problem. But at the time I didn't see what I was doing as anything out of the ordinary. I was working so hard, bringing in good money, and felt I was entitled to use it. I rationalized that I needed it because I had a strong sex drive. And I figured I could take care of everything by hiding my porn better and being more careful next time."

Porn users often employ a number of strategies to avoid looking at the fact that they may have a serious porn problem. They may take a break from using porn for a while, hoping things will cool down and problems will go away. They may change how they access porn and what type of porn they use. When confronted by others, they may deny using porn, refuse to talk about it, or promise never to do it again. Or they may go on the offensive and verbally attack or blame others who call their attention to the serious problems that are going on.

The strategies and self-talk porn users employ to ignore or avoid serious consequences are often effective in buying time. They allow a porn user to continue with his relationship with porn without being constantly reminded that something is wrong. But these strategies don't permanently fix anything, and in time the serious consequences will inevitably grow, multiply, and exacerbate each other. One type of consequence from porn use can inflame another. For example, a long-term sex problem in a relationship can lead to increased isolation and depression. And the need for more intense graphic stimulation can lead to accessing illegal porn or engaging in other criminal behavior.

This is what happened to Rob. He was eventually arrested and jailed for accessing child pornography on his computer. Rob told us, "My porn habit progressed to include downloading pictures of teens having sex. I kept telling myself I would never get caught. I justified my interests saying the girls looked over sixteen years old. Because I never addressed my porn problem, it ended up costing me everything I cherished. I lost my lovely wife, my two beautiful kids, a well-paying job, and a big, beautiful house. As clever as I thought I was, I never saw it coming."

When we ignore serious problems and refuse to deal with them directly, they will invariably fester and build over time. And if we don't address them, the danger to ourselves and the people who care about us will only get worse.

5

Partners in Pain

Twenty-two-year-old Megan woke up in the middle of the night and smiled. Memories of her recent honeymoon with her new husband Jesse—five days and nights of passionate lovemaking in a tropical paradise—flooded her senses. She instinctively moved across the sheets to find Jesse's warm body. But he wasn't there. Thinking maybe Jesse had gone to the kitchen, Megan hurried out of bed to find him. Walking by the spare bedroom she noticed a faint light glowing beneath the door. Thinking he might have fallen asleep, Megan turned the handle quietly and walked in. There was Jesse with his back to her, huddled over his laptop computer, clicking away, staring intently at the screen.

Megan moved closer, looking over his shoulder to see what he was so mesmerized by. "I couldn't believe it," she said. "Jesse was sitting there looking at pictures of naked women with their legs spread open. It was a complete shock. I didn't even know he liked porn. All of a sudden the sex we had on our honeymoon felt cheap. When Jesse noticed me, he looked almost angry that I had disturbed him. I asked him why he was looking at porn. He told me it didn't mean anything. He said I should get used to it and not let it bother me. I felt punched in the gut, like throwing up."

When Megan discovered that Jesse was interested in porn she was devastated. Even though from Jesse's perspective his porn use shouldn't be a problem for her, it was a huge problem. Like Jesse, many porn users think they can keep their porn use separate from their relationship, and if it does come to the surface, they want their intimate partner to accept it or at least tolerate it and not make an issue out of it. It's easy for a porn user to get caught up in rationalizing his own behavior and fail to consider how differently his partner might feel. While Jesse knew that a lot of women don't like porn, he was genuinely perplexed by how hurt Megan seemed. Jesse said, "I was stunned the next day when Megan packed her bags and said she was ready to leave me—get a divorce and everything—unless I could honor her feelings and give it up."

Understanding what intimate partners go through and how they feel is important for anyone who wants to be in a healthy, meaningful, intimate relationship. Porn use and a truly happy partner rarely coexist. This is because a relationship with porn undermines the critical values that are the foundation of a healthy intimate relationship—values such as honesty, fidelity, affection, intimacy, respect, support, trust, and love. Women enter relationships expecting these values to be supported and honored. A relationship with porn signals to a woman that something else has her partner's sexual interest and emotional attention, not her. And the lying and deception porn users often rely on to cover up their porn habit make honesty, trust, and respect impossible.

Even though Jesse didn't *intend* to make his new wife unhappy, she was hurt at a very personal level that undermined her faith and trust in her new husband. Contrary to what many porn users believe, it's highly unlikely that a porn user can maintain an active sexual relationship with porn without it eventually having serious negative repercussions for the intimate partner and the relationship.

In this chapter we will focus on answering the following questions: How does a porn user's habit typically affect his intimate partner? What feelings do women experience as they move from being unaware of a porn problem (or at least how deep the problem is) to being unable to deny the problem exists? And why do intimate partners of porn users feel and react the way they do? Since they do make up the majority of partners of porn users, we focus on women in heterosexual relationships in this chapter. But we know from our counseling work that the feelings and dynamics that occur are similar to what most intimate partners of porn users experience.

We have identified four primary stages intimate partners go through when in a relationship with a porn user. These stages may overlap and a woman may cycle through them over and over depending on what is happening in her relationship and how honest the porn user is with her. The stages are:

Stage 1: Being in the dark
Stage 2: The shock of discovery
Stage 3: Emotional wounds
Stage 4: Trying to cope

Let's look at each of these stages and find out what intimate partners experience.

STAGE ONE: BEING IN THE DARK

Like Megan, some women are completely unaware that their partner likes porn or is engaged in a serious relationship with it. They unconditionally trust that their partner is being truthful and sexually faithful. Most women assume their partners understand that hidden porn use would be as destructive as an affair with a real person. Her trust and faith in her partner, her ignorance about the depth of problems porn can bring into their relationship, and the lengths to which her partner would go to deceive her about his porn use, all combine to keep a woman in the dark for months and, sometimes, years.

For many women partners, however, ignorance is not bliss. Over time, especially as their partner's problems with porn worsen, women experience increasing feelings of inner confusion and distress.

"Something Is Wrong—But What Is It?"

Imagine feeling ill and not knowing what is causing it. Consider what it's like to want a promotion at work, and then not get it and not be told why you were rejected. These are the kinds of feelings that women experience when porn is causing problems but they can't make the connection to it as the cause. They sense that something is wrong in their relationship, but are not able to identify exactly what the problem is.

When a woman is unaware of her partner's porn use, problems with the sexual part of the relationship are often the first to surface and trouble her. Some partners may begin to feel pressured to engage in sexual activities that are emotionally or physically uncomfortable to them, or they may start to feel sexually neglected and rejected. When Debbie, a fifty-three–year-old homemaker, was a newlywed she couldn't figure out why her healthy and attractive husband, Roger, wasn't into sex. "Before we were married," Debbie says, "he seemed to enjoy making love. But soon after the wedding, sex became erratic, and when we did make love, I had to do the initiating." While their sexual contact felt physically good, Debbie was often left feeling unsatisfied. Their sex lacked emotional closeness. She thought maybe their sexual problems stemmed from the fact they were both tired from working their way through school. Or, she worried that perhaps Roger no longer found her attractive and had lost sexual interest in her. "I couldn't figure it out," she said. "I thought guys wanted sex all the time. I wondered what was wrong with him and what was wrong with me that he didn't want to make love."

Some women who are in the dark about porn use first notice changes in their partner's moods and interests. Karen, a twenty-eight-year-old beautician, experienced this in the early years of her marriage to Johnny. While their sex life seemed fine, he suddenly stopped wanting to do many of the things they used to enjoy doing together, such as attending church. "Our belief in God and the importance of faith had been a strong reason why we were attracted to each other in the first place," Karen said. "His sudden refusal to go to church seemed really strange. He said he wasn't sure about his faith. He also started acting angrier and angrier. Up until then, he had always had a pretty gentle spirit and treated me really well. I had no idea what was going on with him." Lacking a clear understanding of what was going on with Johnny's porn use, Karen wondered whether his mental health was okay, and she began to feel frustrated and angry with him.

Debbie and Karen had no idea their husbands' changed behaviors were due to secret sexual relationships with porn. Neither wife saw any porn in the house or heard her partner talk about wanting to be involved with it. It wasn't until later in their marriages that they discovered the truth. In the interim, their lives were filled with stress and unresolved marital problems that intensified for years. Their marriages didn't grow

stronger and more intimate and satisfying, as they had hoped and expected. They felt confused and stuck in a bad situation without having
any clue that porn use was at the root of their distress.

"I Thought It Was No Big Deal"

Even when their partner's porn use is known, some women are still in
the dark about the extent of the use and its significance to the porn
user. They may have some knowledge that their partner likes and uses
porn, but no idea about how much damage porn use can do to both
their lives and their relationship. When Hana invited her boyfriend Ricardo (the man whom she would eventually marry) to move into her
home, she found a box of porn videos, books, and magazines among
his stuff. But as a sexually open-minded person, she thought nothing
of it and never even mentioned it to Ricardo. "I knew that some people
use porn for stimulation, like a sex toy, so it didn't bother me that he
had some," Hana said. "Our sex life was really good, very open and
experimental. I never thought negatively about the idea of him having
or using porn. It was much later that I learned a box of porn like that
is a big red flag."

Slowly, over the course of the first year of marriage, Hana began to
notice that Ricardo was spending a lot of time during the day on the
computer before he went to work in the evenings as an executive chef.
He began neglecting his daytime responsibilities and became emotionally distant and less affectionate. Ricardo's changed behavior bothered
Hana and she began to wonder what was wrong. "Even though I knew
Ricardo had a history with porn, it never crossed my mind that he was
using it regularly on his own or that it could be the reason he was acting
this way toward me. When we were married the label 'porn addiction'
didn't exist. I didn't know that watching porn could be unhealthy and
destroy a relationship."

Paula, a twenty-six-year-old secretary, also knew about her husband
Brad's interest in porn early in their marriage. At the time, when he told
her about it, she didn't think it meant that anything was wrong. "I had
seen sexy pictures in a magazine as a teenager and didn't think it was so
bad," she said. "I just figured porn was something a lot of guys did. Plus,
I assumed Brad was talking about something he had done before we

were married or just a few times since. I didn't want him carrying around a lot of unnecessary guilt so I just replied: 'Thanks for confessing. Don't worry about it. No big deal.'" Even when Brad started demanding things from her sexually that she was uncomfortable with and being insensitive to her needs, she did not realize that porn was the cause.

Hana and Paula were both naïve about porn's negative potential. Like many women, they assumed that porn was something that most men do and was "no big deal." They felt it would be best for their relationships *not* to make an issue of it or "blow it out of proportion." Because they had dismissed porn as a possible problem, Hana and Paula initially had difficulty making a connection between the problems they began having in their marriages and their husbands' involvement with porn. Thus, like women who have no clue that their partners are using porn at all, women who are somewhat aware may also be left wondering what's going on, worrying about the changes in their relationship, and not seeing any solution in sight.

"Could He Have a Problem with Porn?"

Sooner or later, a woman in a troubled relationship will begin searching for answers. She is often motivated by her own distress and by her concerns for the relationship. She may start reading books on relationship problems, talk with a counselor, or begin to discuss her concerns with friends. In some cases, her efforts may lead her to suspect the possibility that her partner has a problem with porn.

Debbie told us that ten years went by in her strained and sexually starved marriage before she considered porn as a possible reason for their troubles. After listening to her talk about her problems, a friend asked her if it was possible that her husband might be involved with porn. "I went home that night and confronted Roger. He went pale and broke down. He told me 'Yes,' he had dealt with some pornography in the past and that he wasn't doing it anymore. And he promised not to do it again."

Debbie was relieved to have gotten an answer to the nagging questions and believed Roger when he said he'd quit. What she didn't realize was that Roger, like many porn users, was so ashamed of and addicted to porn that he wasn't capable of telling her the truth. Most porn users deny or minimize their porn use when they are initially asked about it. "From what Roger told me," Debbie said, "I assumed he had just been buying a *Playboy* now and then. I had no clue how extensive the problem was."

Even though Debbie confronted Roger and he was able to admit to some use, what he didn't tell her was that he was using it every day and masturbating to it. Debbie's lack of understanding about porn's harmful potential coupled with Roger's only partial honesty about his use kept her in the dark for several more years. She told us, "After that night I continued desperately trying to pull things out of him, pulling a relationship together, pulling a connection and it's not there. I was at a loss as to what to do."

Suspicion and confusion also plagued Sue, a forty-five-year-old bank teller, even though she knew firsthand that her husband, Bob, had at one time really enjoyed watching porn. For a few months early in their twenty-year marriage, they had experimented with watching porn videos together before making love. While it was exciting for a while, Sue became disenchanted with it, feeling it got in the way of them feeling emotionally close. She assumed Bob had given up porn when she did.

But last year something happened that made Sue begin to suspect that Bob had returned to using porn. "I got a phone call from someone who said Bob owed him money for a porn video," she said. "I was shocked. Bob laughed and told me it was a mistake, and that he'd take care of it. But a few months later I got another call from someone saying Bob owed money for *more* videos. Come on. How could the same weird thing happen twice?" Sue felt increasingly distressed. When she questioned Bob he gave her vague answers that were hard to believe. "I felt like the wife of an alcoholic who smells booze on her husband's breath, but hears him claim he's sober," she said. "I got really confused and didn't know who to trust. Bob told me he hadn't been using porn. But something inside me knew that something wasn't right."

Even though Sue knew that her husband's answers to her questions didn't make sense, she held herself back from trying to wrestle the truth out of him. "Part of me didn't want to accept he was using porn again. It was just too horrible to think about. I let Bob make his explanations and listened to him promise it wouldn't happen again. Deep down I didn't want to believe that Bob was capable of lying to me. And I didn't want to think that anything could be wrong with our relationship."

Like Debbie and Sue, many women partners of porn users often find themselves wanting to give their husbands or boyfriends the benefit of the doubt. A woman may be desperately trying to avoid seeing her partner as a liar, especially someone who would *intentionally* and *boldly* lie to her. The desire to hold on to a positive image of the partner and the relationship is very common. Janet, a thirty-two-year-old bartender, said, "In spite of my boyfriend's denials, I kept finding evidence that he might be heavily into porn—a strange e-mail account, a *Playboy* in his trunk, a topless female keychain. With everything I came across, I just chose to look the other way. I didn't want to believe he would like that stuff."

In some cases, a woman may encounter undeniable evidence of porn use that makes it obvious to her that there is a strong possibility that her boyfriend or husband is seriously involved with porn. One day Hana came home early from work and found her husband, Ricardo, sitting in the living room at the computer. "The room was dark and smelled like semen," Hana said. "It was really obvious. There were all these wads of toilet paper in the garbage can. I couldn't believe it and I asked him: 'Are you jacking off to pornography? Are you watching it on the Internet?' Ricardo just denied it over and over again. Then he refused to talk about it anymore. I was really upset. I feared he was more seriously into porn than I'd ever imagined. I let the incident pass, knowing the whole subject made him really uncomfortable."

Many intimate partners like Debbie, Sue, Janet, and Hana, tell us that their inability to get satisfying answers to their questions leaves them feeling confused or even "insane." Their instincts and perceptions tell them one thing and their partners tell them the opposite, causing increasing levels of stress and anxiety. Physical problems such as headaches and sleep disturbance are not uncommon. And due to building internal emotional distress, women in these situations may become more emotionally sensitive and reactive.

Looking back on this time in their lives, many women say they were unaware of what to look for in figuring out whether their partner had a serious problem with porn. The symptoms of porn problems are rarely discussed openly in our society. It has been difficult for women to get the information they need to substantiate their instincts and perceptions.

Many women tell us they wish they had paid more attention to certain changes in their partner's behavior that they now see were pointing to the active porn problem. In particular, they would have taken more seriously the following behaviors:

Possible Indicators of a Problem with Porn

____ 1. Unexplained absences and unaccounted time

____ 2. Possessing porn materials or visiting porn sites on the Internet

____ 3. Excessive or late night computer use

____ 4. Demanding privacy when using the television or computer

____ 5. Change in bedtime rituals

____ 6. Social and emotional withdrawal

____ 7. Maintaining a private e-mail address, private credit card, or private cell phone account

____ 8. Vague and nonsensical explanations for behavior

____ 9. Defensiveness when questioned about porn use

____ 10. Evidence of hiding, lying, and secretive behavior

____ 11. Unexplained tiredness, anger, and/or irritability

____ 12. Increased concerns regarding sexual attractiveness and performance

____ 13. Decrease in affection and nonsexual touching

____ 14. Insensitive sexual comments and unusual sexual language

____ 15. Loss of emotional closeness in the relationship

____ 16. Lack of sexual interest and sexual functioning problems

____ 17. Heightened need for sexual stimulation, contact, and release

____ 18. Strong interest in unusual or objectionable sexual practices

This list can help a woman evaluate whether the problems she is experiencing in her relationship may be due to her partner's porn use. However, it's important to keep in mind that many of these items can also be related to other types of personal problems and secretive or addictive behavior.

Coming out of the Darkness

Given how uncomfortable a woman can feel when she suspects a porn problem and her husband or boyfriend denies it and tries to dismiss her concerns, it comes as no surprise that many women in this situation take steps to try and find out what is really going on. Some women repeatedly ask their partner questions about changes in his behavior and then challenge any answers that don't make sense. Other women tell their partner how unhappy they feel in the relationship, in hopes of kindling protective instincts and motivating their partner to be more forthcoming with honest information. Still others plead with their partner to let them in and tell them what is really going on. It's not uncommon for many women at this stage to initiate relationship and marital counseling in hopes that a counselor will be able to help expose the truth.

Due to their overwhelming distress, some women become more assertive and start looking for evidence. A few months after she moved in with her boyfriend, Darlene, a twenty-eight-year-old computer technician, began to worry that her boyfriend had gone back to his pre-relationship porn habits. She said, "He started acting strange. After we made love he'd act sleepy and say he needed to nap. I'd offer to sleep with him, but he'd just smile, give me a kiss, and say he was fine being alone. The napping thing happened several times over a few weeks and I became suspicious. The next day I checked the logs on his computer. Sure enough during the times he said he was napping it showed he'd been visiting porn sites. I was pissed and confronted him about it."

Like many women who similarly snoop around looking for evidence of porn use, Darlene was desperately seeking a way to deal with the internal conflict and distress she felt. She didn't like that she was not being fully honest with her boyfriend about what she was doing, yet rationalized her behavior as better than remaining in the dark about what was going on. And, even though she felt the relief of having her instincts validated, she was very upset when she actually discovered her boyfriend was, in fact, involved with porn.

Stage Two: The Shock of Discovery

At some point the truth about porn use usually surfaces in a relationship. Most often a woman accidentally discovers clear evidence that her partner has been using porn. Sometimes someone else, such as another family member, an employer, or an acquaintance, becomes aware that her partner is accessing porn and fills her in. Occasionally, a porn user will suddenly disclose his problem with porn. Regardless of how discoveries occur, women are usually shocked at not only the extent of the problem but what it means for their relationship. Let's look at a number of common reactions women have when they find out their partner is undeniably involved with porn.

"I Thought He Had Quit"

Debbie was shocked to discover that Roger was still using porn when he had told her he had quit ten years earlier. One morning when she was packing up their camper to go on a vacation, she found a receipt for a porn video rental dated the night before. "I confronted him about it. After denying it at first, Roger finally admitted he had rented some porn videos. I felt lost. Then he admitted he had never quit pornography and had been lying to me for more than ten years. I was furious, very angry. It was just like this hot searing knife had been stabbed into my core. I doubted everything. Every penny that was spent on lunch, was it spent on lunch? Or was he going to the porno place? Was he watching porn when he should have been working and making money? Every time that he was late from work, every time he didn't want to make love—was it because of porn? I didn't know what was real. I no longer knew the person I married."

"I Had No Idea He Even Liked Porn"

Lucy, a graduate student in women's studies, found it unbelievable when she discovered that her live-in boyfriend, Tony, would even be attracted to looking at porn. For the three years of their relationship she had been under the impression that like her, Tony found porn exploitive of women and didn't want anything to do with it. Using porn seemed so out of character for him. "Tony was on the computer a lot one afternoon," she said. "Finally I asked him what he was doing and he said 'government research.' I'd felt he'd always been open with me, but government research? That was a stretch. I got upset and demanded to see what he was hiding. He refused, got angry, and threatened to leave. Finally he told me he'd been looking at porn. I sat at the computer to see for myself. There were swinger sites, escorts, and large-breasted women. He'd always told me he hated porn. But here he was looking at it. Now I wonder, *Are all men jerks? Are all men unfaithful?* I want to be able to trust again, but it doesn't feel healthy to totally trust all the way."

"I Can't Believe He Is Turned on by This"

Even a woman who already has some knowledge of her partner's use of porn can suddenly be shocked to discover the *nature* of what he is watching and masturbating to and the *extent* of his porn use. Paula experienced a major shock when she accidentally saw for herself the actual images Brad had been watching and masturbating to. "I was on the computer looking for a letter in our files and some porn suddenly popped up on the screen," Paula said. "It really shocked me. It looked nothing like the sex pictures I had seen as a kid. This wasn't making love. It was disrespectful, unloving, and cruel. The women on the screen were being treated like rag dolls. It affected me in a totally different way. I remember thinking, *He likes* this? *How can he like* this?

"It suddenly dawned on me that Brad's secret porn use was the reason why he acted so defensive, angry, and sexually inappropriate much of the time and couldn't relate directly with me during sex. The ramifications of how it had affected him and our life together just hit me all at once. Before, when he said the word 'pornography,' it was just a word. Actually seeing the naked women he had been looking at made it real. Suddenly, I saw myself as my husband was probably seeing me: as an object, something to look at and use. Sitting there in front of the computer, I started crying. All of my emotions and all of my pain and hurt in the relationship hit me all at once. I cried for two days."

"My Whole Life Changed in a Moment"

Although not all intimate partners react exactly like Debbie, Lucy, and Paula, feelings of shock, anger, betrayal, and sexual inadequacy are very common responses when a partner's porn use is confirmed. The experience can feel overwhelming. It can be similar to finding out that a partner has been having an affair or has a major drug or gambling addiction. Reality suddenly shifts. Everything—the way they think about their partner, themselves, and the relationship—can change in an instant. And, the shock of the discovery can have a sudden, powerful effect on her emotions and physical reactions.

Visceral reactions, like Debbie's feeling "stabbed to the core" are not uncommon. Some women say they felt a jolt of fear and adrenaline shooting through them. Others said they couldn't breathe and their hearts began to beat rapidly. A number said they felt sick to their stomachs. Some broke down in tears, others screamed and shook. They felt like running away, or destroying the porn. And it's not unusual for many intimate partners to be so upset they have difficulty eating and sleeping for some time afterward. The power of the experience should not be underestimated.

Discovering porn can spin a woman off on an emotional roller-coaster ride that lasts for days, weeks, or months. One moment she's seething with rage and anger, and the next, she's experiencing a numbing sense of despair. Many intimate partners feel helpless and unsure what to do. Some women tell us they were so stunned and overwhelmed by what they learned that they felt completely shut down and out of touch with their feelings for a long time.

The intensity of a woman's reactions can vary depending on her attitudes about porn, the nature and extent of the porn use, and how emotionally attached and committed she is to the porn user. The longer and more involved the intimate relationship, usually the more intense her emotional reactions.

Women like Debbie, Lucy, and Paula, who are in long-term committed relationships, where their lives and dreams are deeply connected to their relationships, are more impacted than women who are casually dating a porn user. Given the time, energy, and emotional investment women in committed relationships make, it's no wonder that when the porn use is discovered, it's a huge blow. But it's not just the fact that her partner is involved in porn that causes the distress—the lies and secrecy that have been rampant in the relationship in order to hide the porn problem are also devastating. Realizing the extent of the deception and dishonesty can destroy any sense of trust she may have felt toward her partner.

"His Porn Interests Scare Me"

For Karen, discovering her husband Johnny's secret involvement with porn was especially upsetting because of the ramifications of *what* he had been looking at. They had been thinking about starting a family. "I opened a file of his on our computer," Karen said, "and it was filled with sexy pictures of young girls. I was devastated. I had no idea what to do. I wondered, *Can I stay married to somebody who is playing this close to the edge of child pornography?* It frightened me. If the pictures had been of thirty-year-old women, it still would have upset me, but my fears would have been different. After seeing his porn, I realized I could not in good conscience bring a child into the world who could be in danger from him. I questioned whether I'd ever be able to have kids. I loved Johnny and it grieved me that someone I loved so much had sunk so low."

Like Karen, women whose husbands or boyfriends are into the more extreme types of porn—involving force, humiliation, torture, or sex with minors—often react to the discovery of the porn habit with extreme alarm. Finding out that her boyfriend or husband is sexually aroused by images of people coerced, tied up, or in pain, can result in a woman fearing for her own safety, or the safety of others.

"It Feels Like Sexual Abuse All over Again"

Women who are survivors of sexual abuse and trauma may be especially upset when they discover their partner's involvement with porn. The experience can re-traumatize them because the way people are treated and the way sex is approached in porn can look similar to the dynamics of sexual exploitation and abuse.

Fran, a thirty-seven-year-old survivor of sexual abuse, had told her boyfriend, David, about her sensitivity to porn early in their relationship, and he had assured her he had given porn up for good before they started dating. Thus, it came as a huge shock one night when Fran accidentally found an Internet porn site saved on David's laptop. "I stupidly clicked on it, thinking that maybe I was wrong, and it wasn't really porn,"

Fran said. "It was. I quickly closed the link, feeling numb and shocked. I scrolled down further and saw another link, this one to teen porn. It devastated me, especially because I had been sexually abused as a teen by men who used pornography and David knew that.

"I was shocked that David was into porn and deeply ashamed for having believed he had stopped. I felt like a fool, utterly devastated. I needed him emotionally, yet I knew I couldn't stay with him. I couldn't think straight and had no idea what to do. I felt dirty and violated like I had when I was abused. I hated him for doing this to me, particularly when he knew so much about my past. I felt lost, confused, dependent, vulnerable, and scared, as well as incredibly hostile, bitter, and full of rage. It helped that he stayed with me that night and accepted my reactions. But given how I continue to feel, I'm just not sure I can stay with him."

STAGE THREE: EMOTIONAL WOUNDS

Feelings of betrayal, disappointment, sexual inadequacy, and rejection can last for many months, even years, well past when the angry outbursts and crying spells have ended. Women often suffer in internal psychological ways that can be difficult for the porn user to see or understand. A woman's self-esteem, sense of security, and ability to feel open and sexually responsive are often profoundly wounded. These emotional kinds of wounds do not heal quickly or on their own. Porn users are often surprised at how much continued suffering their partners report. The length of time a woman feels hurt depends in large part on how well her partner responds to her feelings and what steps he takes to address the porn problem that results in regaining her trust and rebuilding intimacy in the relationship.

Let's look a little more closely at some common ways women experience hurt that can be challenging for a porn user to notice and understand.

"How Can I Ever Trust Him Again?"

When Debbie finally learned that her husband, Roger, had been secretly masturbating to porn for the twenty years of their troubled relationship, she completely lost her trust in him and in their relationship. "All those years I doubted my own sanity, because at times when I questioned him, Roger told me nothing was going on," she said. "I had asked questions, trusted he was telling me the truth, when he was really lying to me. I couldn't trust him anymore. So I think, *Well, am I being lied to this time too? Was I being lied to that time?* I don't know when to trust. It's like trying to tell the difference between one snowflake and another when you are in the middle of a blizzard and everything around you is whirling—it's blackout, it's whiteout. I just don't know."

Like many intimate partners, Debbie had assumed she and Roger both valued and aspired to being emotionally open and honest with each other. Honesty provides a basis for constructing a life together, and when she discovered he'd been lying to her for years, the assumption of honesty was destroyed, making it difficult for her to trust him anymore.

Many women interpret their partner's involvement in porn as a violation of another implied agreement: the understanding of mutual sexual fidelity. The fact that a partner has been or is still in an ongoing sexual relationship with porn destroys the assumption a woman has that she and her partner are committed to directing their sexual interest and energy toward each other. As a result, women lose their ability to trust their partner to be sexually faithful. "I doubt Roger ever to this day had a physical relationship with anyone outside our marriage, but it feels the same," Debbie said. "His sexual attention, energy, and connection—that was mine, it belonged to me and not anyone else. I felt robbed. How can I trust him not to cheat on me again in this way?"

Fran also struggles to be able to trust her boyfriend, David, again since finding his hidden online porn. Previously, she had assumed that he was telling her the whole truth about his sexual life and activities. "Now I'm finding it difficult to believe him and feel safe with him," she says. "He lied to me for most of our relationship, so what else does he lie about?"

"I've Lost Respect for Him"

Loss of trust can quickly turn into loss of respect. It's difficult to continue to respect someone you now know to be a liar and a deceiver, or someone you discover has a problem with impulse control, aberrant sexual interests, and emotional intimacy. In an instant a woman's view of her partner can shift from thinking of him as someone who is worthy of respect and admiration to seeing him as insensitive, hurtful, and frightening.

A woman's loss of respect for her partner can also be related to her realizing he likes a product that is notoriously known for being degrading and insensitive to, as well as exploitive of, women and children. Until she knew he was into porn, Fran had always seen David as a smart and caring person. But since learning of his involvement in porn her feelings toward him have changed dramatically. "He is not the man of integrity I thought he was," she says. "I need a man who values women, not someone who gets off on objectifying, disrespecting, and colluding with an unrealistic view of women. Now I feel he is just like men who abuse women. I can't help feeling he's dirty and nasty and abusive and unhealthy. I've lost respect and admiration for him."

"I Feel Sexually Unattractive and Inadequate"

It is not unusual for a woman to take her partner's sexual interest in porn as a personal criticism of her own looks and sexual attributes. After seeing what types of women her boyfriend, Tony, had been looking at and lusting over on his computer, Lucy started doubting her ability to be found sexually desirable. She laments, "All of a sudden I felt like my boobs aren't big enough. I've never had feelings like that before. Now I look at my relatively flat chest and feel like I have an appendage missing. The porn images feel like poison in my brain."

Like many intimate partners who find out about their partner's porn use, Lucy plunged into a sea of self-doubt fueled by feelings of being unattractive and sexually inadequate. The experience shifted how she thought about her body and sexual worth. "I've always had a healthy image of myself sexually," Lucy added. "When I found out he was using porn and got off on those women, for the first time in my life I questioned it. I really miss how I used to feel about myself."

It's very common for women to feel physically and sexually inferior to the women in porn. "I feel ugly and fat and inadequate next to all those young, slim, overtly sexual women and girls," says Debbie. "I worry that my husband is constantly comparing me to them and that I don't measure up to the porn-queen standard. Those women don't require any emotional involvement or communication or anything. They look perfect and they'll do anything he wants. I feel like I'm not enough, my body's not enough, and I will never be enough."

Knowing that her boyfriend, David, used porn created deep feelings of sexual anxiety for Fran as well. "I can never match the young sexy bodies of the porn images," she said. "I feel bad about my sexuality, because I know that unlike porn stars, there are some sexual things I could never do."

"I'm Uncomfortable Having Sex with Him"

Many women pull back from having sex for a while once they find out about their partner's porn use. The sense of betrayal, distrust, loss of respect, and their own sexual inadequacies and anxieties can combine to create a strong deterrent to physical intimacy. "Even though David and I shared an incredible sex life before I discovered his porn use," said Fran, "now sometimes I find myself not wanting to have sex with him ever again."

Hana lost interest in having sex with her husband, Ricardo, not because she felt sexually inadequate, but because of a continuing lack of trust and faith in him. In spite of growing evidence to the contrary, Ricardo kept denying his porn use and refusing to talk to her about it. "My trust in him was broken down by his continuing lies and denials. It spilled over into our physical life together, and I pulled away from him sexually. Just thinking about his whole cyberspace porn thing turned me off. His sexual world was not based in reality. It was so bizarre, like he was addicted to Pokémon or something."

When sexual relations do occur post porn discovery, they are often less enjoyable and provide less lasting pleasure to partners of porn users. Many women begin to wonder what their partner is really thinking about during foreplay and sex. "To have sex means getting naked," Darlene said. "But whenever I take my clothes off, my boyfriend leers at me like I'm on display. It makes me feel cheap, not cherished."

Debbie concurred. "Now I don't trust that Roger is not thinking of pornographic images while he's looking at me or being sexual with me. I fear that he holds those images in his head long after he's seen them. Sometimes in the middle of intercourse I suddenly realize he isn't there, isn't connecting. His body is there, he is physically engaging with me, but it feels like in his head he's someplace else. It makes me feel I'm not exciting enough for him or worth relating with other than as a warm body."

This feeling of not being the one her partner is thinking about during sex can be devastating to a woman, crippling her openness and spontaneity. "I feel a thousand times more inhibited," said Karen. "I don't want to be associated with what my husband has seen in pornography when we are making love. I get suspicious when he suggests we do something different in sex. He'll request something that would normally be perfectly reasonable for a husband to ask of his wife, but I immediately start wondering whether this is something weird he saw on some twisted site and wants to do with me. I have a hard time just relaxing under these conditions."

Knowing he had looked at a lot of porn, Paula became increasingly sensitive and critical about the way her husband would approach her and act in bed. She said, "There were times when Brad would grab me inappropriately during the day or ask me to do some things in bed that I really wasn't comfortable doing. I wondered what made him want to do *that*. It registered in my mind that he might have seen this in porn and wanted me to act it out. I hated it. It made me feel like an object when we had sex. Sometimes I'd intentionally avoid being near him."

Some women become less interested in sex because they interpret the porn use as meaning that their partner does not honor and respect sexual union in the same way they do. Debbie said, "Roger has taken the most intimate gift he has to offer our relationship, his sexuality, and shared it with countless fantasy women. I thought our sexuality was meant to express the bond of love between us, just the two of us, in private." Similarly, Fran felt David's porn use insulted the special intimate connection she had assumed they shared. She said, "I felt humiliated and shamed, like our sex, which I had seen as so special and sacred, had meant nothing to David."

"He's Emotionally Abandoned Me—I Feel Unloved"

After finally learning that her husband, Bob, had been secretly using porn for most of their twenty-year marriage, Sue said the worst shock now is that she has realized that, in spite of her objections to it, Bob has no intention of giving up porn. She feels unimportant, discounted, and powerless. The experience is leading her to question her beliefs about her husband, herself, and their marriage. "I told Bob over and over again that his using porn really bothers me. It makes me feel disrespected. I don't want it in our home and I don't want him to look at it anywhere else either. He says I'm being uptight and overreacting. I can tell he's still lying to me and doing it. I don't know how we will be able to make this work. He's more faithful to his porn than he is to me. I thought I was supposed to be his priority. There are no words to describe the pain of knowing he is going to use it no matter how bad it makes me feel."

Although Megan hasn't been married long, she experienced similar feelings of being unloved and unimportant. After she caught her husband looking at porn, it upset her that her husband concentrated on defending himself and justifying his porn use instead of being really concerned about *her* pain and concerns. She had to threaten him with divorce just to get his attention. "He seems intent on continuing his porn use in spite of how bad it makes me feel," she said. "It feels like Jesse is picking porn over me. Were all those vows he made about promising to love and honor me just words? If he truly loves me, he wouldn't want to keep doing something that hurts me so much."

Like many intimate partners, Sue and Megan believe that both people in the relationship should sincerely care about each other's feelings. They expected that their husbands would listen to them and take their feelings and concerns about porn seriously. They believed that once they had clearly expressed their objections to porn and communicated how badly hurt they felt, their partners would, without hesitation, agree to give up porn and never use it again. When their husbands were not eager to quit using and seemed instead to ignore the pain that they each felt, the emotional pain was exacerbated.

When a woman fails to get a comforting and caring response from her partner when she is distressed, she often feels alone in the relationship. Fran told us that on top of the betrayal of trust and the sexual insult she experienced, she was hurt most by her boyfriend David's failure to immediately make a full commitment to changing his behavior. "I couldn't believe David continued using porn *after* the night I discovered his online stash," she said. "He thinks he may be addicted to it. He says when things get shitty between us, he stops caring and figures I won't know. While I appreciate his honesty, I feel *repeatedly* abandoned—what I need most emotionally is not important to him. The fact that he would keep doing porn even though he is aware of how bad I feel about it is so devastating. Now David tells me he's giving porn up for good. But I feel like it's too late. If he had been serious about us, and really loved me, wouldn't he have gotten help for himself a long time ago?"

STAGE FOUR: TRYING TO COPE

Once a woman has experienced the roller coaster of emotions associated with discovering the depth of her partner's porn problem, she usually feels compelled to take some kind of action. Often she will not leave the relationship, at least not right away. More often, she is likely to do something to try to control or fix the porn problem herself. This desire for control is completely understandable—it is an attempt to overcome the feelings of powerlessness in a situation where trust, honesty, and fidelity have been destroyed.

Becoming a Porn Cop

A common strategy some women use to try to control the situation and feel safe is to become a "porn cop." She may police her partner's activities and behaviors, interrogate him unceasingly, or even create elaborate sting operations to try to catch hidden porn activity. Most women don't enjoy doing this. They do it out of a desperate attempt to single-handedly restore accountability, honesty, and trust in the relationship.

Nancy, a thirty-six-year-old mother of three, took on the role of porn detective after catching her husband, Logan, watching Internet porn and then learning that he had been into porn for ten years of their marriage. "I became a terrific detective," Nancy said. "I learned how to look for hidden files on the computers. I locked the computers. I wouldn't give him access to anything on the Internet. I went through all the bank statements, the credit cards. I spent the first few weeks driving myself crazy trying to figure out how to stop the pornography use. I thought that would fix it. I didn't want to be deceived and disappointed again."

Obviously porn copping tends to make a porn user angry and combative, because it makes him feel like he's being treated like a child or a criminal and must always be on the defensive. It feels like an invasion of his privacy as well. The partner can also grow weary of being the porn cop because she has to be constantly alert and on watch. Rather than bringing a sense of security, porn copping often increases tension and conflict in the relationship. At best it may give the *illusion* of having control. Because, in today's electronic, sexual image–filled world, it's relatively easy for any determined porn user to surreptitiously access porn.

Competing with Porn

At the other extreme, a woman may respond by trying to compete with porn. She may believe that by acting like a porn star she can once again be the object of her partner's sexual desires. It can also be an unconscious way of addressing her feelings of sexual inadequacy and rejection. Some women go to great lengths to change their physical appearance in attempts to compete with porn stars and models. They dye their hair, get breast implants, shave or wax their genitals, put on long fake fingernails, undergo liposuction, constantly diet, and more. They may also force themselves to have sex more frequently, and try to act more like a porn star in bed. In an effort to please her partner, a woman may submit to sexual activities she is not really comfortable with, such as rough sex, fantasy role-playing, and certain sexual activities that are emotionally humiliating or physically painful.

While some porn users may be happy with these changes in their partner, the partners themselves often start to feel worse about themselves over time, especially if they are doing things that violate their values. And at some point, almost every woman realizes she can't physically measure up to the young, shapely, air-brushed, carefully choreographed women in porn. Twenty-five-year-old Sara said, "I can't compete with porn stars who act like whatever gives the man pleasure drives them wild as well—even if guys are choking them. In porn, women never complain or request the guy do anything different. Helping the guy have a good orgasm is enough for her." Megan told us, "I tried to please my husband by acting like one of those porn girls, but it made me feel like a whore. I want sex between us to be special, not a performance." Carol, a writer, adds, "When I dressed up like my boyfriend wanted me to, I never knew who he was loving. Was it me or the warm-blooded version of his porn fantasy that I'd become?"

Getting Outside Support

A third strategy, and the only one that can actually really help the partner of a porn user relieve her pain, is getting outside support. As we noted earlier, the porn user is usually no longer available as a reliable source of support, so women must turn to friends, family, their church, a twelve-step recovery program, or professional providers to get comfort, reassurance, and advice. Unfortunately, many women are hesitant to talk with others about the porn problem, because they fear it will reflect badly on themselves as sexual partners, or make others negatively judge their male partners. They may also worry that the porn problem will negatively affect the couple's status in the eyes of others.

Karen said, "For a long time I didn't feel I could talk with anyone about what I was going through. I didn't even want to believe it myself. I thought other people would think horrible things about Johnny, because I was thinking horrible things about him. I was afraid it would affect us for the rest of our lives, and I wanted it to go away and not affect us. But eventually, I spoke with a counselor at my church."

Sue also had trouble getting help at first. She later sought advice from a sex and relationship therapist. "I felt a lot of shame around Bob's porn problem. I didn't know whom to tell, and I didn't really want to tell my girlfriends because it felt like I would be violating my husband's privacy and our relationship. I was thinking about his porn use every second of the day and feeling so alone. It would have been easier had he been into alcohol or drugs, because those problems are better understood. This, on the other hand, has to do with sexual behavior and is so private. Who would really understand? It was a big relief when my counselor told me how common porn problems are these days and that I'm not the only woman whose husband is into this."

When her husband, Ricardo, refused to deal with his porn problem, Hana relied heavily on the support of close friends and family members. "It really helped that I didn't keep anything secret from my parents and close girlfriends. They were very sympathetic. Ricardo was becoming more isolated, not taking care of himself, and looking real bad. They noticed the changes and felt concern for him too. We tried couples therapy, but the therapist said he couldn't work with Ricardo unless he would take ownership of his problem and get help himself. I ended up going to a therapist on my own. We dealt with my insecurities and fears about the future. I realized that Ricardo's porn habit isn't my fault and has nothing to do with me. The support of so many strong, caring people meant everything to me. My advice is: *Don't go through this alone.*"

As painful as it was, Hana made an important discovery. She realized that she couldn't keep expecting Ricardo to change unless he could acknowledge he had a problem and was committed to do something about it. If she wanted her life to improve, she had to get help for herself and start making changes that would allow her to live according to her values and her needs.

Whether hidden or out in the open, a serious problem with porn will, like dry rot in a house, slowly destroy the most critical foundations of a relationship. And when left unattended, the results can be devastating. "It saddens me how porn wiped out our marriage," Hana told us. "I'd try and talk with Ricardo and he was just not present. He'd isolate himself and get angry. His porn addiction created an alter ego who no longer cared about me. He emotionally left our relationship, our family, and was just living until his next porn fix. He was completely consumed by it, and my love couldn't reach him."

6

Hitting Bottom

Pornography gives you a false sense of pleasure. It feels good for the
moment and then it just takes you down.

—Rob

What happens when a person continues to have an ongoing sexual relationship with porn in spite of the problems and dangers that come with it? For some porn users, the answer is they crash and hit bottom, experiencing a major life crisis with repercussions that can no longer be ignored. All of the denials, rationalizations, and excuses become meaningless and ineffective, as the porn user is confronted with the undeniable reality that he has been hurting himself and others all along.

Hitting bottom can be the result of an external crisis such as getting caught using porn at work or having an intimate partner leave the relationship, or it can occur internally in the form of a mental, emotional, or spiritual breakdown. Some porn crashes are predictable. For example, someone who uses porn compulsively and experiences many serious negative consequences would be more likely to hit bottom than someone who just sneaks a peak at porn now and then. But other porn-induced events come about unexpectedly. A first-time porn user, for example, can inadvertently download child porn and get busted. And an infrequent porn user's long-forgotten X-rated video can be discovered by his wife and trigger a series of events that ultimately leads to a devastating divorce.

The truth is: *no matter how much you may think you have porn use under control and contained, you cannot absolutely insure that you will not bottom out from it.* Like drinking alcohol, doing drugs, or having an affair, porn use has an inherent destructive potential that is beyond our ability to completely manage and control.

In this chapter we'll present the stories of four people who hit bottom. You will meet Mitch, a fifty-five-year-old former teacher with a wife and three daughters; Hank, a forty-seven-year-old divorced welder; Marie, a forty-three-year-old single mother of two; and Tom, a twenty-six-year-old drugstore clerk. All four believed porn gave them the best, most exciting sex they ever had. And they felt entitled to experience that excitement, that is, until their lives crashed because of it.

We have chosen their stories because they illustrate how people can hit bottom in different ways. You'll be able to see for yourself how porn crashes occur and what it feels like for a porn user to go through one. Although their experiences are unique, Mitch, Hank, Marie, and Tom all share one thing—porn ultimately rendered their lives unmanageable. Their desire for porn, and the immediate pleasures they received from it, tricked them into thinking they could risk continuing to use it without damaging their own lives and those of the people they loved. As you read their stories, you may notice a common theme: *any time they used porn, they were only moments away from one of the worst experiences of their life.*

MITCH'S STORY

Mitch didn't think his life could get any better. He was a happily married man in his early fifties, with three teenage daughters who adored him, and a highly esteemed career as a high school teacher and coach. He served on education committees and boards. Students and parents praised him for his friendliness, talent, and competence. His colleagues respected him. From the outside, he was the picture of a successful American man.

Like many of his childhood friends, Mitch began looking at porn as a teenager after finding some of his father's magazines. As a young man, he would occasionally buy a porn magazine while on a business trip or rent a porn video. In the late 1990s, with the availability of the Internet, he soon discovered that it was easy to get as much porn as he wanted on a computer. He began watching it more frequently and on a regular basis.

"I didn't want to keep any pornography in my house or on our home computer, because we still had our three daughters living at home," he said. "I didn't want to risk exposing them to it. So I started looking at porn at work over the Internet, in my private office alone with the blinds shut and the door locked, long after all the students had left. Looking at it there seemed like a good idea at the time. I thought it was safe."

Mitch considered the porn he was looking at harmless. "It was mostly soft-core stuff," he said. "Naked bodies. Adult men and women having regular sex—nothing out of the ordinary. No kinky stuff. Nothing illegal. I really liked the pictures and videos that had some kind of love story to them where the couple would end up making love. They had silly plots a lot of the time, but lots of sexual action."

Even though Mitch said he and his wife were sexually active and had been throughout their thirty-year marriage, he used porn as a way to supplement his sex life. "My wife doesn't care as much about sex as I do," he said. "She's never felt as passionately about it. That's just the way it is and I had accepted that early in our marriage. Porn is always there, and with the Internet, always available. It makes for incredible sex. It gave me a powerful rush and very intense orgasms. It was an attractive drug of choice."

Mitch realized that his porn habit, as he described it, was compulsive, but it seemed similar to other compulsive activities that were part of his life that he considered benign. "I had to read the paper every morning, I had to watch a little porn after school, and I had to have my late-night snack. If I didn't do these things it bothered me. Porn was the only really bad compulsion I had. And I didn't really consider it bad, just not something I would want anyone else to know about."

One Friday, after the last school bell rang and all the kids had left the classroom, Mitch was sitting at his desk organizing the papers he needed to grade over the weekend. Suddenly, in walked the principal, district superintendent, and an assistant. They all looked grim. "I greeted them pleasantly. I had no idea why they wanted to see me," Mitch said. "Then in a stern voice the superintendent said, 'We've been tracking what you've been doing on the Internet. We know you have been looking at porn on your work computer. We're taking your computer with us today and we intend to have you fired. Turn over your keys to your classroom and the building, now. And get out!' I was stunned. I couldn't believe what was happening. They were treating me like I was some kind of sexual pervert and predator.

"They asked if they could get my home computer. I said, 'Sure, sure—you can have it. There is nothing there. I just did it here.' And then the superintendent said, 'Well, we're going to check every computer you've ever been on and we won't stop until we find something to have you arrested.'"

Realizing that his secret life was about to be exposed to everyone, Mitch decided he should come clean with the people who mattered in his life. "I told my pastor about it first," he said. "And that evening I sat my wife and daughters down in the living room and confessed everything. They were shocked because they never had a clue." Mitch then contacted his union education representative and got a lawyer. They told him he could probably keep his job if he fought the school district.

Instead of fighting, however, Mitch decided to resign. "My school district threatened to destroy me publicly," he said. "They had done it to two other men before me. I got a call from a guy in the district who said, 'If you don't come down here and resign, we're releasing this to the press.' They wanted to make an example of me. It didn't matter that I'd never spoken or behaved in a sexually inappropriate way to any of the kids I'd ever taught or coached. And, the fact that I had an outstanding thirty-year record working for the district didn't matter. They wanted to get me and I knew they could. It would ruin me in the eyes of the community. Whatever people read or hear in the media about you, no matter what the truth is, it can't be changed."

Mitch looks back on his experience of being caught using porn at work as being a "tough, dark time" in his life. His thirty-year teaching career got wiped out in an instant. He lost the respect of his family members, friends, and colleagues. "But," he said, "as unfair as the experience seemed at the time, it did make me realize how lethal it is to have a problem like this and keep it secret. After being put on probation with the school district and voluntarily going through a sex offender assessment and treatment program, I was finally able to get my teaching certificate back. Even though I'm in a new career now, I still keep my teaching certificate with me in my wallet as a reminder of what I went through. I had a problem with porn that I didn't take responsibility for. I just kept it secret. If I had really been courageous enough, I would have told my wife and pastor about it before I got caught, and gotten help. If I'd done that, I'd probably still be teaching now. As it was, my porn habit ultimately overwhelmed and controlled me. It steamrolled my life."

Mitch found out the hard way that porn use can easily cloud your judgment and trick you into taking risks you don't even consciously realize you are taking. As smart and competent as he is, when under the influence of a desire to use porn, he made what he now calls some "very stupid choices." Even though at times he had a nagging sense in the back of his mind that looking at porn at work wasn't a good idea, his desire to do it made it seem okay. He rationalized his behavior by telling himself, "It's only softcore. No one will ever know. I'm protecting my family by doing it here at school." He never had the inclination or took the time to really think out what he was doing and all the ramifications that would occur if he ever got caught. Something about using porn made him feel invulnerable.

When Mitch talks about porn having "steamrolled" his life, he is not only referring to the fact that his outstanding three-decade career as an educator was destroyed in a single day, but also to many other ways in which his life and the lives of those closest to him were profoundly impacted. Mitch's wife was shocked and angry. She felt personally hurt and interpreted his porn use as a serious sexual infidelity. His daughters were disappointed in him. He had to be dishonest with students, parents, and others about why he suddenly left his job. He was forced to find another way to support his family. And for a long time he lived in constant fear that the truth would come out and his reputation would be further tarnished.

HANK'S STORY

Like other kids he grew up with, Hank, a divorced forty-seven-year-old, began looking at *Playboy* regularly in his early teens. Although initially he didn't consider it pornographic, it didn't take long for Hank to make sexually provocative photos the focal point of his masturbation.

At seventeen he had sex with a girl for the first time and got her pregnant. They were forced by their parents to get married. Even though Hank's young wife liked sex and was eager to have sex with him whenever he wanted it, he was surprised to find himself still needing to regularly masturbate to porn. Hank says, "I never found personal sexual satisfaction being with my wife. I was eighteen years old with a normal sex drive and a regular, willing sexual partner. I couldn't understand why I still had to have my pornography, but I did."

Hank got divorced, but his need for porn continued even after he began sleeping with a number of other women. "I kept having the same feelings of sexual frustration. I realized it wasn't that I had needed novelty or variety in sex, it was that I was looking for the *ideal* woman, like the ones who exist in porn. Porn hadn't prepared me to be with a *real* woman. I wanted perfection or nothing."

In the years that followed his divorce Hank got more heavily involved with porn. He says, "After my marriage I felt like a starving man at a banquet. Suddenly I could get all the porn I wanted and not have to worry about anyone else. I got to gorge myself and I did. Even the way I had sex with real women was just another form of porn for me."

Hank describes himself as becoming a "party boy" who just wanted to get laid. "For a while I was fairly sexually active. I had a number of sexual partners, but each one was totally frustrating. My 'relationships' wouldn't last more than a few weeks or a few months because after the initial fascination and mystery wore off or my immediate sexual needs were met, I found the woman inferior. I judged her as below me, not my equal, not someone who I would be proud to be with. I was also ashamed of being with her because I knew I was just using her for sex and didn't really want a relationship with her. I wasn't pursuing an intimate partner, I was looking for a piece of ass, but more often than not my sexual needs were met by pornography use. By the time I was in my late twenties I had pulled back from the dating scene, preferring to use porn and have occasional one-night stands when I needed some human contact."

Hank didn't mind having little sexual contact with real women. His masturbating to porn was completely satisfying on a physical and emotional level. He enjoyed the feeling of having total control over his own sexual experience. He says, "I didn't have to think about anybody else's needs. I could control every level of my own sexual response."

By thirty years old, Hank felt he had learned how to address all his sexual needs in such a way that he didn't need a woman. "All I needed was the stimulation I got from visual and written pornography," he said. "When I felt a fever of sexual need I would turn to pornography and masturbate. I could finish up in ten minutes or prolong the experience with a gradual build-up to a fever pitch that lasted for hours."

But Hank's physical finesse with using porn came at a social price. Hank reflects, "I became less capable and willing to reach out and spend time to build a relationship with a woman. I was way too self-centered. If I went to a party and found someone to have sex with, it was still all about *me*. Sometimes I slept with a woman just to make sure I was okay and still in touch with humanity."

Over the course of the next ten years, strange shifts began occurring in Hank's relationship with porn. Masturbating to porn stopped being something he was *choosing* to do to address his sexual urges. He began *needing* to masturbate to pornography frequently in order to simply feel good. "It became compulsive. I had to do it or risk feeling miserable. I had been masturbating to porn a lot, once or twice a day, every day for years, but it had turned into something more than just a need for sexual release. I started masturbating for longer periods of time and needing newer and different types of porn. I progressed from *Playboy* and soft-core magazines to the very edges of child pornography. And the progression was almost unnoticeable to me. It felt natural. I needed different and deeper stimulation. *Playboy* didn't satisfy me because it's too plain, too common. I wanted magazines that were barely legal. I also began using porn in combination with alcohol and other drugs to heighten the effect. My experience of porn changed drastically."

Hank increasingly found himself in a bind. "Visual images no longer worked for me. I'd get a tingling or a tickling of a sexual response, but my sexual needs became more internalized, based on ideas in my own head. I felt like I could write my own script for my perfect sexual response. So I began writing my own pornography for myself, starting from my own sexual desires. Writing enabled me to justifying my continued porn use. I told myself this is intellectual and I'm learning how to write by doing this."

Hank would hide away in his room for days at a time, writing pornography while getting high on methamphetamine and drunk on frozen vodka martinis. "I could maintain an erection for hours, literally for hours. And I did this for months. Every weekend I'd lock myself in my room and do this stuff. It started out as something great, but quickly became very, very unsatisfying. I started feeling bad for staring at a picture of a woman, for using her body parts this way, and not caring a thing about her. I'd use her image until I no longer found her interesting and then drop her in the trash. I felt ashamed for her and for myself.

"I understood what I was doing, how selfish and self-centered it all was, how little I got out of it. But it's almost like it was feeding itself. I was no longer in control of my sex life. I had become the object of the pornography. We'd switched places. The pornography had a life of its own. It was the dictator. It was running the show and I was just the whipping boy."

Hank's preoccupation with porn and the exhaustion that resulted from his weekend binges started to cause him trouble at work. "I'm a welder and you have to be very precise and very careful. After all, I'm working with fire and dangerous gasses. One wrong move and you can hurt yourself or even die. One day after I'd just come off of a three-day run of writing porn, getting high, and getting off, and had maybe three hours of sleep, I went to work and just stood there. It was like I had forgotten this job and who I was. I just stood there and broke down. It was almost as if my conscience *wept*. I felt this very deep level of shame. It was like I had reached the point where my conscience was giving up, my conscience was reaching out to me in the only way it could.

"It's odd that I've never talked about this and I've never really been able to verbalize it, but in that moment, I could no longer drink, I could no longer do drugs, and I could no longer do pornography. It all came to an end in an instant and I just broke down. I broke down physically while I was at work. I broke down emotionally. I broke down spiritually. I was so bereft of any positive self-image that I just wept. It was almost like part of me died and I was grieving that death. I was no longer able or willing to do that to myself anymore. No longer willing to give that much of myself away. I just wanted to feel whole again."

Unlike with Mitch, Hank reached bottom from the inside. No one caught him using porn. No intimate partner threatened to leave him. He didn't lose his job. Porn use sent him on a gradual slide into a psychological and spiritual abyss where he lost touch with his values and who he was as a human being. He came to realize that no matter how cocky he'd been, believing he could fool others about his secret behaviors, he wasn't able to hide what he'd been doing from himself. He reached his own personal and moral limits.

Emotional breakdowns are often the result of an unresolved internal conflict about what we are doing or not doing in our lives. The psychological pressure we feel inside gets so intense that it explodes from our subconscious, where it has been lurking all along, to our conscious state. And as it does, it triggers mental exhaustion and collapse. Hank's mental/ spiritual breakdown was a natural consequence of having ignored his core values, feelings, and needs. His breakdown triggered the realization that he no longer wanted to be doing porn and other behaviors that weren't healthy and good for him physically, emotionally, and spiritually. Hank's hitting bottom experience allowed him to see that his life had become unmanageable. He could no longer deny the fact that his problems with porn, drugs, relationships, and masturbation had spun out of control. As Hank reflects, "The line between extreme self-indulgence and inevitable self-destruction is very thin."

MARIE'S STORY

Marie is a middle-aged single working mother with two teenage children who slid into the porn trap when she discovered that masturbating to porn helped her cope with difficult life experiences. Like Hank and Mitch, Marie got involved with porn when she was a teenager, starting with detective stories and pulp fiction that featured something sexual on every page. In her late teens she worked at a motel as a housekeeper. "I could get my hands on just about anything when I worked there because people would buy porn and leave it behind in the room. I collected everything I found and had quite a stash of different kinds of magazines. I had so many, I'd act kind of like a dealer, giving them away to friends and family members. I looked at them first, but mostly found them boring—the same thing all the time. The greatest excitement was that they were forbidden. When I stopped working at the motel I gave up my porn collection."

Marie's parents got divorced when she was fairly young, and she alternated her time living with each of them. Both her parents dated a lot and watched porn on cable. Marie would watch their porn when they weren't around. "I was drawn to it. It gave me a buzz. If I had the chance to find something or see something, I would." She now realizes that part of the reason she was drawn to porn was that she grew up in a highly sexualized atmosphere. Not only were both parents involved with porn, she was molested several times, including by her father and one of her mom's boyfriends when she was just fourteen.

Marie married in her mid-twenties and became a born-again Christian. During her marriage she would occasionally watch porn on cable. "As a Christian I didn't want to be doing that kind of stuff, but I couldn't stop thinking about watching porn when I was switching the channels. If there happened to be a sex scene, I'd just stop on that channel."

She watched despite the fact that her sexual relationship with her husband was very active. "When I was married I used sex like a drug to relieve stress. It was my 'legal fix.' I could legally go ahead and have sex and do whatever, because I was married now. I loved my husband, but I never really knew what healthy sex was. Sex was just a way of getting stress relief."

Seven years into her marriage, with two children—one five and one eighteen months old—her thirty-two-year-old husband died suddenly from an asthma attack. "I called an ambulance and tried to do mouth-to-mouth resuscitation, but it didn't work. He died in my arms just as the paramedics put the oxygen mask on him. My son's first day of kindergarten was the day of the funeral. My husband's dying was the worst pain I have ever experienced."

After her husband's death, Marie became more and more isolated. "I didn't want anything to do with anybody. I hurt so bad I vowed I wouldn't hurt like that again. I didn't have any friends to go out with, so I stayed home and went back to using porn. That's when my addiction to porn just took off. When I was involved with porn, I didn't have to feel the pain of losing my husband and my loneliness. I didn't keep much around the house, like books or magazines, because I didn't want my kids seeing it. Plus, since I live in a small town, I didn't want anyone seeing me buy porn. I didn't subscribe to cable, but the Showtime channel came through, it bled through, anyway. I could see the pictures pretty clear and hear the voices."

Marie soon discovered that masturbating to the scrambled porn was a lot more thrilling than just watching it. "Then it got to a point where I didn't even need to see the pictures. If I just heard the sex scenes and knew what they were doing it was enough. I started masturbating to scrambled porn as a reward, and as something to do to help me relax and fall asleep. If I had a bad day or didn't feel good I would go into my fantasy world replaying scrambled porn in my head. Or I would go view it and masturbate. The pornography always enhanced the masturbation. I thought, *This ain't right!* But I'd still do it anyway."

When Marie discovered Internet pornography, the problem worsened. "The kids would be asleep and I would go on the Internet and spend hours clicking away, just looking at all the free porn," she said. "I'd look at practically anything. Whatever popped up I would click into, except for the really perverted stuff. After a while, though, I found myself going places on the Internet I never thought I'd ever go to. For example, I would go into the homosexual chat rooms. It wasn't so much to see what they were saying. I never talked to anybody. But they had pictures that were just unreal. I couldn't believe them. Some were pretty bizarre, but mostly they were groups of men, all aroused, sometimes in unbelievable positions. I didn't think of them as being homosexual. I thought of them as just a bunch of guys."

Seven years went by with Marie masturbating to porn on cable and on the Internet as a regular routine. "I'd do it mostly every day, sometimes a couple of times a day," she said. "It was a craving, like a drug. I'd think about it and I'd have to go do more and more. It was taking over. Sometimes I'd get real emotionally involved with the people I was seeing on TV and the sexual acts they were doing—whatever that might be —imagining I was there with them, one of them. Then, I started thinking about getting involved sexually in real life with other people to act out these porn scenes. The idea dangled there in front of me. I didn't want to go there. I didn't want to be like my mom, bringing men home to sleep with when there are children in the house. But after a while the pornography and fantasy and the masturbation were not enough, not exciting enough. I began to want more. When I found myself thinking this way, it scared me. I knew I had a real problem.

"In addition, I began feeling like I was losing control of my mind and my body during masturbation. I would start clicking away and two or three hours would go by. Next thing I knew it was three or four in the morning, and I had to get up early. Several times I'd be looking at porn on the Internet, clicking wherever I could, and suddenly I'd climax, without ever having touched myself—a 'no hands orgasm.' All I did was click and view and think about what I saw and boom. I lost control, something else took over and my body reacted. I was scared by the power porn had to affect me like this.

"I felt very ashamed because of the porn. It affected my relationship with God. I could not follow God and continue viewing pornography, fantasizing and masturbating. In the Bible, there is a verse that talks about how we cannot serve two gods. For a while, my god was pornography. There were times while sitting in church that I would go off in my head and have X-rated thoughts, or I'd look at someone in church and think sexual thoughts about them. I spent a lot of time thinking and fantasizing about what I saw on the Internet and on cable television. I felt a lot of guilt and shame. I felt God could not love me because of what I was doing."

While her self-esteem, sexuality, social life, and relationship to God were suffering due to her porn habit, Marie also became concerned about how porn was affecting her relationship with her children. "I kept retreating further and further into myself. I met my basic responsibilities as a single parent—holding down a job, getting them fed and off to school, but I wasn't capable of really connecting with them. All I could think about and get excited about was when I would get my next porn fix and how I would do it. I lived in the same house as my kids, but I really didn't know how they felt or who they were. We never played games together. As I discovered later, both my kids were pretty depressed, probably because I wasn't really there for them."

One day, Marie's eight-year-old daughter got upset with her. "She started crying and saying that I didn't even know her. She wondered if I even loved her," Marie said. "It broke my heart and made me start realizing how much I was living in my head instead of connecting with her and my son. They had lost one parent to asthma, and now because of my preoccupation, they were losing another to porn. I knew I had a problem. And I knew I needed help. But I had no idea where to go or what to do about it and was way too ashamed of it to even try to find out."

Shortly after her experience with her daughter, Marie says "fate intervened." Her computer had stopped working and the youth pastor from her church just happened to be at the house visiting her son. Knowing he had a lot of experience with computers, Marie asked if he would help fix hers. "I didn't know a lot about computers. I didn't know that your computer saves your Internet history, keeps a record of all the Web sites you visit. I also didn't know you can delete this stuff. So it was all there.

"The youth pastor started working on my computer and suddenly I could see that he was looking at my Internet history. His eyes widened and his jaw dropped as he read through this long list of triple-X-rated porn sites I'd been visiting. I just about died on the spot! Neither of us said much. It was incredibly embarrassing. I thought, *Oh my God, now what am I going to do?* I just told him, 'I will go talk to pastor about this.' I was totally humiliated and embarrassed. But that's what it took for me to wake up and realize I had a very serious problem with porn and it had to stop. Now I was exposed. Somebody else knew that I was going to all these sites. It wasn't a secret anymore."

Unlike Mitch and Hank, who hit bottom suddenly with one major incident, Marie's life had already begun crashing in multiple ways that were troubling to her. She felt isolated from her children and other people, and alienated from her faith. Her sexual responses and interests had become more extreme and were scaring her. Even though Marie could tell that these areas of her life were suffering, she didn't know what to do about it. She was sure no one would understand. "I felt a tremendous amount of shame being female and using porn," Marie said. "People expect men to be into pornography and all that sexual stuff, but they never dream of a woman doing it. The fact that I had a problem masturbating to porn made me just want to keep it a secret that much more."

Marie's ordeal of having her porn use discovered by the youth pastor was an important part of her bottoming-out experience. It was the final blow and broke the shell of her isolation. It triggered such intense embarrassment and humiliation that it was no longer possible for her to not get help. A week after the incident, Marie met with her pastor and his wife. She told them what she had been going through with her porn use. They listened without judging her and gave her information on healing from sexual addiction. Marie said, "Talking to them was uncomfortable, but in a weird way, it was a relief."

TOM'S STORY

Twenty-six-year-old Tom lives alone and works in a drugstore. He has been in recovery for three years. His life had revolved around porn for as long as he can remember. "My dad kept a stash of hundreds of *Playboys*, *Hustlers*, and *Penthouses* in a cabinet in our garage," Tom said. "I stole from his stuff to make my own secret stash. My dad never said anything, so I figured it was okay. Apparently my mom got upset one day and made him get rid of his stash. He did, but it wasn't long before I found a new collection of porn hidden in a compartment under his waterbed. Sometimes I'd even hide behind my dad's recliner and watch the *Playboy* channel with him without him knowing I was there."

It upset Tom that his dad did not pay attention to him. "Dad was gone a lot, and when he was home, he never spent time with me. We never played sports or worked on a car together. I was angry that he didn't seem to care about me, so looking at his porn kind of gave me a feeling of connection to him. This secret is what we shared in common."

When Tom was eighteen he got a job as a security guard and had some extra money of his own. "I'd stop by the adult bookstores and watch the videos there. It was something completely new. Suddenly I didn't have the desire for *Playboy* and the like any more. They were too soft. I was still a virgin and seeing actual intercourse fascinated me more. I'd buy a whole bunch of videos. I ended up getting a blow-up doll and stuff like that. I was surrounded by it. I still lived with my parents, but I was lost in my little porn world.

"I had a strong desire for porn, but it was just eating me up," Tom told us. "A couple of times, I remember breaking the videotapes, ripping all the tape out, and taking everything and throwing it in the trash can. I didn't want to become like my dad. I felt disgusted with myself. I desired porn physically, but in my heart I knew it was not what I wanted to do. My porn abstinence would last for maybe a month and then I would tell myself, *It's okay*, and then I'd rent a movie and watch it at work. Since I worked security, there was nobody around, so I would masturbate to porn at work."

Tom started watching and hiding porn videos at his parents' house too. He was masturbating to porn five or six times a day and it was taking a toll on him emotionally. "I remember leaving the adult bookstore with my stack of videos, going to work, and crying because I felt like this huge weight was bearing down on me. I wanted to change and I couldn't. I didn't know where to go for help. I was only nineteen and I couldn't get away from it. Even when I stopped for a while, I still had problems with the pornography in my mind. All the images I'd seen were still there. I still struggled with it. I couldn't sleep at night because my mind would be running everywhere with thoughts of porn."

The constant exposure to porn started to affect Tom's ability to set healthy sexual boundaries in the real world. "I began fantasizing about the women around me. I had sexual thoughts about my three sisters. I fantasized about the women who worked for the security company. I felt so much shame. I thought if my sisters and other girls knew what I was thinking about them, they'd want nothing to do with me. The shame was overwhelming. I struggled with it a lot."

When Tom found out that one of his married coworkers was depressed and that her husband went out of town a lot, he justified beginning an affair with her by thinking he could make her feel better. He was still a virgin. "She was twice my age and married, but she was open to it. I ended up in an adulterous relationship with her for quite a while. After the first time I had sex with her, I started crying because it just wasn't what I'd expected. I thought there was going to be a lot more pleasure. I thought sex with a real woman was going to fill all my being and it was just going to fully engulf me and make me completely happy for the rest of my life. But it didn't. It was just like masturbating to pornography.

"That first time, and for most of the sexual encounters that followed, I had a really hard time reaching climax. My girlfriend said it was probably because I had masturbated too much. But I know now it was because I had so much junk in my mind that came from having watched porn. I had a hard time focusing on one woman, being with her. I felt so much shame for all the masturbation, all the images I'd seen, and the thoughts I'd had about women. I didn't feel worthy to actually be with a woman. I felt I didn't deserve to reach climax and have pleasure because of how I victimized women in my mind.

"When I was masturbating it was easier to handle the shame. I'd tell myself: *This is part of life. It's okay. I've dealt with this before.* I'd feel the shame for a split second and then I'd automatically just stuff it deep inside. But with a woman it was more challenging. Porn kept me focused on my genitals. I didn't have to focus on a person. So even though I had a girlfriend, an actual person there, I still wasn't happy. I blamed the woman for not making me happy, even though I was the one who wasn't able to really be intimate."

Tom's involvement with porn soon intensified even more. He began accessing it on the Internet on his girlfriend's office computer at work and on his dad's computer at home. Since his dad was now retired, Tom had to wait until his dad was done looking at porn before he could go online himself. "It made me really angry at times," Tom said. "I'd justify my own porn use by telling myself: *He has no right to do it, but I'm not married and I do.*"

Tom's relationship with his girlfriend broke up and he immediately became involved in another adulterous relationship. It lasted only a few months. "At this point my parents were divorced and my dad had remarried," Tom said, "so I was living on my own, alone. I was always on the Internet. I'd come home and would spend eight hours after work on the Internet looking at nothing but pornography. I was looking for the perfect picture. I never found the perfect picture, but I would find one that suited me in the moment, that helped me reach climax. I never returned to the same one. Every night it was a different picture. Each one I looked at quickly got old and lost its power. I became really desensitized.

"My head was so full of garbage, thoughts of porn. One evening I was at my dad's house giving my twelve-year-old stepsister a backrub and ended up massaging her breasts. At the time, in my mind it wasn't bad, it seemed natural. After all, she looked eighteen. But then, I had an attack of conscience, just like the times when I threw all my porn away. I thought, *WAIT A MINUTE! THIS IS WRONG!* I left the house and on the way home I stopped my car, burst into tears, and cried uncontrollably. That was really the only time in my life that I ever seriously contemplated suicide. I felt completely controlled and ruined by the porn. I didn't plan on doing what I did to my stepsister, but it ended up happening that way. It was like I got tunnel vision and just went into that same state I did when I used porn, in which none of my surroundings seemed to be there. I was just focused on doing this one thing. I was being sexual and gratifying myself and thinking only of myself.

"My dad and stepmom confronted me about it. That was just what I needed, them saying, 'What's going on? What kind of life are you living?' I broke down in tears and said, 'Dad, I'm struggling with this, too.' He started crying and said, 'I thought I'd kept myself far enough away from you that my porn habit wasn't going to affect you, but it did.'"

Tom turned himself in, and he was arrested for molesting his stepsister. At that time, he felt his life had been destroyed. "But now, looking back I can see that it turned out to be the biggest blessing of my life, the answer to so many prayers. I hated myself. I was turning into my dad and being controlled by porn. Bottoming-out like I did helped to set me on the road to recovery."

Tom found out the hard way that a serious, long-term problem with porn can set a person up for sexually abusing someone else. His internal sexual fantasy world kept slipping into his real life. In his self-centered mind-set, his own sexual gratification temporarily overruled concerns about the impact of his actions on anyone else.

Looking back, Tom can see how he steadily progressed in his porn addiction to where he was bound to do something extremely inappropriate sexually. He knew he had a problem with porn that was beyond his control. He had already crossed healthy sexual boundaries by having sex with married women and masturbating to sexual fantasies involving sibling incest. Porn had influenced his sexual thoughts and behaviors to the point where he was primed for committing a sexual offense. "I wish I could rewind time like you can rewind a video," Tom said. "I'd do anything to have never stepped over that line and victimized my stepsister."

A s unsettling as hitting bottom is, all four of the people in this chapter eventually came to realize that there was also a positive side to their crashes. The one event that sent them sinking to the bottom of the porn pit was also the event that started them on the journey that eventually gave them back their freedom. After losing his job, Mitch got involved in counseling, successfully started a new career, and later went on to help found and run a porn recovery program for men at his church. Following Hank's breakdown at work, he entered an inpatient residential addiction recovery program and got help for his multiple addictions. He has been porn-free and clean and sober for more than three years. Marie became involved in counseling, healing workshops, and a twelve-step sexual addiction recovery program especially designed for women. She has reconnected with her children and has been making new friends. And, after fulfilling his legal responsibilities, Tom went into individual, twelve-step, and group counseling to help him quit porn and learn about healthy sexuality. He now feels confident that he can set appropriate sexual boundaries and has healed his relationship with his family.

Rather than ending in tragedy and more pain, Mitch, Hank, Marie, and Tom used their hitting-bottom experiences as something to push off from and begin a journey out of the porn trap.

II

Healing

In the end these things matter most:
How well did you love?
How fully did you live?
How deeply did you learn to let go?

—Jack Kornfield, Buddhist teacher

7

Getting Motivated
to Quit Porn

*Nothing can stop the man with the right mental attitude from
achieving his goal; nothing on earth can help the man with the
wrong mental attitude.*

—THOMAS JEFFERSON

We don't need to tell you it's a good idea to quit porn. You've probably already considered this yourself. When the negative consequences of porn use begin to outweigh the pleasures, most porn users start wanting out of the trap they're in. They are tired of lying to others and to themselves, tired of pretending to quit in order to simply pacify someone else, and tired of worrying that they might get caught. When people have a genuine desire to quit using porn they often want something better for themselves, like a deeper relationship with a partner, feelings of personal integrity, and being respected by family and community. They want to take back control of their lives.

The decision to quit porn is a positive, life-affirming milestone in a person's life. It represents a new level of maturity and self-responsibility. It signals the beginning of a person's recovery from porn and the gateway to a porn-free lifestyle. Unfortunately, the actual task of quitting porn is not easy to accomplish. As we've discussed in earlier chapters, porn is extremely powerful and can quickly pull people into a trance-like state, restrict their thinking, and impair their judgment. Porn habits become a learned way of coping with stress and a familiar way of expressing sexual energy.

When people start out with the intention of no longer using porn they often discover, much to their own dismay, that porn is extremely difficult to give up. It's not enough to simply make a promise to stop using porn, throw out a porn stash, or disconnect the Internet service in order to succeed at quitting. In spite of a genuine intention to stop, the desire to continue accessing porn can remain strong. Early attempts at quitting frequently fail.

Dale, a forty-year-old doctor, was shocked at how much trouble he encountered when he first tried to go without porn. "I wanted to stop using porn for the sake of my marriage. I thought it would be easy," he said. "A few nights after I decided to quit, I got in bed and felt an intense urge to watch porn. I forgot about my commitment and got up to go to the computer to get on the Internet. I stopped halfway down the hall and remembered my decision. After thinking about it for a few minutes I thought, *Screw my commitment*, and kept walking toward my computer. Then I changed my mind again, turned around, and headed back toward my bedroom. This seesawing went on for a few hours, with me going back and forth from my bed down the hall. I got through that night without using porn, but it was a nightmare. A week later I went back to using it. I was horrified that porn meant that much to me. It made me realize the extent of my problem and that giving it up wasn't going to be easy."

It is discouraging, as well as exhausting, when a person gets caught in a revolving door, attempting to stay away from porn and then going right back in to using it again. Nick, a sixty-two-year-old former porn user, told us, "For a long time in the beginning of my recovery I was stuck in what felt like a never-ending cycle. I'd use porn, feel miserable, and tell myself I was never going to use it again. Then I'd use it again and feel terrible, guilty, and ashamed. Then again I'd tell myself, *I'll never do that again*, but break my promise to myself within days. It was amazing how quickly I would forget my vow and go back to porn again."

Dale's and Nick's initial unsuccessful attempts to quit were not only disappointing to them, but brought up strong, conflicting emotions. This is a common experience for many porn users who want to quit. But why? Why is it that a porn user who has gotten to the place in his life where he strongly wants to quit can have so many competing feelings in trying to do so?

The starting point in answering these questions is to understand the key concepts of *ambivalence* and *motivation*.

Ambivalence is the coexistence of opposing attitudes and feelings within an individual. Although the person may think he has made a decision, there is a mental conflict that brings about uncertainty about his choice. Ambivalence is a very normal human experience that universally occurs whenever we are trying to quit something that has given us pleasure, excitement, or fulfillment in the past. For a porn user, it is not uncommon to have the simultaneous, opposing thoughts and feelings of "I want to sometimes use porn because of all the pleasure and excitement it gives me," and "I want to quit porn because of all the problems and pain it causes me and those I care about." Ambivalence is a big reason why people who initially want to stop using porn can end up bouncing back and forth between quitting porn and returning to it.

To be completely successful in quitting porn, ambivalence eventually has to be resolved. It means the thoughts and feelings of "I want to quit using porn" have to significantly outweigh the thoughts and feelings of "I want to use porn." This is where a person's motivation comes in and can tip the scales. Motivation is not only having the desire and willingness to accomplish something, it requires directing your behavior in a clear and focused way, with intensity and persistence, to achieve a desired goal. A strong and enduring motivation is a prerequisite for successfully recovering from any powerful habit or addiction. In quitting porn it creates a stable foundation upon which all the other recovery steps are built. Your desire to quit needs to be conscious and strong for it to prevail when you're up against the powerful pull of porn. The stronger the motivation, and the more consistently that motivation is sustained over time, the more likely ambivalence will be resolved. "I want to quit" will prevail over "I want to use."

In this chapter we discuss ways that you can effectively address your ambivalence and strengthen and sustain your motivation. We present methods and exercises to help you become more consciously aware of *why* you want to quit porn, *what* goals are more important to you in your life, and *how* you can develop the right mental attitude in order to successfully accomplish your goals.

With less ambivalence and more motivation you will be ready and able to persevere in the face of challenges ahead. Rather than spending your time and energy battling with yourself over whether or not you are really ready to quit, you can devote your resources to taking the basic action steps described in chapter 8 that can help you move forward in your recovery. When you have a clear vision for your future, the process of quitting will feel more straightforward and your goals more achievable. And during those times you feel vulnerable to slipping back into using porn, you'll have a way to channel your thoughts and feelings to help you avoid the porn trap and stay inspired and focused on healing.

There are four strategies that are essential in helping to resolve ambivalence and strengthen and sustain motivation to quit porn—each are discussed in detail in this chapter. Once you've read each one, we recommend spending time contemplating your situation and how you can implement that particular strategy to improve your level of motivation. The strategies are:

1. Acknowledge how porn use causes you problems
2. Identify what matters most to you
3. Face your fears
4. Take responsibility for your own recovery

STRATEGY #1: ACKNOWLEDGE HOW PORN USE CAUSES YOU PROBLEMS

This strategy involves recognizing and staying connected with the serious consequences and problems you have already experienced, as well as identifying what future problems continued porn use could bring. The more you are consciously aware of the specific ways porn has hurt you in the past, continues to damage your life in the present, and threatens your well-being in the future, the more motivated you will be to stay on track in your efforts to quit using porn. This is an important step, because many porn users have become accustomed to turning a blind eye to many of the problems associated with their habit.

When a porn user automatically dismisses from his awareness the negative consequences of his porn use, he is operating in denial. Denial can be a very effective method for someone who wants to focus on the benefits of porn and, at the same time, keep problems that porn use causes out of his conscious awareness. In order to stay motivated and be successful in quitting porn, the denial process must be deactivated. Identifying and acknowledging the problems that porn use has resulted in for you and others brings these problems into conscious awareness and consequently can go a long way in helping to neutralize denial, especially if this is done on an ongoing basis over time.

There are a number of ways to stay in touch with the negative consequences of porn use. Talking with a trusted friend or counselor about current and potential problems, writing down your experiences and concerns in a journal, and taking regular time for self-reflection can be helpful. You may also want to refer back to the list of negative consequences of using porn in chapter 4, on page 72, and identify which repercussions from porn use apply to you. In addition, you may want to do the following exercise, "How Porn Is a Problem for Me."

How Porn Is a Problem for Me

Set aside an hour when you won't be distracted by anything else to answer the following questions:

1. What problems has porn caused me in the past?

2. What problems am I experiencing today because of my porn use?

3. How has porn changed me in ways I don't like?

4. How does my porn use hurt my intimate partner and others?

5. What problems could occur in the future if I continue to use porn?

We recommend writing down your answers on a piece of paper. Keep the answers nearby, perhaps in your wallet, on your desk, in a nightstand, or next to your computer so you can access them easily. Reread your answers frequently, especially during times you feel the urge to use porn and could easily forget your commitment to quit. Add to and elaborate on your answers as you become more aware of the negative consequences of porn in your life. You can also discuss your responses with a counselor or a trusted friend.

Many people who are successful in quitting porn tell us that they frequently think about the painful consequences their porn use has caused, both for them personally and for the people they care about. Ethan, for example, often reflects on a specific incident in his life that was particularly painful and humiliating. Several years ago habitual use of both marijuana and porn had led him to act out his favorite porn scenarios. These sexual practices involved tying up and sometimes urinating on female sexual partners. He thought that the women he had sex with were accepting of his behavior, but after acting out one of his porn fantasies, a girlfriend became extremely upset and cautioned other women in their small town to avoid him. One day when he was in a busy store, a friend of the girlfriend's loudly chastised him for his sexual behavior. "I was stunned to have my private life broadcast publicly," he said. "I felt shocked and humiliated. But it made me realize how dangerous my sexuality had become and how emotionally disconnected I was from myself and my sexual partners. As uncomfortable as it is, I regularly conjure up this memory. It's an important reminder to myself why I no longer want to use porn."

Laura, a thirty-five-year-old former porn user, thinks back to the most frightening situations her porn habit led her into in the past. "I had developed a habit of watching pay-per-view porn in my hotel room when I was on business trips," she said. "I'd get sexually excited and masturbate to it. After a while this stopped being enough to satisfy me. I began following up my porn watching with picking up men in the hotel lounge for a one-night stand. Porn gave me the ideas sexually, and I wasn't content with just having sex with myself. Things got pretty scary. One man gave me a sexually transmitted disease and another got physically violent with me. I constantly remind myself of how bad things got and remember that sick feeling of fearing for my life."

Porn users also develop their motivation to quit by thinking about all the negative consequences that could happen in the future if they continue using porn. Identifying and thinking about possible—even likely—problems down the road can be a powerful way to strengthen your motivation to stick to your goal of quitting porn. Examples of possible future consequences include: getting caught using or hiding porn; developing unhealthy sexual interests; losing an important intimate relationship; losing a job; losing respect of friends, family, or coworkers; being publicly humiliated; becoming involved in harmful, illegal, or abusive sexual behavior; exposing children to the harmful influence of porn; becoming addicted and not being able to live without porn; and getting in trouble with the law. You may be able to identify other possible problems from your porn use.

Bill, a thirty-five-year-old stockbroker, developed a strong interest in quitting porn because he was tired of living with the fear of being caught. "I would be masturbating to porn in my office in a public building, and even though my door was locked and the windows were closed, I knew someone walking around the building could get up close to the window, peek through the blinds and see me. At home I was always afraid that at any minute my wife would catch me, or a police officer would knock on my door and arrest me for the pictures of children I had downloaded on my computer. I knew I could face charges that would put me in jail. All the worrying about getting caught was making me ill."

When Alex was nineteen and heavily into porn, he looked ahead to the future and could see that porn was eventually going to cause him problems in forming a serious relationship and getting married. He said, "The only purpose for pornography is to develop sexual feelings that you're directing at someone other than your wife or girlfriend. I knew in a few years I'd want to get married. I just had a sense that I needed to stop using the stuff. I didn't want to have a wife and a family, and then be hiding in my office somewhere with these fantasies." As a young man Alex also worried that continuing to use porn was going to seriously harm his ability to be sexually healthy and able to act as a leader in his spiritual community. "I came to a point in my life where the complications that came with pornography far outweighed the pleasure I got out of it. Sure, it's very pleasurable. But, I came to see that using it would only hurt my relationships and warp my sense of what sex is really all about. I attribute much of my recovery success to the fact that I remember this and constantly remind myself that porn is capable of ruining my life."

Whether you focus on past, present, or future problems to get past denial and stay motivated to quit porn, you may find this exercise will cause some degree of emotional discomfort for you. Rather than avoid this discomfort, you should keep in mind that it can actually help to strengthen and sustain your resolve. A moderate amount of emotional distress is needed in order for anyone to successfully make a major change in their life: not enough emotional upset, it's hard to stay motivated; too much, we can shut down and go back to old habits in order to sooth ourselves and cope.

STRATEGY #2: IDENTIFY WHAT
MATTERS MOST TO YOU

Another compelling way to strengthen and maintain your motivation to quit porn is to be honest with yourself about how using porn prevents you from living up to your core values and beliefs and meeting your life goals. We know from our counseling work that former porn users are well on their way out of the porn trap when they start saying things like: "Porn is absolutely incompatible with what I really want in life," "It's come down to a choice, and I choose to quit porn," and "It's impossible for me to be the kind of person I want to be and still be using porn."

In order to recognize the inherent incompatibility of porn with things that are important in your life, first take the time to identify what you really want out of life, what principles you believe in, what kind of contribution you want to make to your family and your community, and how you want others to think of you. One might think that everyone knows what matters most to them, but many regular porn users have been so preoccupied in the imaginary world of porn that they haven't taken the time to get clear and stay focused on their important life goals and values. Those who got involved with porn at an early age may not have ever decided who they'd like to be and what they'd like to accomplish.

Establishing and maintaining a connection with our own values is important for all of us. But, as a current or former porn user, clarifying your values can be an especially beneficial process for you. It not only can help illuminate the inconsistencies of who you are when you've been using porn and who you actually want to be, it can also highlight your own inner conflicts about your behavior. Additionally, connecting with your values can provide you a foundation for strengthening your commitment to your goal of quitting porn by giving you something positive and personally meaningful to move toward in your recovery.

There are many ways you can become more aware of and connected to the things that matter most to you in life. You can take time every day to think about your values and goals; read books on values, ethics, and goal-setting; and discuss what's important to you in your life with a family member, counselor, or good friend. You can also become more consciously aware of what is important to you by doing the following writing exercise, "What Really Matters to Me."

What Really Matters to Me

The following questions can help you identify your values, beliefs, and goals. In answering these questions in writing, you can become more consciously aware of what's important to you. Make sure to give yourself plenty of time to really contemplate and explore your principles and ideas. Be as concise or elaborate with your answers as you like.

1. What are the top six things that matter most to me in my life?

2. What personal goals do I want to achieve?

3. What are the morals and values I believe in?

4. What are my religious or spiritual beliefs?

5. Who is most important to me in my life and how do I want to treat him or her?

6. What personal traits do I want to convey to others?

7. How would I like to contribute to the lives of people I care about?

8. How would I like to contribute to my community and society?

9. In what ways does porn use conflict with my values, beliefs, and life goals?

Once you've finished this process, keep a copy of your responses somewhere you can easily access them. You may even want to discuss your answers with a friend, partner, counselor, or other support person. While no one can tell you what is important to you, conversations you have on these issues with people you respect and admire can help to stimulate your awareness, insight, and convictions. Frequently look at the questions and answers you have written. You may find yourself wanting to revise or add ideas as you move forward in your healing process.

Many clients and former porn users tell us that regularly thinking about what really matters to them helps sustain their desire to quit porn. Sean found a huge discrepancy between his role as a church youth group leader and his compulsive porn habit. He said, "I recognized the contradiction between what I said I believe and what porn was putting into my head. Even though I wasn't physically committing adultery or breaking any of the big sins, I was doing it in my mind. I realized my spiritual beliefs and my porn use cannot coexist peacefully in my life. I can't lead a youth group where I have a meaningful spiritual experience, drive to the store and pick up a *Penthouse*, and go home and masturbate to it. It isn't congruent."

Corey identified his desire to be in a good long-term relationship. He explains, "It finally dawned on me that using porn would only further isolate me and keep me from being emotionally available to anyone. Porn gives a sexual charge and gratification, but it can't give the acceptance and love I want. It actually makes it *more* difficult for me to have a healthy sexual relationship. Porn increases sexual tension and makes me crave sex, like it's a drug. I'd like to experience what it's like for sex to be natural and comfortable, for it to be about loving and caring for a real person."

When Max started becoming more aware of his values, he was shocked at the discrepancy between his porn use and his desire to respect the women in his life. "In college I met a number of female students and coworkers. We got together regularly to work on projects and just talk. Our relationships weren't about sex. I got to know these women as equals, as friends. Then, when I'd watch porn, I started noticing how porn consistently disrespects women and puts them down. I couldn't be with my women friends and then go home and masturbate to scenes of females being treated as complete and utter sexual objects."

As you become more aware of your personal values and goals, you can also see more clearly how porn use conflicts with the type of person you want to be in the world. Nick quit porn after he realized how his dishonesty was harming his view of himself. "I was sick of lying to myself and other people," he said. "My whole life felt like one big lie. As long as I kept using porn I couldn't have integrity. It's essential that my private actions be in line with what I say and with my heartfelt beliefs."

As Sean's, Corey's, Max's, and Nick's comments reveal, understanding how porn doesn't fit with your core values can provide you with a compelling reason to make a change and stick with it.

In the following exercise, "I Want to Be Someone . . . ," you will find a list of personal traits former porn users have shared with us that they found were incompatible with using porn. Staying conscious of this incompatibility has helped them to succeed in their recovery. Read through this list of traits to identify the ones that are important to you. Then take some time to consider how porn interferes with the traits you checked and your ability to actualize your personal goals and values.

I Want to Be Someone . . .

___ who is honest and trustworthy.

___ who keeps my word and follows through with my commitments.

___ who values others through both my words and my actions.

___ who loves with my heart as well as my sexual desire.

___ who has a high degree of integrity.

___ who spends time in productive and meaningful activities.

___ who is a positive role model in the community.

___ who feels he is a good person.

___ who has self-confidence and self-respect.

___ who is in control of his impulses.

___ who is ethical and respects the law.

___ who feels proud of himself.

___ who demonstrates respect for women and children.

___ who can be looked up to and respected by others.

___ who doesn't emotionally or physically hurt his intimate partner.

___ who lives according to religious and spiritual values.

___ who protects family members from hurt and harm.

___ who is free of addictions and compulsions.

___ who isn't supporting the porn industry.

___ who is physically and emotionally healthy.

___ who connects love with sexual expression.

___ (other traits)

_____

_____

_____

Take the list above and make a clear statement that reflects the *absolute incompatibility* of each trait you checked off with your use of porn. For example, you might say, "I can't use porn and be someone who is honest and trustworthy." It can also be helpful to say out loud why you can't. "I *can't* use porn and be someone who is honest and trustworthy, *because* using porn requires me to be secretive and lie about what I'm doing. I can't expect someone to trust me if I'm lying." And, if you identified that you want to be someone who feels proud of himself, you might tell yourself, "I *can't* use porn and be someone who feels proud of himself, *because* whenever I use porn I end up feeling ashamed and guilty." Write down your explanation of incompatibility for each desirable trait you identified. Read your responses out loud every day. The process of getting clear on your values and goals, and then shining a light on how porn use is incompatible with those values and goals, is an invaluable tool for strengthening your motivation to quit using porn.

Strategy #3: Face Your Fears

One of the reasons so many porn users start to feel ambivalent about their decision to quit porn, and lose motivation to continue the healing journey, is fear. Fear is a common emotion that arises when someone tries to quit porn. The idea of making any kind of major life change and facing the unknown is often initially frightening, even when we are fairly certain the change will improve our lives. In the early stages of porn recovery, many people feel afraid to give up porn because it has provided them instant pleasure and emotional consolation. Quitting means making significant lifestyle changes, such as saying good-bye to well-established sexual habits, finding new ways to cope with emotional stresses, and learning how to relate to others more openly and honestly. Needless to say, porn users with the strongest emotional and sexual attachments to porn often have the most fear when faced with quitting.

Many human fears lie below our consciousness and are masked by other emotions. For example, many porn users feel anxious and depressed when they begin the process of quitting porn. They don't realize that fear is actually driving those feelings. When fears are not identified and resolved, they can sabotage your recovery efforts by continually undermining your motivation to quit porn. Like a nail you are unaware of in one of your car's tires, an unidentified and unaddressed fear can slow your healing journey down without your even realizing what is happening. And the more unconscious fears you have, the more challenging and difficult it will be to stay on track with effectively dealing with your porn use issues.

Identifying and being able to admit your particular fears about quitting porn is an important first step in ultimately resolving those fears. Many of the people we have counseled and interviewed found it beneficial to do this as they started out on their healing journeys. Below is a list that includes their responses. You may find this list useful in helping you identify your own fears.

Common Fears of Being without Porn

Put a check (✔) next to each item with which you agree:

___ I'm afraid of becoming depressed.

___ I'm afraid of getting angry and upset.

___ I'm afraid of feeling lonely.

___ I'm afraid of getting stressed out.

___ I'm afraid I won't be able to masturbate without it.

___ I'm afraid of losing my sense of sexual power.

___ I'm afraid of losing interest in sex.

___ I'm afraid of having less enjoyment in sex.

___ I'm afraid of feeling sexually frustrated.

___ I'm afraid I'll get involved with even riskier sexual behaviors.

___ I'm afraid of becoming more dependent on my partner for sex.

___ I'm afraid of feeling "less of a man" or less sexually liberated.

___ I'm afraid I'll have to tell others about my problem and they'll reject me.

___ I'm afraid no one will understand and be able to help me.

___ I'm afraid I will fail if I try to quit.

___ Other

_____

_____

_____

As the list demonstrates, fears of quitting porn fall into the categories of emotional well-being, sexual enjoyment, and relating to others. These fears make sense given that porn use can play an important role in temporarily fulfilling needs in any one of these three areas. Go back over the list and look at the specific fears you identified. Notice which of your fears have to do with emotional, sexual, or relationship concerns. Do you have some fears in each category or do your fears tend to concentrate in one area or the other? Understanding the type of fears you have can help you become aware of what particular issues you'll need to focus most on in your recovery; by doing so, you can ensure you meet that need in some other way than by using porn. For example, if you identified that you are afraid of feeling lonely if you stop using porn, then you have a legitimate *need* to not feel lonely. You can tame this fear by planning things to do so you won't feel alone without porn.

In addition to the loneliness factor, emotional experiences such as the fear of feeling depressed, angry, and stressed out often accompany the loss of any significant attachment. These emotional reactions are usually the most intense during the first six months of going without porn. When you stay committed to the process of staying porn-free over time, these fears usually subside in intensity, duration, and frequency. If, for some reason, they persist longer than feels right or interfere with your day-to-day functioning, you can always reach out and get medical and psychological help to deal with them.

Many porn users are afraid of how quitting porn will affect them sexually. They may worry that quitting porn will in some way mean losing out on sexual opportunities or no longer being a sexually active person. This fear is understandable and often strongest in people who have come to rely on porn as a primary sexual stimulant and outlet. You can minimize this fear by remembering that while quitting porn does involve closing a door on one type of sexual outlet, it also opens doors to other types of sexual experiences that can be enjoyable and fulfilling. Sexual behaviors that involved porn and caused you problems can eventually be replaced with new sexual behaviors that support healthy self-esteem and emotional intimacy. By thinking of porn use as just one of a number of sexual possibilities (and a problematic one at that), and anticipating a life that provides more sexual options rather than less, it's possible to reduce your fears that relate to sex.

When Ed began his recovery process, he confronted his sexual fears in writing. In his private journal he reassured himself of his ability to handle the changes to come. "I'll probably go through natural dips and adjustments in my sex drive," he wrote. "I need to be prepared. They're to be expected with this change. I'll make sure that I learn new ways of getting excited and being sexual that I'll enjoy and don't lead to problems. I can create my own sexual fantasies." You may want to consider regularly addressing your fears and your plans for dealing with them in writing too.

Identifying the false beliefs that underlie some of your fears and countering them with truth and reality is another way to help maintain your motivation to quit. For example, some male porn users are afraid that giving up porn will mean giving up part of their self-identity, even their manhood. They think, *I'll be less of a man if I don't use porn.* This fear can relate to false ideas about what it means to be a man that were learned in childhood, which were reinforced by porn's messages and never altered. Looking at this belief closely and challenging its assumptions can reveal its inaccuracies. For example, Randy, a recovering porn addict, said, "I grew up thinking that 'real men' looked at porn. When I quit porn, for a while I worried what other guys would think if they found out I wasn't looking at it anymore. Then I realized the truth of it is it actually takes a *strong* man to overcome a powerful addiction like this. And only a real man who isn't into porn can love a woman deeply."

Saying each of your fears out loud can also diminish their power. When you say a fear out loud to yourself or talk to someone else about it, the fear can start to feel less absolute and imposing. Out in the open some fears may suddenly seem irrational. You may start to realize that, like anyone else, you have a natural ability to adapt to change and that despite years of doing porn, you are still capable of learning new ways of dealing with your problems. You can call upon friends, support professionals, and other resources to help you. The more you identify and express your fears, the clearer new options for getting your needs met will become.

Regardless of the nature of your fears, getting them out in the open weakens their influence and helps you stay motivated to quit porn. When you start to challenge your fears and counter them with ideas for making valuable changes to improve the quality of your life, you'll feel emboldened and empowered to continue on your healing journey. Remind yourself that anyone who has been brave enough to quit porn has faced similar fears and came out stronger, because they had the courage to move forward and did not allow their fears to hold them back.

STRATEGY #4: TAKE RESPONSIBILITY FOR YOUR OWN RECOVERY

Probably the most important mental preparation you can do to stay motivated to successfully break free of the porn trap is to take full responsibility for your own recovery. It's very difficult to stay motivated if you believe you are quitting for someone else, or because you've been pressured into the decision and don't feel you are in control of your choice. When this is the case, bitterness and resentment will come between you and success.

While other people can be important in providing encouragement and support, when it comes to breaking an emotional and physical attachment to porn, you need to make it happen yourself. Hank said, "One day, pornography is not gonna come up to you and say, *Look, it's okay if you don't want to use me anymore.* Change has to start from within. It's up to you to make it happen. You have to tell yourself, *I'm not gonna have to do this anymore. One day I will change to the point where I won't ever use porn anymore.*"

Taking responsibility involves developing new skills so that you can be your own coach, quarterback, referee, and cheering section for your recovery. You are in charge of coming up with the plan, executing the maneuvers, setting and following the rules, picking yourself up, and trying something new when you encounter setbacks, and rewarding yourself for your successes.

In order to become the leader of your own battle plan to quit porn, one of the best strategies is to start by making a list of successes you have had in overcoming other difficult challenges in your life. Everyone has encountered tough times, whether giving up a bad habit, dealing with a chronic illness or injury, or facing financial difficulties and other hardships. As a result, we all develop unique strategies that have a high likelihood of working for us when we have to tackle new problems. Some people talk things out with their friends or professionals, others prefer to handle a problem on their own. Some like to experiment with different approaches until something works, while others create a plan and stick to it no matter what. Simply reviewing your own successes can reassure you that, although change can be stressful and challenging, you have been successful at facing up to it in the past.

When Ethan decided to quit porn he was able to stay motivated by adopting a "fake it till you make it" approach that gave him a sense of ownership and control over his own recovery. He had used this kind of approach before in overcoming his addiction to marijuana. "I started out just staying away from porn for a while," he said. "I acted as if I *did* want to quit rather than waiting to want to quit. This gave me the space I needed to find out for myself how much healthier I felt without it. You know, you don't make a dog drop what's in its teeth unless you can offer it something else. I don't think I'm that different than a lot of other human beings. If someone tells me I should give up something because it's bad for me, and I'm still really enjoying that thing, I'm not going to give it up. I need to experience for myself why I'll be better off for giving it up. Giving up porn initially felt like a renunciation, but just by coaching myself to stick with it, within weeks I started feeling it was the right thing to do."

Some people find that they can assume more responsibility for quitting porn simply by changing their mental "self-talk." When they notice they are telling themselves things like, "I have to use porn," "I have no control over it," or "I'll never make it," they quickly counter the thoughts with more positive statements, such as, "I can do anything I set my mind to do," "I know where to get the help I need," or "I've made big changes in the past and I can do it again."

The truth is you can't climb uphill thinking downhill thoughts. As simple as it sounds, changing the words you repeat over and over to yourself every day can change how motivated you feel during your recovery. Rob, whose porn addiction cost him his marriage, quit porn and turned his life around by continually reminding himself of his own inner goodness. "I have strong spiritual beliefs," he said. "And one of those beliefs is that I am the loving child of a higher power that I call God. I am an expression of this energy and in that energy there is good and there is love and there is light. And because of this I can be a good person and have a good life free of porn."

Whether through words, thoughts, or actions, the more you are able to take control of your own porn recovery, the more you will feel empowered and in control of your life. "Porn recovery is not about having a simple formula for quitting porn," said Nick, a former porn user and men's group leader in his church. "It's about making a commitment. You have to be determined and resolute, and take responsibility for yourself. You have to get clear on what you want and insist on right behavior for yourself. When you're not committed, there's nothing else in your mind to counter longings for porn. Being determined means at that very moment when you think about porn, you take control over your own experience and fight it."

D eveloping the ability to strengthen your motivation to quit porn through acknowledging porn's problems, knowing what is most important to you, facing your fears, and taking responsibility for your recovery is critically important to your future success. But it is also important to understand that you don't have to be motivated at an extremely high level before you can take action steps to heal. Motivation grows and intensifies as you become more proactive in separating yourself from your porn behaviors. The recovery steps we present in the next chapter can help you move out of isolation, experience firsthand how much better it feels to be out from under porn's stranglehold, and realize the satisfaction of being involved in new and healthier activities.

As you will see in upcoming chapters, healing results from a combination of changing your attitudes as well as changing your behaviors. Healthier attitudes and healthier behaviors reinforce each other. A positive mental attitude helps you make important behavior changes and positive changes in behavior help you shift and develop better attitudes. Either way, the common denominator in porn recovery is the fact that the choice to change is yours alone. A proven process for quitting porn exists, but it's up to you to decide when to engage it and get the ball rolling.

As Hank said so well, "If in your heart you want to quit porn, do it. By taking just the first step toward a porn-free life, you start the chain of events that will eventually allow you to quit for good. But it's not gonna start unless *you* start it yourself."

8

Six Basic Action Steps

Porn recovery takes time, love, and understanding. It also requires truth and accountability and taking the right steps at the right time.

—MITCH

Every former porn user we spoke with for this book had a different story to tell about how they quit. Some had phased out porn gradually, using less each week until they had finally weaned themselves from it. Others told us they shifted from hard-core to soft-core porn and then later gave it up altogether. Some quit cold turkey, riding out their discomfort with sheer willpower until the cravings diminished. However, while the initial strategy used to quit may have differed, each former user followed specific action steps to stay committed to quitting and to keep the journey out of the porn trap on track.

In this chapter, we will introduce you to six basic action steps that will help you be successful in quitting porn. These steps—which are based on our counseling experience, clinical research, and the interviews we conducted for this book—show you how to reach out and get support from others, reduce your exposure to porn, and develop healthy new skills and behaviors that will create a more fulfilling life without porn. By focusing your time and energy in new directions using the steps presented here, you will find porn's pull naturally lessens and becomes easier to resist. In later chapters you will have an opportunity to learn more advanced strategies and techniques that can further reinforce your goal of staying porn-free. Knowing all your options and how best to move forward can help you take the right steps at the right time as you travel toward a deeply rewarding life without porn.

THE SIX BASIC ACTION STEPS

We refer to the six action steps as being "basic," not because they are particularly easy or simple to do, but because they are necessary in order to ensure success in quitting porn. Without these action steps you can't make the kinds of thorough and systematic changes needed to assure that you can stay away from porn for good. These basic steps are essential in creating a regimen of self-nurturing and self-care that is essential for getting out of the porn trap. Only by learning to take care of yourself and giving yourself time and space to heal, can you find the emotional and physical resources you'll need to recover. Taken together, these six steps reduce many of the factors we've discussed in previous chapters that contribute to and accelerate serious porn problems, such as social isolation, easy access, stress, addictive tendencies, and sexual insecurities and frustrations.

The six basic action steps in quitting porn are:

1. Tell someone else about your porn problem
2. Get involved in a treatment program
3. Create a porn-free environment
4. Establish twenty-four-hour support and accountability
5. Take care of your physical and emotional health
6. Start healing your sexuality

Some steps may be easier for you to do than others. Ironically, the steps that seem the most challenging are often the ones that can be the most rewarding and effective in helping you quit porn. If you initially balk at the idea of trying a particular step, you may want to ask yourself the following questions: Why am I having this reaction? What does the step require of me that I am not used to doing? What am I afraid will happen if I attempt the step? What do I need to deal with or do so that I can follow through on the step? When faced with a challenging step, we recommend you consider a way, no matter how small, that you can move forward and do it in spite of your initial reluctance. To help make it easier for you, each step offers a number of options from which you can choose to help you get started.

It's important to understand that these six steps aren't separate— they complement each other and work together. Don't think of them like stepping-stones across a creek, but rather as sections of a bridge. The stronger each section is, the sturdier the whole bridge, making it more likely to stand up to difficulties that may lay ahead. For example, it's easier to attend a treatment program when someone who cares about you and your struggle encourages and supports you. Neglecting a particular step can weaken your recovery process. In fact, we have found that many people who have chronic difficulty quitting porn can point to one or more of the basic steps they haven't yet followed through with. Therefore, it's a good idea to evaluate how you are doing with each step from time to time throughout the course of your recovery. If you find you haven't fully committed to a step or two, you should focus more time and energy in that specific area of your recovery for a while.

Let's take a closer look at each of the six basic action steps.

Step One: Tell Someone Else About Your Porn Problem

"I have a problem with pornography and I want to quit." When a porn user first says words like these out loud to another person, he takes a significant first step in climbing out of the porn trap. As we've seen in previous chapters, most relationships with porn thrive on isolation, secrecy, and denial. By talking openly and honestly with another person about your problem you automatically weaken your connection to porn. The need to lie and deceive feels less necessary. The strategies you have developed over months or years to hide a porn habit and keep it separate from the rest of your life begin to have less importance. The simple fact that someone else now knows about your porn use usually makes the porn lifestyle less appealing. Many former porn users told us that purposefully "blowing their cover" in this way helped ignite their motivation and commitment to quitting.

Disclosing a porn problem is not easy for anyone. It involves admitting a personal weakness, a lack of control over a particular part of your life, and a sexual behavior that may be seen by others as unacceptable or even deviant. As a result, talking about it for the first time (and even the second and third) can trigger many uncomfortable feelings such as shame, guilt, fear, and anxiety.

Like most people, porn users are not comfortable with and haven't had much practice talking about sexual matters openly and honestly. You may worry that the people you talk with about your porn problem will judge you, criticize you, lose respect for you, and ultimately reject you. This is a common and understandable concern. Ed, a forty-seven-year-old former porn user, summed up his initial fears about disclosure this way: "I felt so ashamed of myself. I thought if someone else knew of my involvement with porn, they wouldn't like me. I worried they'd feel contempt for me, think I was a deviant, and not want to be around me." Ed eventually found a way to tell others about his porn use problems. Although he was reluctant at first, he opened up because the time had come for him to quit using porn, and he realized he had to take this step if he was ever going to succeed in achieving his goal.

The fear of being judged as sexually perverted or abnormal may be especially strong for women because porn is generally thought of as a guy thing. Other women may be less accepting of women users than they are of men who use porn. And anyone, male or female, whose porn problems involve unusual or violent content or child pornography, may also understandably be reticent about disclosing their porn struggles. For all of these reasons, taking this first action step takes a lot of courage and determination. It can be helpful to remember that you are disclosing your problem to other people not because it will feel good to get it out in the open (it may or may not), but because you know it is an absolutely necessary thing to do in order to be successful in quitting porn.

Picking a supportive person. When the time has come for you to talk, whom you tell, when you tell, where you tell, and how much you tell is entirely up to you. To help you feel less uncomfortable, you may want to choose someone you believe will be reasonably understanding and supportive as the first person you open up to.

One option is to disclose your porn problem to a trained professional. Our clients often tell us that we are the first people they have ever talked to about their porn problem. The confidential setting of a therapist's office can feel relatively safe, especially if you choose a therapist experienced in working with sex and addiction problems. Clergy and health professionals are also likely to be receptive to hearing about your porn problem. In recent years, an increasing number of ministers, rabbis, priests, and physicians have developed a sympathetic attitude toward people who have become caught in the porn trap. You may also consider calling a trained counselor at a confidential national sexual addiction or mental health hotline (see listings in the Resources section). The hotline worker can also be helpful in directing you to counseling and support resources in your local area.

Some porn users prefer to first disclose to someone they know well and frequently talk with, such as an intimate partner, a close relative, a teacher, or a good friend. If this is an option you are considering, asking yourself the following questions will help you pick someone who could be supportive:

- Who is likely to accept me in spite of my porn problem?
- Whom can I trust not to shame me or condemn me?
- Whom have I been able to confide in previously, with positive results?
- Who does not gossip about others?
- Who has respected confidentiality in the past?
- Who has compassion and sensitivity about personal problems?
- Who is understanding and knowledgeable about addiction and recovery?

Choosing someone you trust who has enough life experience and maturity to understand issues related to porn and give wise counsel can help you make disclosure a positive experience. There are no guarantees, however, that you will feel good after disclosing your porn problem to someone, no matter how carefully you choose. It's a calculated risk, but it's not only a risk worth taking, it's a risk all porn users who want to quit *must* take.

Former porn users we interviewed were passionate about the importance of self-disclosure in breaking free of a porn addiction. George, a fifty-six-year-old former porn user, offers this advice: "If you have a problem with porn, find someone you can be honest with about it. It could be a minister, a healer, a counselor, a trusted friend, and it might be a spouse or a partner. And tell them. Tell them because it is the aloneness and disconnection that makes you want to do porn and spend your time that way." And, Tom recommends, "You just have to take that first step. You have to find someone you feel is safe and trustworthy. Go through that door, overcome the fear, and confide in them. Once you do, it is so much easier to be honest with other people and yourself. You no longer have to hide."

Disclosing to an intimate partner. If you are in an intimate relationship, you will at some point need to disclose your porn problem to your partner. While you may not choose to have your partner be the first person you tell, for the sake of trust-building in the relationship, she or he should at least be one of the first people you tell.

When you tell your partner about your porn problem, don't expect support and understanding, at least not right away. As we discussed in chapter 5, it is common for intimate partners to have strong emotional reactions when first learning about an ongoing involvement with porn. Partners can initially feel shocked, angry, anxious, and sexually betrayed. No matter what your partner's reaction is to your disclosure, it is important that you stay focused and not allow yourself to be deterred from taking this step. As much as your partner may be upset at first, disclosing is the right thing to do because it allows you to break through old destructive patterns of isolation and secrecy, and thus pave the way for a healthier relationship with each other in the future. Later on in chapter 10, "Healing as a Couple," we will provide you with guidelines on how you can help your partner and work together to heal the wounds caused by your porn problem.

Kirk experienced a sense of inner satisfaction when he finally disclosed his porn use to his wife. "It took me six years to admit to myself that I had a problem. I wasn't able to live with the lies I was telling myself anymore. I told my wife for the first time that I was addicted to Internet porn. It was uncomfortable confessing to her, but it was the first step I took in being able to reclaim my dignity, spirituality, and self-respect."

Ways to disclose. Some people disclose their porn problem impulsively, without giving it much thought beforehand. Something unexpected happens, and they suddenly feel compelled to divulge what's been going on.

For example, Brad had no intention of telling his wife, Paula, about his porn habit when he returned from a sales trip during which he binged on pay-per-view porn in his hotel room. But that's what he ended up doing. "I'd been so totally engulfed with porn on the trip that when I got back I couldn't reconnect with Paula," he said. "We started fighting and then we stopped fighting. I think on some level I finally saw how my addiction was ruining our marriage. That night I had a kind of nervous break-down. I was curled up in a fetal position on our bed and began shaking uncontrollably. It was really bizarre. At the time I didn't know what was going on and felt horrible. Paula got concerned and tried to help me. She asked, 'What's wrong? What's going on?' I just spilled. I told her about my porn addiction. We talked about how I could get help. The shaking stopped and I actually felt better afterward."

Other porn users work up to admitting their addiction to porn slowly, with lots of preparation and planning. They give much thought to choosing whom to talk to, what to say, and how to take care of them-selves afterward. If you like the idea of thoughtfully approaching a dis-closure, here are some suggestions that can help in your planning and preparation:

Tips for Disclosing a Porn Problem

- Consult with a mental health professional or pastoral counselor who can help guide you through an effective disclosure pro-cess.
- Make sure that you pick a time when the person to whom you are disclosing is not distracted by something else. For example, turn off the phone and talk in a private setting that feels safe to you.
- Let the other person know you have something personal and confidential to share.
- Ask if the person is open to listening. Even when it appears to be a good time for you, it may not be for the other person.
- Share how difficult opening up is for you. Let the other person know you have struggled to reach the decision to talk about your problem. Tell them that you chose to reveal your problem to them because you trust them, feel safe with them, and re-spect their opinions.

- Let the other person know why you are revealing this now. You might say something such as, "I am telling you this now because I no longer want to keep this a secret; I don't want to continue hurting myself and others; I'm ready to admit I've got a problem and do something about it."
- Let the other person know what you most need from them. Do you want them just to listen, to offer advice, to share their thoughts and reactions, or help you in some specific way?

Reactions will vary. Following these suggestions can help you increase the likelihood that the person you talk to will feel some empathy and respect for you. But it is impossible to control or predict anyone else's reaction. Dave told us, "There were some people who did withdraw. My guess is they were either genuinely disgusted by the topic or it put them in touch with something they were afraid of, felt humiliated by, or hated in themselves. They had to reject me because they didn't want to deal with what my issues brought up for them. Once I understood that, their negative reactions didn't really bother me. I just focused on and appreciated those people who were understanding and supportive to me."

Many former porn users tell us they were able to find acceptance and understanding from the people they admitted their porn problems to. Kevin decided to start talking about his problem when he went on a fly-fishing trip with two guys he had known for years. "During the trip I had plenty of time to think about how my porn use was affecting my wife and family," he said. "I really wanted to quit and knew I needed to reach out to other people for support. At dinner one night, I told my buddies about it. It was amazing. They supported me. One of the guys said that he had problems with it too. I realized that we all have our struggles with our compulsions, fears, and secrets. Whatever the problem, someone else can relate. I found out that when you honestly start talking about your issues, people feel empathy and often open up to you in return."

Alex was also moved by the support he received from a small group of close friends in his church group when he first revealed his porn addiction to them. "When I told them about my problem, everyone in the room cried," he said. "No one was disgusted with me, rejected me, or called me sinful. It was a huge relief to be honest with them. They cared as much about my problem as I did. My life really mattered to them. I didn't feel alone."

Hopefully, you will have a positive experience when you tell someone else about your porn problem. But, regardless of whether your initial disclosure is met with support and empathy or anger and rejection, it is an essential step you have to take if you want to free yourself from the isolation and pain of a problem with porn.

Step Two: Get Involved in a Treatment Program

If you have a serious porn habit and want to successfully quit porn, eventually you will need to participate in some type of ongoing treatment. Without the focus and direction of a treatment routine, it's easy to lose sight of goals, become overwhelmed by stress, and slip back into old ways of thinking and responding that increase the likelihood of continuing your porn use.

The idea of going to counseling or attending group meetings devoted to porn recovery can be frightening and off-putting at first. Taking the step to find treatment requires a level of openness and vulnerability that is higher than just telling a few special people about the porn problem. It takes time and energy to research and locate counselors and organizations that provide porn recovery services. It can be inconvenient to rearrange your schedule in order to attend counseling or group meetings. You may have to spend money on a treatment program. There has to be a willingness to explore a number of different options because you can never know in advance whether something will suit you and your needs until you give it a try. You'll also have to learn to put your trust in a person or group of people you most likely have never met before.

Getting involved in treatment is a powerful and important step to take. Many of the people we spoke with said ongoing treatment changed their lives in profoundly positive ways. Through their participation in individual or group counseling, they were provided concrete tools for quitting, found role models for recovery, got insights and new ideas about their own behavior, and were able to evaluate their progress as they moved through the process of recovery. Participating in a treatment program also helps make the recovery process feel normal because you meet people who are on a similar healing journey. Contact with others provides emotional support, reduces feelings of shame, and inspires a porn user to stick with the process of change.

Corey told us that the support and encouragement he received in his men's recovery program for sexual addiction is what finally enabled him to quit porn. "It's difficult to stop doing something you get that kind of sexual reward out of. I needed to hear other people constantly remind me that it wasn't all right for me to keep using it. That was a key in my success. I could no longer justify in my own mind that porn was in any way good for me."

Treatment programs for people with porn problems vary in approach, format, and cost. Some involve one-on-one meetings with a counselor, health-care provider, or other specialist, while others involve attending group meetings with people who share a desire to quit porn and overcome other forms of sexual addiction. In order to find a treatment option that is most likely to help you, it's important to do some research and spend some time thinking about what's available and what types of programs resonate with your values, beliefs, and lifestyle. You may have to try out more than one approach before finding one that fits your needs and personality.

Some of the most common treatment options for porn recovery include:

- Individual counseling
- Couples/marriage counseling
- Therapist-run group counseling
- Twelve-step addiction recovery groups
- Faith-based recovery groups
- Residential treatment programs
- Special programs and workshops

A good way to begin your search for the best treatment program is to set up a confidential consultation with a mental health counselor, religious leader, or addictions specialist. This should be a person you feel comfortable discussing your situation with, and he or she should also be knowledgeable about the types of services that are available in your area. With their help, you can begin formulating a treatment plan tailored to your individual situation, concerns, and goals. (See the Resources section for treatment programs and organizations that provide referral information for counseling.)

After meeting with a mental health counselor, Ed came up with the following treatment plan:

1. I will see a counselor who specializes in sexual addiction recovery once a week for at least three months;
2. I will attend at least one Sex Addicts Anonymous meeting a week for at least three months;
3. I will reevaluate how I am doing in three months and revise my plan to move on to the next steps in my recovery.

The combined individual counseling and a group recovery program Ed chose is an approach that has a high rate of success for people in the process of quitting porn. Different approaches often complement each other and can help you make steady progress over time. Even so, keep in mind that the plan you start out with may change several times as you reach new levels of recovery.

Let's look at the characteristics and advantages of each of the different approaches to porn recovery.

Individual work. Individual counseling involves meeting privately with a professionally trained counselor, clinical social worker, psychologist, or other licensed mental health practitioner. Someone who is specifically trained in sexual addiction recovery would be most beneficial. Sessions may be weekly or bimonthly for several months to several years. A therapist can provide guidance and support in addressing underlying emotional wounds and unresolved issues from your past that have fueled your porn use. Meeting with the same person privately over an extended period of time also provides an opportunity to sharpen interpersonal skills and become more comfortable opening up emotionally.

While hesitant to try individual counseling at first, Bill was later glad that he took this step. Of all the options, individual counseling seemed like the safest and most effective place for him to address his problem of being attracted to child pornography. "When you're like me and you get turned on by looking at children, the biggest problem is isolation," he said. "I worried that I'd be condemned as a 'pervert' or 'animal' if I admitted to anyone what I was doing. Talking with a counselor allowed me to break out of my isolation. It was the best thing I ever did. The counselor helped me start seeing myself as separate from my problem. And he gave me strategies for being able to change my behavior and focus my sexual interest in a more positive and appropriate direction."

Couples work. Couples counseling can be beneficial when relationship stress is high, because both partners get an opportunity to discuss porn problems in a neutral setting. This type of recovery work can help a couple understand how porn has harmed their friendship, trust, and intimacy. With the help of a trained marriage counselor or relationship therapist, the former porn user and his intimate partner can work together to repair the damage porn use caused to their relationship.

While couples counseling is recommended for any recovering porn user who is in an intimate relationship, it works best as an adjunct or follow-up to individual therapy. Some couples counseling early on in the recovery process can help stabilize the relationship as both partners try to cope with the intensity of each others' feelings and reactions. Couples counseling can also enable the porn user to more fully understand the destructive impact of his porn use on his partner and on their relationship and provide insights that help him stay on track with his own recovery. However, the porn user needs to make progress in his healing and recovery before the relationship can heal. Ongoing couples counseling is usually most effective once the porn user has been able to make a solid commitment to recovery and has experienced some success in staying away from porn for a period of time. Only then there will be a strong enough foundation from which the couple can work together to heal the damage porn has caused in the relationship.

Ongoing group work. Group counseling and other types of group experiences, such as twelve-step recovery groups, are often an essential part of a porn recovery plan. After all, it is much easier to stay committed to recovery goals over an extended period of time when you are regularly connecting and interacting with other people who have similar goals.

Group recovery programs include therapist-led counseling groups, religious faith-based recovery groups, and twelve-step programs such as Sexaholics Anonymous (SA) and Sex Addicts Anonymous (SAA).

Many of the standard ongoing group recovery programs are relatively low cost or free. Group size can vary from five or six people to over twenty. Many groups use a structured format for sharing personal experiences and follow an agenda that concentrates on a different aspect of recovery each week. This approach usually helps make everyone in the group feel more comfortable and secure discussing their porn problems and learning from others.

Porn users who attend group programs say the experience can be truly healing and satisfying, because it helps them feel part of a community that not only provides support, but also puts a high value on personal responsibility and honesty. It is easier to stay away from porn when you know that you will be checking in with others about your progress on a regular basis. "The idea that other people know the struggle I'm going through helps me a lot," Ivan said. "I'm committed to quitting, but there are many times that I want to go back to porn. Every once in a while other people in my group will check up on me. They'll ask, 'How are you holding it together?' Knowing that they might at any time ask me certainly helps me stay with the program."

Group treatment also has the advantage of helping keep you honest about your own feelings and behaviors by providing regular exposure to the experiences of other porn users. As you listen to stories about the destructiveness porn has had in the lives of the other members of your group, you start to develop a new consciousness about your own problems. Twenty-seven-year-old Brad has been part of a men's porn recovery group at his church since he was twenty-three. "It's the reason I was able to quit porn," he says. "After several group meetings I stopped feeling tempted to use porn. I had no desire for it. I didn't even crave the porn fantasies or masturbating to it. I've heard other guys say they had a similar experience. It felt so great to step away from the addiction. I could see more clearly what I had been doing, how it had affected my life, and just how far down it had taken me. I started to understand what I had been dealing with and how I could go about getting it under control."

Group treatment programs can also help in the development of interpersonal skills that are often a problem for people who've been caught in the porn trap for a long time. Justin told us, "My porn addiction had stunted my growth emotionally and kept me from entering into trusting relationships with women and other people in general. In Sex Addicts Anonymous we spent time identifying our emotions. The men and women in the group essentially taught me how to have a relationship and share on a feeling level. Once I was able to relate more emotionally and connect with people, I didn't feel the need to compulsively masturbate anymore. Masturbating to porn just seemed like a cheap substitute."

When you realize that everyone in the group has similar problems to yours, it can also help you deal with your feelings of shame. Thirty-four-year-old Dick said, "In my men's group we go beyond the pride and macho bullshit of not ever admitting we have weaknesses and are capable of feeling hurt. New guys come in the group and try to rationalize using porn in some way, and the rest of us in the group say, 'Give me a break. We're just like you. We all get horny! Don't give me that.' We're able to call our behavior for what it is, while not censuring or shaming each other. We are deeply committed to each other. We trust each other and respect confidentiality. I think there is a camaraderie that is almost like being in the military. It's like we've been through a war together, have suffered together, have pain and casualties together, and it's really bonded us. We're also helping each other communicate better and treat our intimate partners with more respect. I feel much better about myself because of this group of men."

Finding a group to go to can be challenging if you don't live in a metropolitan area. Marie has to drive three hours each way to attend the nearest Sexaholics Anonymous meeting. She told us the trip is definitely worth it because the advantages of the group process are so vital. "I stay over and see my counselor in the morning," she says. "Sometimes I'm the only woman at the SA meeting. It used to feel strange, but now I'm just one of them. I feel safer there than I do in a lot of places. The men are working on their issues and I'm working on mine. We're all there for the same thing: to stay away from porn, manage our lives better, and help each other heal."

Residential treatment. Residential treatment programs can be especially helpful for porn users who are out of control with their sexual behavior and who are experiencing overwhelming emotional distress. Most programs are located on campus-like hospital settings and provide intensive services that include assessment of therapeutic needs, individual counseling, group counseling, educational information, and the development of an ongoing treatment plan upon discharge. Though the financial cost is high compared to other treatment options, this type of concentrated individualized care can give some recovering porn users what they need most—distance from their porn habit and established routines, focused clinical attention, and time to rest and recover emotionally and physically.

Special programs. A variety of other special programs and services are available for recovering porn users. These include short-term intensive outpatient programs and workshops that participants attend daily for several days or several weeks in a row. Less expensive than residential programs, these programs frequently are held in classroom settings and are attended by other porn users and sex addicts in recovery. Laura was able to get started on her recovery after attending the Bethesda Workshops, a sexual addiction treatment program for Christian women in Nashville, Tennessee. "I had always thought of myself as a female kind of 'Lone Ranger' in regard to having a problem with porn," Laura said. "It wasn't until I took the workshop that I realized there are other women out there who struggle with the same issues."

Only you can determine the treatment plan that will work best for you, but it is important that you find a program that helps you maintain a level of honesty and commitment to change, and that builds a layer of emotional and spiritual support to guide you through your porn recovery process.

Step Three: Create a Porn-Free Environment

Getting pornography out of your immediate environment is, of course, a very practical step toward recovery. Obviously if you want to quit porn, you will need to get it out of your house, your office, and any other locations where you have typically used it. Just as a smoker who wants to quit needs to completely dispose of his cigarettes and an alcoholic has to pour out his booze, a recovering porn user needs to get rid of his porn. When your environment is porn-free, it is not as easy to fall mindlessly back into using it. You get both the physical and psychological distance needed to help you break free. Without porn in your environment, you are more motivated to develop new healthy pursuits that bring you pleasure.

Unlike cigarettes and alcohol, porn is not just a product that sits on a store shelf waiting to be purchased. It is easily accessible all the time, for little or no money, in a variety of forms, through a multitude of sources. You can't keep it out of your life simply by ridding your personal spaces of it and staying away from the places that sell it. It takes a serious ongoing effort to separate from porn. You have to be willing to actively push it away any time it tries to come back into your life.

When it comes to creating a porn-free environment, the options can be summed up simply: *Clear it out. Keep it out. Turn away from it.* Let's see how to accomplish each one.

Clear it out. Locate and completely get rid of any type of porn you have been keeping in your home, at work, in your car, and anywhere else in your personal environment that you have come in contact with it. Get rid of magazines, books, videos, DVDs, computer files, and cable porn channels. Think of this as a toxic substance removal effort—porn has been poisoning your life, and the only way to improve your health and the health of your environment is by getting rid of it entirely.

While throwing things out is straightforward enough, the act of clearing out porn can be emotionally upsetting and challenging. It is not uncommon for feelings of sadness, fear, and anger to emerge. It can feel just like the end of a relationship, a relationship that provided pleasurable sexual experiences. Some porn users have spent years cultivating porn collections that cater specifically to their individual interests and tastes, and they may have a strong emotional attachment to their stashes. In addition, some people feel they may need some porn as a safety net in case this "recovery stuff" ultimately doesn't work out. Clearing out porn makes quitting porn real. It's a very concrete physical act of separation.

Former porn users liken getting rid of their porn to "saying good-bye to an old friend," and some say it was "terrifying," and "the hardest thing I ever did." The intensity of their feelings often reflects the strength of the emotional and sexual attachment they had with porn. Anyone whose porn habit is casual will clearly have an easier time clearing out porn than someone who used it regularly and for an extended period of time. For those who find throwing out porn to be emotionally challenging, it can be helpful to discuss with a counselor or members of a recovery support group how to best do it and handle the feelings that come up. Once the porn is gone and they have adjusted to it being gone, many former porn users say they feel an overwhelming sense of relief, as well as pride at being able to detach from it. There is comfort in knowing it would take an intentional, concerted effort to get that involved with it again. "It gets easier to stay away from porn when it's not always there before you," Marie said.

Keep it out. Once your environment is clear of porn, the job becomes one of keeping it out. Porn and porn-like images can pop up unannounced on the Internet, on television, in movies, in print media, and in dozens of other places we may frequent. Advertising and entertainment industries rely heavily on using sexually provocative images. Many corporations are deeply invested in maximizing their customer base for products with "adult content," whether through pay-per-view television, magazines, satellite and cable TV, and a multitude of high-tech electronic devices. Many Web sites that have nothing to do with porn will use sexually charged pop-ups to keep users on their sites.

Staying away from porn requires diligence and effort. We've found that the best strategy for keeping porn out of your life is to construct barriers. When you keep in mind the fact that porn use thrives on anonymity, low-cost availability, and easy access, anything you do to reduce these factors will help you keep porn out of your life. Consider the following options and identify the ones you think will help you create and maintain a porn free environment:

Options for Reducing Exposure to Porn

___ Cancel all subscriptions to porn (Web site, magazine, cable, cell phone, etc.).

___ Change to a family-oriented Internet service provider.

___ Change your e-mail address.

___ Install cyber controls on your computer.*

___ Move your computer to a public area in your home.

___ Cancel Internet service altogether.

___ Buy a new hard drive or computer.

___ Use the computer only when someone else is nearby and can see the screen.

___ Subscribe to television programming packages that are completely porn-free.

___ Get rid of your television, VCR, and DVD player altogether.

___ Block out television channels that carry porn.

___ Avoid driving by adult bookstores and strip clubs.

___ Avoid stores that sell porn magazines and other porn products.

___ Avoid video stores that carry X-rated movies.

___ Avoid anyone who you used to watch porn with or who enabled your porn use.

___ Call ahead when staying at hotels to make sure they don't subscribe to channels with sexual content, and if they do, request that these channels not be available to you in your room when you check in.

___ Tell friends, relatives, and coworkers not to send you porn or links to porn.

*See "Organizations, Programs, and Web sites" in the Resources section.

Taking steps to block your exposure to porn is something you do to make it easier to quit. "I think of porn as a narcotic," says Wes. "The more you allow it into your system, the more you want it there. When I did porn it would stay in my head for several days and I'd feel compelled to binge with it. I quit smoking ten years ago and it taught me that the desire to use an addictive substance lessens with time spent away from it. You just have to get the time in. Keeping porn out of all areas of my life has really helped to reduce the cravings."

Tom found that by changing some of his routines at work, he could keep a healthy distance from porn. "I work in a major drugstore and we have a large magazine section filled with magazines that I find pornographic, like *Maxim*, *FHM*, and *Cosmopolitan*. The magazines are all over the place. They feature half-naked women on the covers. I make sure I distance myself from the racks. My coworkers are sometimes there and will grab a copy and start going through it. It would be easy for me to get distracted by that too, so I just stay away and don't engage with them when they are doing that. I don't watch TV anymore because of some of the images and the many sexual jokes and innuendos that are involved. I eliminate as much of that stuff from my environment as I can, so it doesn't trigger me into thoughts of wanting to use porn."

Turn away from it. It is important to recognize that no matter how diligent you are at getting porn out of your environment and taking steps to keep it out, you will still be exposed to it from time to time. You may see a sexually explicit billboard while driving. You may be watching television and click onto a music channel with singers and dancers whose moves remind you of porn stars. You may open your Sunday newspaper and find a women's lingerie insert that looks like a strip-club advertisement. Then what do you do?

Since it's impossible to totally avoid all exposure to images that can stimulate your desire for porn, your best bet is to have a strategy to shut it out as quickly as possible. Just because something exists doesn't mean we have to keep it in our consciousness. Whether we are aware of it or not, every waking moment of every day we make decisions to either pay attention to or ignore hundreds of different things in our environment. You can put porn-oriented images on your "ignore this" list and not give it any energy. You can simply close your eyes, click on another channel, click off a device, or get up and move somewhere else. It's important to remember that you always have options for actively putting visual and emotional distance between you and porn images.

Hank uses what he calls an "eye bounce" whenever he unexpectedly encounters porn images or materials that remind him of porn. "My mind and my eyes instinctively go to porn because I've always gone there and they're trained to go there," he said. "So when my eyes see something sexy now, I bounce away. *Oh there's a picture of a sexy girl,* BOUNCE, I look elsewhere. If I watch TV I find I bounce my eyes away a lot because practically all of the advertising segments include some form of female body and it's usually very suggestive. I hear the ad, but I'm not watching it. It felt strange doing this at first, but now looking away has become a new habit. The more I do it the easier it is. For most of my life I walked around with a kind of low-grade sexual fever. But lately, for the first time, it's starting to diminish and almost disappear because I'm no longer feeding it. It feels like a part of me has been set free to do other things and it's fabulous."

Removing porn from your environment and developing your own personal approaches for coping when you are accidentally exposed to it can help you move further and further away from a life dictated by porn. And the more distant porn becomes, the easier it is to live a life that is happier, healthier, and more in tune with your personal values and goals.

Step Four: Establish Twenty-Four-Hour Support and Accountability

Just as you need to be prepared to handle sudden unplanned exposures to porn, you also must be ready to deal with a desire to use porn, which can strike at any time. Taking a deep breath and counting to ten may work for some people, but this doesn't work for most porn users. The impulse to use porn can be too powerful to manage on your own—it helps to have a support team to whom you can turn to when you are struggling to escape the urge.

After Mitch lost his job as a teacher and coach because of using porn on school grounds, he decided to quit using porn for good. "Was I tempted? Did I have a habit I had to break? Absolutely! But my men's sexual addiction recovery group at church helped me stay on track." As he moved forward in his recovery plan, Mitch found that he needed more support to help him resist his strong urges to use porn again. "I established an understanding with my pastor that I could call him any time I needed. That first year of my recovery I ended up calling him three to four times a week. I'd tell him, 'I'm really struggling right now. Can you pray for me? Do you have any suggestions for what I can do?' My pastor would listen, say something soothing, and give me ideas. His support and the strength of our friendship got me through the rough times and helped me break my habitual patterns."

You may want to consider any of the following people as members of your support team—professional counselors, clergy members, twelve-step program sponsors, recovery group members (sometimes referred to as "accountability partners"), your intimate partner, family members, friends, or counselors at local and national hotlines (see Resources section).

It's good to have several options to call upon as needed so you don't overwhelm any one person, and in case that person is not available when you need them. Tom told us that both his mother and sister have been the most important people in his recovery. "They are there and they listen. They know my history and know how much I was exposed to porn as a child through my dad's problem with it. They understand the magnitude of how it can affect a person and the kind of struggle that I've had to go through to get porn out of my life."

Tom doesn't limit his support to his mom and sister, however. He said, "I also talk with my brother-in-law who is a real strong supporter. It's nice having the guys in my twelve-step group and the people at church aware of where I've been and what I'm going through too. I've told so many people. I thought that I would never tell anybody. I thought people would hate me if they knew. But that isn't the case. I have some awesome friends who know, really care about me, and back up my recovery."

Intimate partners can also be helpful supports, but the extent to which it is productive for them to be involved in the recovering porn user's healing work varies. Many intimate partners become easily upset hearing details about porn cravings, contents, and slip-ups. It's often difficult for them to not fall into old dysfunctional patterns of wanting to control, pass judgment on, or monitor the recovering porn user's behavior, especially in the early stages of recovery. Intimate partners are often most effective as supports when they are not relied on as the primary or sole support person, and when they feel confident about the former porn user's commitment to healing.

Alex found his wife Alisa's support extremely helpful in his recovery. He married her at twenty-two years old, several years after he realized he had a problem and had stopped using porn. Alisa never felt betrayed by him or competitive with his interest in porn. As a result, she felt comfortable being a support person for him. "I told Alisa about my past porn problem before we were married. I had an inkling porn might continue to attract me from time to time, since it had been such a strong habit. Sure enough it has. When I get a craving for porn I talk with my wife and tell her I'm struggling with the thoughts. She'll hold and comfort me until I feel better. Alisa doesn't shame or judge me. Knowing she's there and cares helps a lot."

Adam, an SAA sponsor, has years of experience talking with porn addicts who call him when they are feeling vulnerable to using porn. This is his advice: "I encourage people just to be gentle with themselves. Just try and figure out what it is they feel and need. I'm always reminding people to become aware of what they are feeling in their bodies. So much of our pain comes from having feelings trapped in our bodies that we are unable to express. Recovery is all about increasing self-awareness and options, and having someone to help you when you need it."

Step Five: Take Care of Your Physical and Emotional Health

Quitting porn can be emotionally and physically stressful. People who are used to using porn regularly and compulsively may experience withdrawal symptoms similar to those experienced by drug addicts who stop using cocaine or other hard drugs. Like recovery from prolonged drug use, it can take a period of time to completely heal changes in brain chemistry that may have been caused by extensive porn use. During this period of recovery and physiological readjustment, it's not uncommon to experience increased irritability and insomnia for a while.

One of the best ways to cope with the emotional and physical problems that are common among people quitting porn is to take positive steps to stay healthy. Not only do people with strong bodies, minds, and spirits recover faster, they also have more energy to explore alternatives to porn and move forward toward a new life and improved relationships.

Many of us are familiar with the basic principles of good self-care, but if you've been trapped in the world of porn for a while, chances are you've been neglecting your health and could benefit from a few reminders of what's important. Here are some suggestions:

- *See a doctor or other health practitioner to evaluate your current health status.* Obtain recommendations for dealing with stress and staying healthy as you resolve your issues.
- *If you don't have a daily exercise routine, now is the time to begin one.* Develop a routine that improves strength, stamina, and flexibility (for example: weight-lifting, running, and stretching). Being in shape will help you strengthen your nervous system and help you manage stress. Whether you start jogging,

swimming, or take up boxing, exercise itself can also help you defuse many negative emotions, such as anxiety, anger, frustration, and depression, which you may experience while quitting porn.

- *Find a workout partner to help you commit to exercise.* You may even want to find a porn recovery support person who is also a regular exerciser so that you can accomplish two goals at the same time. Having a partner can help you stay motivated during those times you don't feel like exercising.
- *Try to get at least seven hours of quality sleep every night.* Good sleep improves your physical well-being and your ability to make good decisions. In addition, you may find that you actually need more sleep during the quitting process to deal with any added stress.
- *Evaluate your eating habits and make necessary improvements.* Consider consulting a nutritionist and getting advice on what you need to do to improve your dietary habits to help you feel better physically and emotionally.
- *Identify several stress management techniques you can use on a regular basis to feel less tense.* These can range from simple things such as listening to your favorite music or taking your dog for a walk, to more structured techniques such as yoga or meditation.
- *Seek evaluation and treatment for any underlying conditions that can hamper porn recovery,* such as drug and alcohol problems, clinical depression, obsessive-compulsive disorder, and hormone imbalance. It's hard enough freeing yourself from porn—doing so without dealing with other serious issues can make the process significantly more difficult.

Improving your health while quitting porn can be a reward on its own. Tony said, "I work out at the gym nearly every day. I avoid junk food and eat well. I'm getting at least seven hours of sleep a night. I'm in better physical and mental shape now than I've ever been before. Exercise and all doesn't just feel good, it keeps me in a self-improvement head space where the thought of doing porn is not so appealing."

Part of the process of improving your health is to keep track of your emotions and work to make sure you deal with them as they arise. Desires to use porn tend to increase when people slip into unpleasant emotional states, such as feeling bored, lonely, anxious, hurt, angry, or stressed out. Your ability to successfully quit porn will be affected by how well you are able to recognize how you're feeling and respond effectively.

Bill noticed a pattern of craving porn during his lunch breaks at work. When he tuned into how he was feeling emotionally, he realized that the underlying culprit was boredom. This information gave him a direction to go in to reduce the cravings. "I started engaging myself with fun activities during my lunch break," he said. "Instead of thinking about porn, I play video games. It doesn't totally eliminate my interest in looking at porn, but it helps and gives me something better to do. Other times, I call my wife, socialize with coworkers, take a walk, or go on a short bike ride."

It's a lot easier to stay away from porn when you are actively doing positive things for yourself that make you feel good both physically and emotionally. Any healthy activity that you enjoy doing, such as playing sports, gardening, playing a musical instrument, hiking, or solving a Sudoku puzzle, can boost your self-esteem while giving you the strength to deal with the stress of quitting porn.

Marie told us, "In the past, I didn't feel I deserved to take care of myself or nurture myself. Now I take yoga classes and I exercise every other day. And I get a therapeutic massage every month whether I need it or not. If I want to take a nap, I take a nap. I never used to let myself do that. I never thought I had time. I'm learning that making my health a priority is essential to my recovery."

It may seem a little overwhelming at first to try to quit porn at the same time you begin other healthy habits. But you'll soon find that the energy you devote to taking better care of yourself is more than worth the effort. It will make the process of quitting porn not only easier, but more likely to be successful in the long run.

Step Six: Start Healing Your Sexuality

The last of our six basic action steps involves understanding and addressing the impact pornography use has had on your sexual attitudes and behaviors. As we discussed in chapter 2, exposure to porn often occurs early in a person's life, so many porn users learned about sex from porn instead of appropriate sex education sources and real-life experiences. As a result, you may have developed sexual habits and patterns that work with porn but don't work in real intimate relationships.

If you have been involved in porn for a long time or used it every-day, it's likely that the way you think about sex and the sexual behaviors you desire have been significantly influenced by your contact with porn. Unfortunately, pornography is self-serving—it encourages a continuing involvement with it. The sexual messages in porn don't help the user de-velop skills for breaking away from it and experiencing healthy, intimate sexual experiences with a real partner. Even when you rid your environ-ment of porn and take other steps to get it out of your life, you will have a difficult time making progress if porn's messages still influence your sex life. Even if those messages are just in your head.

Sexual attitudes and behaviors don't miraculously transform once you've stopped using porn. You'll need to make an active effort to dis-cover new ways to define sex, change the images you associate with sex, and learn new approaches to self-pleasuring and sex with a partner. Ex-amining and shifting your attitudes and behaviors about sex is time well spent, because it's much easier to remain porn-free when you have satis-fying sexual alternatives to take the place of porn.

There are numerous ways you can work on developing new attitudes and understandings of sex. You can read articles and books on healthy sexuality (see suggested readings in the Resources section), take a sex education class offered in your community, or consult with a sexual ad-dictions recovery counselor, certified sex therapist, or sexuality educator. You may also want to talk about healthy sexuality with a trusted friend whose sexual values and conduct you admire, or discuss sexuality con-cerns with leaders in your faith or spiritual group who have positive at-titudes about sex.

It can also help to become familiar with the conditions that need to be in place for healthy sexual experiences and positive emotional inti-macy. The article, "The Maltz Hierarchy of Sexual Interaction," posted on our Web site, www.HealthySex.com, and referenced in the Resources section, can help you accomplish this. You'll be able to recover from porn quicker and more thoroughly when you have a good sense of the differ-ences between porn-driven sexuality and healthy sexuality.

The following chart highlights key differences between the sexual attitudes and behaviors porn promotes and those that exist in healthy sexual intimacy. Pay attention to any concepts that surprise you or that you would like to better understand and address.

DO YOU KNOW THE DIFFERENCE?

Porn-related Sex	*Healthy Sex*
Sex is using someone	Sex is caring for someone
Sex is "doing to" someone	Sex is sharing with a partner
Sex is a performance for others	Sex is a private experience
Sex is compulsive	Sex is a natural drive
Sex is a public commodity	Sex is a personal treasure
Sex is watching others	Sex is about genuine connection
Sex is separate from love	Sex is an expression of love
Sex can be hurtful	Sex is nurturing
Sex is emotionally distant	Sex is emotionally close
Sex can happen anytime	Sex requires certain conditions
Sex is unsafe	Sex is safe
Sex can be degrading	Sex is always respectful
Sex can be irresponsible	Sex is approached responsibly
Sex is devoid of morality	Sex requires morals and values
Sex lacks healthy communication	Sex requires healthy communication
Sex involves deception	Sex requires honesty
Sex is based on visual imagery	Sex involves all the senses
Sex has no ethical limits	Sex has ethical boundaries
Sex requires a double life	Sex enhances who you really are
Sex compromises your values	Sex reflects your values
Sex feels shameful	Sex enhances self-esteem
Sex is impulse gratification	Sex is lasting satisfaction

Besides developing a healthier way to conceptualize sex, this last action step also involves stopping sexual behaviors that perpetuate porn use. Recovering porn addicts often ask: *Should I quit masturbating? Should I stop having sex with a partner?* They worry that engaging in certain sexual activities will reinforce old porn-related ways of approaching sex that pull them right back into using porn again. And they want to know how and when they should begin expressing their natural sexual drives and impulses in positive ways. Rather than leave it up to chance, they wisely realize that their success in recovery may depend on knowing ahead of time how to respond to their sexual feelings and urges.

Decisions about sexual expression vary from person to person. What is appropriate for one person may not be for another. Given the powerful lure of porn, and its strong link to compulsive sexual behavior, we recommend that you seek the advice of a trained counselor in figuring out what is best for you to do. A trained counselor can take into consideration the nature and extent of your porn problem as well as your personal lifestyle, religious/spiritual beliefs, and treatment history, and then help you decide on a safe and productive strategy for dealing with your sexual feelings.

If your sexuality has been deeply entangled with your porn use, you may want to consider taking a break from sex altogether, or from certain types of sexual expression for a while. Some type of break from sex is often recommended, especially for people with sexually compulsive behavior and/or interests in risky, illegal, and dangerous sexual activity. Many twelve-step, faith-based, and sexual addiction treatment programs strongly advocate an initial period of sexual abstinence, which we refer to as a "vacation from sex." This break from sex, lasting anywhere from several weeks to several months or more, can be extremely beneficial, if not necessary, for someone who is struggling to overcome a porn addiction. Knowing that sex in any form is off limits for a while can help a person to create a clear and firm boundary. "The three-month break I took from sex was a lifesaver," Ed told us. "Because I knew I just wasn't going to go there, I wasn't plagued by thoughts about sex and porn."

A vacation from sex can quickly put a halt to negative patterns of sexual expression that are centered around and contaminated by porn. It can give you a chance to realize you can survive just fine without porn-fueled sex, and that your sense of yourself as a sexual person extends well beyond your former relationship with porn. Following the break from sex, you can learn new ways of approaching touch and sex that are free from porn's destructive influence.

Some former porn users are able to continue having sexual experiences while quitting porn without it harming their recovery. For the most part, these are people who have already established highly pleasurable patterns of sexual behavior that have nothing to do with porn. Their sexual interests are not compulsive and do not involve fantasies or thoughts of porn. For example, Derek, a thirty-five-year-old bus driver, is recovering from a sporadic porn problem that he had developed just in the last few years when his marriage was strained. "I prefer fantasizing about my wife when I masturbate and when we make love," he said. "If I were to stop having sex now, just when we're healing our relationship, it would seem silly and unnecessary."

It takes time to undo old porn-related concepts and sexual behaviors and replace them with healthier approaches to sex. This sexuality-focused action step helps get you started and moving in a positive direction. Taking this step helps you avoid sexual issues that, when left unaddressed, can undermine your recovery efforts. As we will discuss more in chapter 11, "A New Approach to Sex," a deep and lasting recovery from porn involves developing new sexual habits that decrease your interest in porn and expand your ability to experience sexual pleasure in new ways. With patience and practice, you can develop a new approach to sexual arousal that enhances your self-esteem and ability to be sexually intimate and loving with a partner.

The six basic action steps presented in this chapter help you build a strong bridge so you can move away from the world of porn. Once you start taking these steps, you'll be able to avoid common recovery obstacles and cultivate new attitudes and behaviors that increase your chances of success in quitting porn. But it is important to recognize that these six steps are not the entire healing process. As we'll see in upcoming chapters, porn recovery also includes knowing how to deal with setbacks, address underlying problems caused by porn, heal a wounded relationship, and develop new sex and intimacy skills.

9

Handling and Preventing Relapses

I am always only a day or an hour away from the same old habit.

—Ed

Long after Drew, a thirty-five-year-old father, thought he was done with porn, he suffered an unexpected setback and started using it again. The experience was upsetting and took him by surprise. "I had three years of recovery with no real cravings or temptations to use porn," he said. "Then one night my wife was out of town, and I started looking at it on the computer. I ended up masturbating to porn basically all night. It was easier than before, because my Internet connection was so fast and I didn't have any porn-blocking software on my computer. I fell right in."

Corey was extremely distraught when he slipped gradually into a major relapse during the first year of his recovery. "I was surfing the Internet and ended up looking at the lingerie advertisements," he said. "After looking at a few of those I thought, *Well, this is just lingerie.* Of course, I ignored the fact that it was turning me on. Then I went to a swimsuit site and figured, *Hey, they're just swimsuits.* Feeling turned on, I kept thinking that I could masturbate to it because technically it wasn't porn. Over the next five to six days I slowly wormed my way into looking at pornography again."

Both Drew and Corey were shaken and disappointed in themselves when they relapsed. Although they knew from talking with other recovering porn users that relapse is often a normal part of recovery, they didn't expect that it would happen to them. Each felt ashamed and worried about what his relapse meant. Was it a temporary slip-up? Were they headed back to using porn again? Fortunately, both men had good support systems in place, and they were able to get help immediately and continue to move forward in their recovery. With guidance from their counselors and the other recovering porn users in their groups, they were able to evaluate and discuss how and why their relapses happened, and develop strategies that further strengthened their recovery efforts.

In this chapter we explore the phenomenon of relapse—what it is, why it happens, and how you can deal with it. Our goal is to give you the information and tools you need to empower you to avoid being pulled back into the porn trap. We'll help you identify factors that trigger your desire for porn, find new ways to reduce your risk of relapsing, and show you how to move away from porn in time to prevent a relapse from happening in the first place.

We'll also provide you with constructive ways to cope if a relapse does happen to you. The fact is the process of quitting porn doesn't usually follow a straight line of progress but, instead, often involves a series of successes and setbacks. Keeping this in mind can help you face the reality of a relapse with a combination of self-compassion, forgiveness, and inquisitiveness, which will make you much more likely to stick to your recovery goals. When you remain kind to yourself and curious, you can learn important things about letting go of your relationship with porn. And by becoming proactive, you will be able to quickly rebound when a relapse occurs and get back on track in your healing journey.

To be successful at quitting porn, you'll need to become an expert at effectively handling relapses and ultimately learning how to avoid them. With the right attitude and approach, you can then transform what could have been a potentially destructive relapse experience into an opportunity for strengthening your personal integrity and being able to stay away from porn for good.

What Is a Porn Relapse?

We define porn relapse as *falling back into the former problem behavior of using porn*. If you have become re-involved with porn after experiencing problems with it and after making a commitment to quit using it, then you have had a porn relapse.

There are many types of relapses, from minor slip-ups such as picking up a porn magazine and glancing through it for a few minutes, to full-scale setbacks that involve seeking out and using porn for sexual release on a regular basis. For most people the briefer, less frequent, and less sexually involved the relapse, the less danger it poses to recovery. When responded to quickly and effectively, a minor slip-up can actually serve as a wake-up call for a recovering porn user to pay closer attention to his behavior and shore up vulnerable areas in his lifestyle.

Relapses that continue for weeks or months, involve sexual arousal and orgasm, and are essentially a return to regular porn use can be quite difficult to extinguish. Once someone has spent time away from porn, reestablishing the emotional and sexual attachment to it can actually strengthen a porn addiction. A relapse that continues over time can restimulate the desire for porn and result in problematic behavior being more intense, time-consuming, and damaging than ever before. As Brad shared, "When I went back to porn after months away and started using it regularly again, it felt as if I was trying to make up for lost time."

WHY DO PEOPLE RELAPSE?

When people have a history of having used porn to cope with emotional pain and stress and for sexual pleasure, they are particularly susceptible to wanting to use it again, no matter how motivated they have been to quit. Porn addiction is a chronic condition that doesn't automatically go away just because someone stops using porn. As we discussed in chapter 4, long-term porn use—like alcoholism and other drug addictions—changes brain chemistry, and those changes take time to heal.

Former porn users often live with a powerful, underlying hunger for porn that can linger for months or even years after they've quit using it. They are particularly susceptible to feelings, thoughts, and situations they have previously associated with porn, because powerful memories of past sexual excitement can bring the underlying desire to use porn back to life. Brad explains, "Alcoholics know they are 'alcoholics for life': as long as booze exists, they want to drink it. And people who quit smoking cigarettes are the first to admit they are 'smokers for life.' Well, the same is true for us porn addicts. When you've had a sexual relationship with porn, you *never* completely stop being tempted by it."

Recovering porn users are especially vulnerable to relapse because the cultural environment in which we live is filled with sexually stimulating messages and images. It is challenging to steer clear of porn for extended periods of time when provocative images that can arouse the desire for porn are everywhere—in ads for beer in magazines, in the scantily clad performers featured on television, in the sexually suggestive links that pop up unexpectedly on nonporn Web sites, and so on. But even if a proliferation of sexually explicit images weren't present in the real world, they can still be ever-present in the former porn user's mind. It's been more than ten years since Alex used porn, and he told us, "Staying away from porn is still hard. My mind is still full of the stuff. I can call up my favorite stories and pornographic pictures at any time. The images feel burned into me."

Drug addicts and alcoholics who are also recovering from porn addiction told us that because of the compelling nature of porn, its abundance in the environment, and the sexual pleasure it offers, they often feel more prone to a porn relapse than a drug or alcohol relapse. Ralph, a thirty-six-year-old recovering alcoholic, told us his cravings for porn are stronger than his cravings for alcohol. His memories of using porn don't serve as a deterrent like his memories of alcohol. "When I think about my drinking days," he said, "I remember throwing up in drunken binges, not being able to drive, and hangovers. But with porn, it's different. I never had an orgasm with porn that I didn't find extremely pleasurable. It takes more thinking to stop myself."

Kirk, a former marijuana and porn user, shared that he has had a harder time avoiding relapses with porn than with pot. "With stopping marijuana all I had to do was not buy it and stay away from people who use it," he said. "One whiff of a joint at a party or friend's house was all it took for me to slip. Now I don't hang out with those people. With porn it's not so easy. Sexual images are everywhere. I can get to porn anytime I want. I have to work much harder at staying away from it."

Many users underestimate their bond with porn, believing they can avoid or resist the urges that plague other people in recovery. But believing you're invulnerable can work against anyone's ability to avoid relapse. Pastor

Jim Thomas cautions the newcomers to his men's porn recovery groups: "Every one of the men in this room has relapsed to some extent. Don't get cocky and believe that relapse won't happen to you, because once you think you can avoid it, that's probably when it's going to blindside you."

Even when their motivation is genuine and they are receiving competent care and support, recovering porn users can relapse anywhere in the recovery process. Some former porn users said they were more likely to slide back into porn early on because they were ambivalent about their decision to quit or assumed quitting porn would be easier than it actually was. They hadn't replaced old porn patterns of sexual pleasuring and dealing with stress with healthier porn-free patterns, and they still held attitudes about sex that made it extremely difficult to turn their backs on porn.

Other former porn users told us that relapse became a serious issue for them in the later stages of recovery when they thought they had the problem under control. They forgot how emotionally and sexually attached to porn they had been, how many problems porn use caused them, and how serious and risky even a little contact with it could be. Successful time away from porn led them to let down their guard. "I thought I could handle it," Corey said. "I was testing myself to see what kinds of sexual images I could still enjoy." As Corey and others discover, these "tests" increase exposure and vulnerability to triggers and can result in a serious relapse before a former porn user realizes what's happening.

WHAT IS THE PROGRESSION OF A RELAPSE?

Going into a relapse is not like accidentally stepping in a hole in the ground. A recovering porn user doesn't suddenly, without reason, drop back into a state of being sexually re-involved with porn. Like other events in life, a relapse occurs in stages and is really not a single event, but a process that happens over time and has many different levels of experience. You shift from a state of being uninvolved with porn, that we refer to as being in the "Porn-Free Zone," to being vulnerable to relapse in the "Trigger Territory." From there you can enter the "Relapse Zone" in which you can become progressively more involved with porn again. As Diagram 1, "Getting into a Relapse," shows, porn relapses actually start well before a person physically renews his involvement with porn materials.

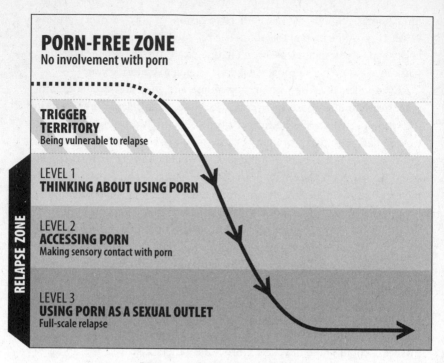

PORN-FREE ZONE
No involvement with porn

TRIGGER TERRITORY
Being vulnerable to relapse

RELAPSE ZONE

LEVEL 1
THINKING ABOUT USING PORN

LEVEL 2
ACCESSING PORN
Making sensory contact with porn

LEVEL 3
USING PORN AS A SEXUAL OUTLET
Full-scale relapse

Diagram 1: Getting into a Relapse

The ultimate goal of porn recovery is to be in and stay in the Porn-Free Zone. This is where you have absolutely no involvement with porn, mentally or physically, and are not troubled by porn in any way. Diligently working the basic action steps described in the last chapter will enable you to spend increasing amounts of time in the Porn-Free Zone.

When you are in the Porn-Free Zone, something external in your environment or internal with the way you feel, emotionally or physically, can suddenly send you into the Trigger Territory. This is the level where you are more vulnerable to using porn again, even though you haven't taken any concrete steps toward using. External triggers include accidental exposure to sexually explicit material and ideas, being around sexually provocative people, and having contact with porn delivery systems such as the Internet and cable TV. Common internal triggers include feeling stressed, upset, lonely, angry, depressed, anxious, run down, sexually-frustrated, or being under the influence of alcohol or drugs. Richard said, "I know I'm in Trigger Territory and in danger of entering the Relapse Zone when I'm doing something like watching MTV or reading the personals in the newspaper, and I start rationalizing by telling myself, *This isn't as bad as looking at porn.*"

Triggers differ from individual to individual. For example, seeing an R-rated movie with an intense sex scene might trigger some former users into thoughts about wanting to access porn, while the same sex scene might have absolutely no triggering effects on other former porn users.

It is quite common for many people attempting to heal from a relationship with porn to enter the Trigger Territory without even knowing they are there. Many triggers occur outside of our conscious awareness. You may not even be thinking about using porn, but you may in fact be in a state of mind where you are much more susceptible to a relapse than you were days, even moments before. "I didn't understand that I was being set up for relapse," Brad said. "I'd feel a certain way and then something would trigger me. Before I knew it I was just reeling with desire to get off on porn. Then I was either white-knuckling it—holding on for dear life and trying my best not to do it—or I'd plunge in head first and just land right on my face. The trigger could be something as simple as driving by a beer advertisement on a billboard with busty women on it."

Trigger Territory holds the key to relapse prevention. If you know what your triggers are, you can take steps to deactivate them when they come up, and therefore prevent yourself from sliding into the Relapse Zone. And, it can be a lot easier to pull yourself out of a potential relapse from the Trigger Territory, than try to make your way back to the Porn-Free Zone once you have slid further down into the Relapse Zone.

The first level of the Relapse Zone, Level One, involves thinking about using porn. Memories of past porn use may surface. You may start contemplating how pleasurable it would be to use porn, or begin planning how you could use it again. "A sexual thought would enter my mind, and I'd entertain it and begin to play with it," Nick explained about his past relapses. "When I did that even for a microsecond, I was a goner. The fantasies of porn were so pleasurable and I didn't have a mechanism to shift out of that thinking. When you're in the middle of a relapse, the harmful consequences of using porn are in the distant future. I thought I could toy with pleasurable thoughts of porn, but that was dangerous. It was just like touching two wires together. I couldn't pull them apart fast enough to keep them from setting off a spark. And once the spark ignited, I felt driven to seek out and use porn again."

When thoughts of using porn go unchecked, and there is a reigniting of a sexual desire for porn material, it is often just a matter of time before a person moves to the next level of the Relapse Zone, Level Two, and makes actual contact with porn. Then, whether thumbing through a magazine, renting a DVD, or logging onto an online porn site, for most recovering users this return to accessing porn often drops them further into the Relapse Zone, Level Three, where they use porn as a sexual outlet. When a person is in Level Three, he or she is using porn to experience sexual arousal, masturbation, and/or orgasm. This intense re-involvement with porn is extremely dangerous, because the pleasurable sensations of sexual arousal and release that porn facilitates reinforce a person's desire to have contact with porn again in the future. Repeated Level Three relapses can easily stymie a person's long-term efforts to recover from porn.

The further a person slides down in the Relapse Zone, the more difficult it becomes to turn around and get out. Like sinking into quicksand, the forces pulling you down intensify the deeper you slip. The drive to return to porn on an ongoing basis increases as sex with porn is first entertained, then anticipated, pursued, and finally carried out.

How to Reverse a Relapse

Unfortunately, there are no external warnings and alarms—no sirens or red lights—to tell you when you're heading into the Relapse Zone. As a result, you may not become aware that you are relapsing until you are already thinking about using porn, in sensory contact with it, or actively involved with it. Regardless of where you are in the relapse process, your best strategy is to take the appropriate steps to get yourself headed back toward the Porn-Free Zone as quickly as possible.

You can effectively reverse a relapse by implementing the following five-part intervention:

1. **Stop** what you are doing and admit you have entered a danger zone
2. **Get away** from porn thoughts and materials

3. **Calm** yourself physiologically and emotionally
4. **Reach out** for supportive help as quickly as possible
5. **Reaffirm** your commitment to your recovery

The diagram below shows that you can apply this five-part intervention at any point in time to stop yourself from sliding further down into relapse and get yourself back into the Porn-Free Zone.

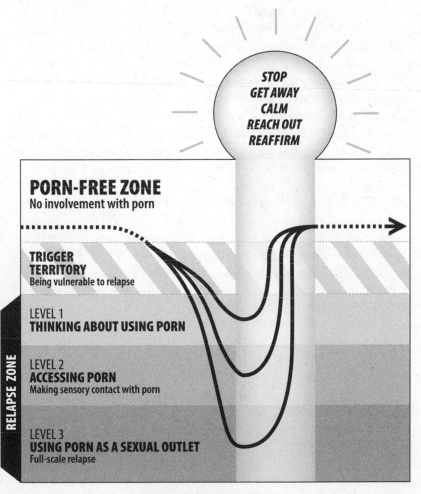

Diagram 2: Reversing a Relapse

Let's explore each of the five parts of the relapse reversal intervention in detail.

1. Stop what you are doing and admit you are in a danger zone. As soon as the thought crosses your mind that you are doing something that could make you susceptible to becoming actively involved with porn again, you need to stop. If you dismiss or rationalize away warning signs of danger, you set yourself up to plunge further down into the Relapse Zone. On the other hand, validating your awareness of being in vulnerable territory and choosing to immediately disengage from your porn-oriented thinking and behavior helps you to break out of the trance-like state that often accompanies a relapse. Stopping is a way of giving yourself an opportunity to acknowledge that what you are doing is dangerous and will lead to problems. "When I realize I'm looking at something that is similar to porn," Corey told us, "I stop, and tell myself, *This is porn and I need to stop!* Hearing myself say it out loud brings me into reality again. It keeps me from lying to myself, which, obviously, I had gotten pretty good at doing when I was watching porn."

The skill of stopping your behavior and honestly admitting to yourself what is happening is vital for being able to successfully deal with relapse at any level. If you find yourself thinking about using porn, STOP! If you find yourself purchasing or looking at porn, STOP! Even if you are in the middle of masturbating to porn, just STOP! Interrupting old patterns of porn use allows you to resume control of your thoughts and behavior and make good decisions about what to do next.

2. Get away from porn thoughts and materials. Once you are aware that you're in a Relapse Zone, take immediate action to create as much distance as you can between yourself and porn. If you had been thinking about using porn, focus your thinking on something else. Keep your distance from sources of porn.

If you're at a computer, turn it off and walk away from it. If you're watching television, change channels, turn it off, or get up and leave the room. Take a walk, call a friend, listen to music, spend time in nature . . . do whatever it takes to shift your consciousness away from porn. (See exercise, "Shifting Your Attention.")

Shifting Your Attention

A simple sensory awareness exercise can help you shift your attention away from what you've been thinking about and on to something else in your environment. Begin by saying the phrase, "Now I'm aware of . . . ," and then complete it by stating something you *see* in your environment. For example, "Now I'm aware of the sun coming through the window." Repeat and complete the phrase "Now I'm aware of . . . ," until you have identified five different things that you see. Continue the exercise stating five different things you are aware of hearing, then five things you are aware of touching or feeling inside your body. This exercise can help center you sensually in the reality of your present environment and take you farther away from the fantasy world of porn.

No matter where you are at any given time or how sexually aroused you might feel, you have many choices for changing what you are thinking about, looking at, and doing. Shifting her thinking and her behavior helped Marie stop herself in the midst of a relapse. "I drove all over town one day with this big plan how I was going to buy porn magazines, take them home, and read them from cover to cover. I passed different stores where I used to get porn and I stopped at one place to make a purchase. When I got to the checkout counter, I suddenly thought, *This is really stupid.* I saw that I was caught in some kind of a little ritual thing. I left the magazines on the counter and walked out of the store."

3. Calm yourself physiologically and emotionally. While shifting your attention away from porn is essential, you also need to deal with the fact that you may have already been stimulated by your thoughts or actions. Just thinking about using porn can trigger certain physiological reactions, such as changes in heart rate, blood pressure, genital blood flow, and pupil dilation, which can set you up for a full-blown relapse. In addition, anticipating using porn can trigger the release of dopamine and other pleasure-related chemicals in the brain that can also propel you toward wanting contact with porn. These physiological and brain chemistry changes start to subside and your body can begin to return to normal when you stop thinking about using porn or break off contact with it. In the meantime, you may feel some discomfort while your body readjusts to the lack of stimulation from porn. This is why it is so important to figure out how to calm yourself, both physiologically and emotionally, once your sexual energy has become activated.

There are a number of ways to calm yourself after thinking about or beginning to use porn. Sitting or lying down in a resting position, breathing slowly, and resting a hand over your heart can help lower your heart rate and lull you into a quieter state. Breathing slowly and deeply through your left nostril for about five minutes while blocking off your right nostril can facilitate relaxation. Another helpful approach is to massage the outer area of your ears, a spot that can induce relaxation and calm. Massaging your feet can also quiet your agitated mind and body by helping move your attention and energy away from sexual excitation and toward feeling good in a non-sexual way. Some people find that quiet prayer or meditation helps create feelings of calm and relaxation, while still others prefer burning off excess agitated energy through vigorous exercise, such as jogging, lifting weights, or riding a bike.

4. Reach out for supportive help as quickly as possible. One of the most effective ways to handle a relapse is to contact someone for support. Calling on a counselor, accountability partner, friend, church leader, or intimate partner who is aware of your recovery goals and efforts can help you pull away from porn again. Pastor Jim Thomas explains, "When you notice you are relapsing, that's a good time to make a phone call, reach out and make connection, and intercept the relapse process. Make contact quickly so you don't get pulled further in."

By reaching out to his pastor, Mitch was able to pull himself out of a Level Two relapse. "One day I got on the Internet and started going to the old sites," he said. "I knew if I didn't deal with it right away I would bury it, nobody would know, and I would act like I was okay. I called my pastor immediately and said, 'I want to come in and see you as soon as possible, and I want you to pray for me. I want to confess it, renounce it, and rebuke it in my own life.' My pastor helped me recognize that in spite of the slip, I had made progress. Before I wouldn't even worry about being there, but now I'm very concerned about it."

Reaching out for support during or after a relapse is not without its challenges. Brad had to overcome his habit of wanting to hide. "When I relapsed, I instinctively wanted to go back into hibernation—hiding from others and being secretive," he said. "I couldn't believe I had failed. There were all these guys from my recovery group to whom I was accountable, to whom I had committed, and I failed. I wondered, *How on earth can I face them?*" When Brad did return to his group and disclosed his relapse, he discovered that all the men were compassionate and understanding, were familiar with the relapse process, and had very helpful ideas on how to prevent future relapses.

Alex turns to his wife when he finds himself on the slippery slope of relapse. "If I see something that is sexually stimulating for me, I tell her. She likes that I turn to her. It definitely helps knowing she's a partner in this with me and a part of my recovery." It is important to remember, as we noted in chapter 8, whether or not a partner can be relied on for support and accountability is something that will differ among couples.

Whomever you reach out to for support in handling a relapse, it should be someone you feel will understand your challenges, hold you accountable for your actions, and offer positive suggestions and continued encouragement in your quest to quit using porn.

5. Reaffirm your commitment to your recovery. Once you have stopped your porn-seeking behavior, shifted your attention away from porn, calmed yourself, and reached out for help, the final step in reversing a relapse is to firmly reestablish your commitment to become porn-free. This important strategy involves remembering why you wanted to quit porn in the first place, and what you are striving to accomplish by no longer having porn in your life. When you refocus and recommit to your recovery goals, you will find yourself back on a trajectory toward the Porn-Free Zone.

A good way to reaffirm your commitment to quitting porn is by reviewing your responses to the exercises in chapter 7 for strengthening your motivation to quit porn. Remind yourself of the problems that come with being involved with porn, how it can keep you separate from others and feeling bad about yourself, put you in danger, and limit sexual learning. Go over your values and goals to re-familiarize yourself with what really matters to you and the kind of person you want to be.

Just as you did when starting out in the recovery process, it's important when you relapse to take responsibility for your own behavior and to take concrete steps to no longer be involved with porn. For ideas and direction to get yourself back on track with your recovery, look over the six basic action steps we presented in the previous chapter. Identify any steps that you may have ignored or have not been following through on sufficiently. Brainstorm how you can move forward more successfully with taking those steps now.

Some recovering porn users find it beneficial to create a ritual or habit they can turn to that helps them reaffirm their recovery when they find themselves in or close to relapse. Ken, a forty-year-old married man, didn't like how he would get automatically triggered to return to porn whenever he saw a particular type of attractive woman. With the help of his counselor, he developed a ritual to quickly recommit to his recovery. The ritual consisted of immediately touching and looking at his wedding ring. Touching his ring reminded him of his love and devotion to his wife and his interest in keeping porn completely out of his life. After several months of using this reaffirmation ritual, Ken was only rarely troubled by thoughts of wanting to use porn again.

The five strategies—stop, get away, calm, reach out, and reaffirm—give you a proactive and effective way of getting out of a relapse. Next, we'll see how through greater self-awareness and building additional skills, you can learn how to keep yourself securely outside of the Relapse Zone.

PREVENTING FUTURE RELAPSES

Whether you've relapsed in the past or not, it is important to develop strategies for preventing future relapses. Your recovery will have a much greater chance of success when you can identify that you are approaching or have just entered Trigger Territory, and you have reliable methods in place for

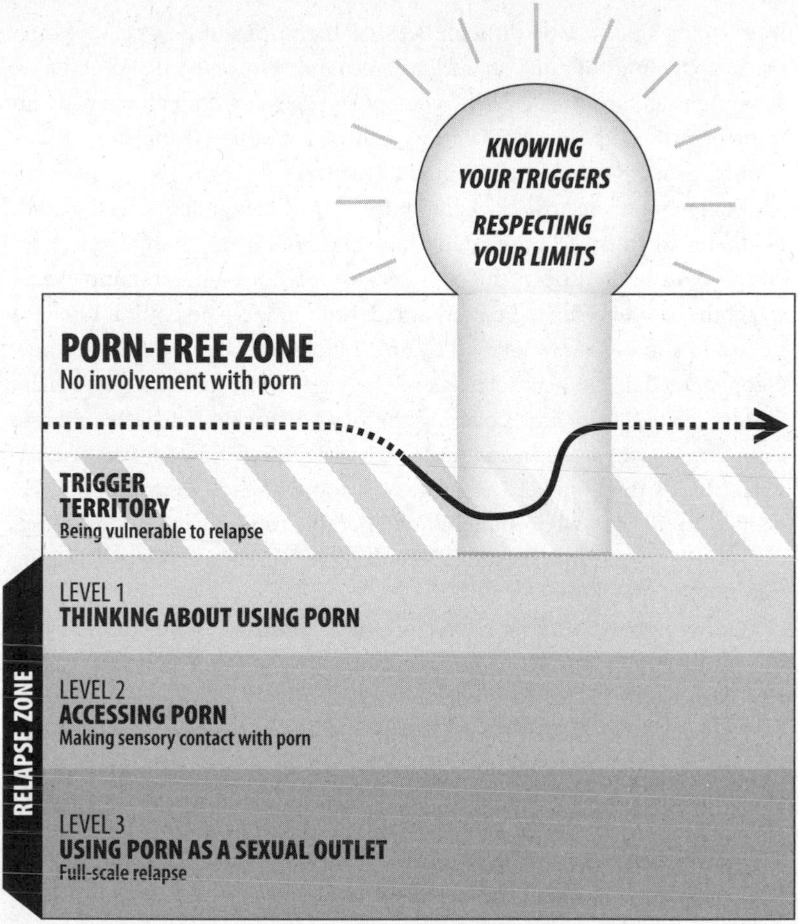

KNOWING YOUR TRIGGERS

RESPECTING YOUR LIMITS

PORN-FREE ZONE
No involvement with porn

TRIGGER TERRITORY
Being vulnerable to relapse

RELAPSE ZONE

LEVEL 1
THINKING ABOUT USING PORN

LEVEL 2
ACCESSING PORN
Making sensory contact with porn

LEVEL 3
USING PORN AS A SEXUAL OUTLET
Full-scale relapse

Diagram 3: Preventing a Relapse

getting yourself quickly and safely back into the Porn-Free Zone *before* you even reach the Relapse Zone. (See Diagram 3: "Preventing a Relapse.")

There are two primary methods you can use to prevent future relapses from occurring: knowing your triggers and respecting your limits. Let's look at each of these.

Knowing your triggers. One of the best ways to understand what triggers your desire to return to porn is to look at past relapses and learn from them. This can be difficult because memories of past relapses can bring up feelings of guilt, shame, and remorse. However, if you can look at any past relapses as part of your porn recovery education, you can transform the experience of feeling bad about yourself into one of becoming proactive and hopeful in your recovery.

Following his relapse back into porn, Corey scheduled a session with his therapist to try to understand how and why it had happened. After all the pain he had been through because of porn—his unhappy marriage, the sexual offense he committed, time in jail—he couldn't believe he would slip back into using it again. "I knew if I didn't figure out how I got there, I'd just go there again," he said. With his therapist's help, Corey created a timeline covering the period shortly before his relapse until after it was over. In his timeline he identified how he was feeling, what he was thinking, and what he was doing at each point in time. He wanted to identify what made him vulnerable to relapsing and might in the future indicate that he had entered Trigger Territory and was slipping into the Relapse Zone.

Corey figured out that his relapse had begun when he started playing mind games with himself when he was feeling lonely and sexually frustrated. "First I convinced myself that I was only looking at swimsuit ads," he said. "Then I began to look at catalogs that included lingerie. I tricked myself into believing all of it was safe and allowable. By the time I got to the porn sites, my sexual excitement had kicked in and I was already so caught up, it didn't matter to me what I was doing." Corey learned that even though lingerie and swimsuit ads are not technically porn, they gave him the same rush he used to get from porn. He didn't even have to masturbate or have an orgasm, just searching for those pictures and thinking of searching brought on feelings of euphoria. It became clear that it wasn't what he was looking at, but *why* and *how* he was involved that mattered in terms of triggering his relapse.

Analyzing her most recent relapses for clues to prevent future occurrences, Marie discovered that what triggered her relapse back into using porn was feeling emotionally vulnerable and looking for something to soothe her feelings. "When I get really stressed out and feel like a failure in life, it's like a little movie projector in my brain kicks on and starts showing the porn I've already seen to make me feel better. Then I get triggered into wanting to go buy and look at more porn. I've learned to pay attention to when I get stressed out and shift immediately into reducing stress and taking care of myself emotionally so that I feel better inside."

Drew looked back on two prior relapse experiences for clues as to how he could prevent new ones from happening. "When I had my first relapse, my counselor thought it occurred because I was isolated and not committed enough to my recovery. She suggested I join a men's recovery group, but I wasn't interested. A few months later I had another relapse with porn. Taking my counselor's advice more seriously, I got involved in a group. I've gone weekly to it for the last four years and it's helped tremendously. I haven't had another slip."

You can draw on Corey's, Marie's, and Drew's examples to start learning from your own past relapses. Take a closer look at a relapse you may have had in the past and construct your own timeline of events related to it. Identify how you were feeling, what you were thinking, and what you were doing at various points in your relapse process. What triggered you into the Relapse Zone? What could you do differently to prevent yourself from getting triggered in the future?

Another good way to know your triggers is to *imagine in detail* what type of situation could lead to a relapse. This visualization process allows you to identify a broad range of factors that could contribute to your being triggered into thinking about porn, acquiring it, or using it for sex. You can benefit from this healing strategy whether or not you have relapsed before.

The following exercise, "If I Were About to Relapse," is designed to help you become aware of a wide variety of experiences that increase your vulnerability to relapse. It is a powerful tool in helping you to gain control over relapsing behavior. However, the process of contemplating and answering the questions in the exercise can stir up some unexpected thoughts and emotional reactions. Therefore, you may want to do this exercise with the assistance of a counselor or other support person.

If I Were About to Relapse

This exercise guides you through a process of imagining a hypothetical relapse experience. It helps you think through the different factors that could set you up for relapse.

Imagine that you are just about to relapse with porn. Answer each of the questions below based on what you envision. It can be helpful to reference to your past experiences when you've felt urges to use porn to guide you with your answers. Identify as many factors as might apply for each question.

Where are you likely to be (home, work, car, hotel, school, and so on)?
_____

What porn delivery systems would be readily available to you (computer, television, porn magazines, cell phone, and so on)?_____
_____

What time of day would it be (morning, midday, afternoon, evening, or late at night)?_____
_____

Who would you be with (alone, friend, intimate partner, stranger, a group of people, and so on)?_____
_____

What activities would you be doing (working, studying, eating, traveling, resting, relaxing, being entertained, exercising, reading, socializing, and so on)?_____
_____

How would you be feeling physically (tired, hungry, agitated, sexually excited, in pain, exhausted, sick, cold, overheated, disheveled, out of shape, fit, and so on)?_____
_____

What, if any, other addictive or problem behaviors would you have been doing (smoking cigarettes, drinking alcohol, taking drugs, gambling, shopping, staying up late, overeating, overworking, and so on)?

_____

What would have just happened (a disappointment, a rejection, an accomplishment, a reward or payment, an argument, a missed opportunity, a physical parting from someone, and so on)?_____

_____

How would you be feeling emotionally (lonely, depressed, angry, anxious, frustrated, sad, happy, bored, disappointed, powerful, and so on)?_____

_____

What unmet needs would you be feeling (the need for companionship, excitement, novelty, competition, friendship, recognition, love, validation, relaxation, comfort, and so on)?_____

_____

What core emotional wounds would be activated (feeling abandoned, betrayed, rejected, incapable, unattractive, humiliated, powerless, inadequate, and so on)?_____

_____

What types of sexually explicit content would you have inadvertently been exposed to (sexual image on television, sex scene in a movie, pop-up ad on the Internet, advertisement, billboard, magazine cover, written sexual description, and so on)?_____

_____

In what ways might you be "pushing the envelope" by involving yourself in activities that are similar to or remind you of using porn (going online when no one else is around, channel surfing for sexual imagery, looking for sexual images in regular magazines, watching

R-rated movies, staying in hotels with pay-per-view porn channels, participating in chat room activity, being secretive about other behaviors, being alone with free time, and so on)?_____

_____

If you were in the midst of the relapse, what strategies for reversing it might you fail to take (stopping what you are doing and admitting you are in a danger zone, getting away from porn thoughts and materials, calming yourself physiologically and emotionally, reaching out quickly for supportive help, reaffirming your commitment to your recovery)?

_____

_____

Any of the items you have identified in this exercise have the potential to trigger you into a relapse. Review your responses and think about changes you could make that would strengthen your ability to remain porn-free. Do you need to take better care of yourself physically? Do you need to learn to better handle your emotions? Do you need to improve your relationships with other people?

It is not uncommon for multiple triggers to be linked together and to reinforce each other when activated. For example, being alone, exhausted, bored, and in front of a computer late at night, may combine to create a high-risk situation. Use the space below to write out the triggers that link together that you need to pay attention to in order to avoid a porn relapse in the future: _____

_____

_____

Finally, based on all that you have learned by doing this exercise, use the following space to list a number of healthy, constructive alternatives you could use to meet your needs when you are vulnerable to using porn: _____

_____

_____

_____

When Jesse, a twenty-five-year-old married recovering porn user who had never gone into a full-scale relapse before thought about how it might happen, he pictured himself alone in his car parked in his garage after work before his wife got home. He imagined feeling nervous and insecure about his job. He saw himself stopping at a convenience store on the way home on the pretense of getting a cold drink and then impulsively grabbing a porn magazine as he passed from the soda dispenser to the cash register. Jesse identified his unmet needs as being a need to physically relax and get emotional reassurance that he was doing well at work and was appreciated.

Jesse used these revelations about himself to devise a plan to avoid relapse. He started calling his wife, Megan, on his cell phone when he left work every day. This practice had an unexpected side benefit of making Megan more amorous toward him at night. If he wanted a cool drink or a candy bar after work, he shopped only at stores that didn't carry porn magazines. He decided to cut back on his caffeine intake during the day so that he would feel less nervous and agitated. He gave himself permission to ask Megan for a neck and shoulder massage at night to help him calm down. Making these changes has helped him cope with and manage his feelings in ways that don't send him impulsively longing for porn.

It can be challenging to sit down and try to imagine yourself becoming susceptible to a relapse. No one likes to admit the possibility of falling back into using porn or picture in detail how it might happen. However, recovering porn users who do this exercise tell us it works as a prophylactic measure, because after completing it they feel better able to recognize when they are vulnerable to using porn again and know what steps to take to prevent an actual relapse from occurring.

Respecting your limits. Another important skill in relapse prevention is to know your own limits and avoid putting yourself in situations where you could be pushed past them and fall back into using porn. Once you've gotten a better understanding of your triggers, you have an idea of where you need to draw the line when it comes to your actions and choices. "I'm learning to stay away from the cliff edge rather than seeing how close I can get to it without falling," Kirk explains. "There are certain things—some sexual, some not—I just don't do anymore because I know they set me up for relapse. I pay attention to where I am and what

I'm doing so I can keep myself safe. I'm like the weather channel, constantly updating my situation."

Here are some examples of changes other recovering porn users made to honor their personal limits and reduce their risk of relapse:

- Tom loves lifting weights and reading articles about it. But because bodybuilding magazines also have pictures of half-naked women in them that he used to masturbate to, he doesn't buy or look at these types of magazines any more.
- Justin doesn't drink beer any more because he used to drink beer whenever he watched porn.
- Laura limits herself to PG–13 movies because the R-rated ones contain all kinds of triggers, like sex scenes, crude jokes, and violence that could set her up for going back to watching porn.

Knowing your relapse triggers and knowing and respecting your limits are vital elements for preventing future relapses. Take some time to consider what you could do to modify your behavior to reduce or eliminate your cravings to want to use porn. Try these changes out for a while and discover for yourself if they further assist you in your goal of more consistently being porn-free.

Going Deeper into the Healing Process to Prevent Relapse

For some people who are working to overcome chronic, long-term porn problems, it's not enough to simply become aware of and avoid obvious relapse triggers. They require a more potent strategy for preventing themselves from sliding back into using porn again. As we discussed in chapter 2, for a large number of porn users, their involvement began in childhood or adolescence when they were in emotionally stressful situations. As adults their attachment to porn may still be fueled by the confusion and stress they felt when they were youngsters.

When this is the case, chronic porn users can help themselves prevent future relapses by addressing the connections between their unresolved childhood issues and their recurring desires to use porn. Nick struggled with chronic relapsing during the first few years of his recovery from porn. "At first, all I could see was the outward manifestation of my problem, which was the sexual attraction. That's all I thought I had to deal with. But then I realized that my continuing interest in porn must be due to something else that was more significant."

With the help of his pastor and men's recovery group, Nick figured out that the driving force behind his recurrent porn use had to do with a profound need to feel adequate and accepted by others. "In the third grade, kids began to tease me mercilessly. I felt worthless, terribly inferior, and ashamed of myself. I found relief in reading lurid paperbacks and looking through porn magazines. Porn was my attempt to fill something in me that was missing. Whenever I felt inadequate and different from others, I'd fall back on porn, and it just became a deep-seated pattern throughout my life. Now, since making this connection to my unhappy childhood, I'm a lot less interested in porn."

Like Nick, Laura has also been able to reduce her vulnerability to porn by understanding her deeper psychological issues. "I'm now exploring the origin of my attraction to porn in therapy," she said. "I've mostly been drawn to written porn about risky sex in which a woman is weak and physically threatened. It's pretty clear that my attraction to this scenario has something to do with how powerless I felt when my brothers molested me when I was a young girl."

Analyzing the types of porn fantasies you are most attracted to is a useful way to learn more about the deeper issues that may be fueling your porn relationship. You may find it helpful, especially with the assistance of a trained mental health professional, to answer the following questions:

- What type of story line and plot are you primarily attracted to in porn?
- What are the characters like, and how and why do they relate to each other in the way they do?
- Is there anything about your ideal porn fantasy that relates to unmet needs or painful events that you experienced in your past?

Ethan told us, "My desire for porn greatly diminished after I took a close look at the porn fantasies I'd treasured since I was eight years old.

They were all about a woman being degraded, humiliated, and treated roughly by a man. No matter what he does to her, the woman thinks the guy is great and doesn't want to leave him. When I really looked at the fantasies, I discovered they weren't about sex, at all. They were about how angry, powerless, and insecure I felt as a child with my mom gone a lot."

As Ethan explored the relationship dynamics in his old porn fantasies, he saw that they defied common sense and were in contradiction to what he really wanted in an intimate partner. "The kind of woman I wanted as a kid doesn't exist," he said. "Any woman who would stick around for that kind of treatment isn't a person I really want to be with. Trying to live out this kind of fantasy is no longer a direction I want to go in real life—I've lost interest in it. These days, I'm more interested in reality and pursuing a healthy intimate relationship."

When a relapse happens, it can generate feelings of disappointment, frustration, confusion, failure, and shame. But, when you use a relapse experience to learn more about yourself and what underlies and triggers your relationship with porn, it can actually help you move forward in your pursuit of a porn-free life. Corey wisely told us, "A relapse is only a failure if you let it be. I've learned that a relapse can be seen as merely a *temporary* step back. Regardless of how disappointed you may feel about it at the time, it always has something important to teach you."

10

Healing as a Couple

Recovery from my porn addiction was what finally motivated us to deal with the underlying problems in our marriage and become the couple we'd always wanted to be.

—LOGAN

When Debbie's husband, Roger, lost his job because of a serious porn problem, she considered divorcing him. "I was so mad," she said. "I told him, 'This is the deal. If you want to stay married to me, you'll have to get professional help and quit porn for good. I don't trust you anymore.'" Determined not to lose Debbie and see his twenty-year marriage come to an end, Roger agreed and began attending a weekly sexual addiction recovery group. He also started seeing an individual therapist.

For months Roger and Debbie were estranged from each other while still living in the same house, both feeling insecure and waiting to see what would happen next with their relationship. "I felt so hurt and angry." Debbie said. "The only positive thing was that I knew he was in a recovery program."

It was a difficult time for Roger as well. He struggled with giving up porn and missed feeling close to Debbie, missed the fun they used to have together. "Finally, one night I sat down with Debbie," he said. "I looked her in the eye and told her, 'I just don't know what to do anymore. I have done everything you asked me to do and I've been making progress. It seems like you're angry with me all the time and nothing I do is going to make you happy. In the beginning I understood your reactions because I betrayed you, but now I feel you're punishing me and things aren't getting any better between us.'"

Debbie remembers that night clearly. "I listened to Roger and saw the truth in what he was saying. If we were going to have a healthy marriage some day I had to be willing to let go of my anger and forgive him." Inspired by their conversation, Debbie got started on her own healing. She read books on sexual addiction, codependency and relationship healing, and got counseling for herself. "With both of us working on getting whole and healthy, it made such a difference," Debbie explained. "We started understanding each other better and talking more about how we really felt. It was a big turnaround and enabled us to get the help we needed to rebuild our relationship."

Roger and Debbie's experience shows just how profound the consequences of a porn problem can be on a relationship. Even when the recovering user makes a sincere effort to quit, there are usually many other issues that need to be dealt with in order to fully heal the damage to intimacy in the partnership. True healing only happens when both partners take steps to reestablish honesty, trust, communication, and affection in the relationship.

In this chapter we explore how couples heal from the aftermath of porn. We'll present stories of couples who have successfully worked through the negative repercussions of porn and ultimately improved their intimate relationship. We provide specific steps you and your partner can take to transform your own problems into opportunities to begin healing the deeper wounds, and eventually create a relationship that is more nurturing, mutually satisfying, and deeply fulfilling than ever before.

There are four important steps couples should take to mend the damage porn has had on their relationship:

1. Restore trust
2. Understand your partner's experience
3. Move from anger to forgiveness
4. Improve communication to build intimacy

While we have arranged these steps in a logical order, they often overlap and complement each other. Let's explore each of these steps in detail.

1. RESTORE TRUST

Restoring trust is fundamental to healing as a couple. The dishonesty that is almost always involved when there's a porn problem affects the very core of a couple's relationship. It destroys the intimate partner's ability to believe anything the recovering porn user says or does, including his promises of quitting. She's afraid if she believes him, she may just be setting herself up for more hurt and disappointment. At the same time, the recovering porn user who is sincere in his desire and efforts to quit porn, may be overwhelmed by his partner's loss of belief in and respect for him. He may also feel that her continuing anger and distrust are harming their ability to move forward together.

Since the breakdown in trust in a relationship was caused by the porn user's choices and behavior, it is primarily up to him to restore the trust. As Roger told us, "I laid the foundation of distrust for so many years, I know it is up to me to be the one to build it back. I can't expect Debbie to trust me again just because I want her to or think she should. I have to show her in big and little ways over a long period of time that I have become someone worthy of her trust."

The difficult truth about trust is that while it can be wiped out in a matter of minutes, such as when an intimate partner discovers a file full of Internet porn, it generally takes months or sometimes even years before it can be fully reestablished. This means that the recovering porn user has to not only work on ways of rebuilding trust, but must do so with patience and perseverance. It is unrealistic to expect an intimate partner to automatically trust her partner again simply because he is being "good" by not using porn. He also needs to demonstrate his dependability and credibility in everything he does for as long as it takes.

Walk the talk. When it comes to rebuilding trust, actions speak louder and truer than words. Pastor Jim Thomas explains, "A woman who is healing from a betrayal of trust is thinking: *You can say whatever you want, but you better 'Show me the money' here. I need to be able to see change through your behavior. Your words mean nothing to me.*"

Actions that demonstrate trustworthiness can include: getting involved in a treatment program, taking steps to avoid porn triggers such as accidental exposure to porn or porn-like materials, practicing good self-care, creating a support system, and engaging in honest communication about the recovery process. Although Nancy was extremely upset when she caught her husband, Logan, using Internet porn, it meant a lot to her that within three weeks of the discovery he started individual counseling, joined a men's group for sex addicts, and agreed to couples counseling. "The fact that Logan immediately sought help and went to all the sessions and meetings showed me that he was serious about quitting porn. It reassured me to see how hard he was working to understand the issues underlying his porn problem and to address those issues. His words and actions were consistent. After about six months of his being involved in recovery, I realized I had begun to trust him again."

Recovering porn users who follow through on agreements and recovery activities, even during times when the relationship is strained or other obstacles surface, have a good chance of eventually re-inspiring their partner's trust.

Tell the truth. Honesty and openness are essential in restoring trust, in large part because it was the porn user's dishonesty and deception about using porn that broke the trust in the first place. Your partner needs to know that not only will you tell the truth when she asks you questions, but that you will also volunteer important information about your recovery process. Being up front about porn-related issues and personal behavior is absolutely necessary in order for your intimate partner to believe you can be trusted.

A recovering porn user may be anxious about being completely honest and aboveboard with his partner, however. He may fear that any bad news about his behavior will cause his partner to get angry, emotionally withdraw, or push him away. While these concerns are understandable, the likelihood of these reactions is even greater if the recovering porn user tells half-truths or doesn't fully disclose what he is thinking, feeling, and doing in his recovery process. When a recovering porn user is honest and committed to healing, it is much more likely that his partner will be able to handle setbacks and continue to work together on mending the relationship.

To avoid disagreements and unwarranted accusations of dishonesty, it can be helpful, especially when assisted by a therapist or clergyperson,

for a couple to reach a mutual understanding about the following important aspects of recovery:

- The steps the recovering porn user will take to quit porn;
- How long and how frequently the recovering porn user will attend any treatment programs;
- The specific sexual behaviors that will be avoided;
- What details will be disclosed to the partner regarding thoughts about and/or actual contact with porn;
- The actions that would constitute a relapse; and
- The amount of time following a relapse before it will be disclosed to the partner.

Although many intimate partners say they want to be kept informed, it is often difficult for them to listen to setbacks and disappointments that occur during recovery. It helps when an intimate partner has a realistic understanding of the challenges of quitting porn. "I asked Logan to let me know when he has been struggling a lot with thoughts of porn," Nancy said. "In asking him to be vulnerable with me I have to accept the fact that it might hurt to hear what he has to share. I can't use what he tells me as a hammer against him, to hurt him back, because that would just dissolve the type of healthy communication I want us to have. Wanting your partner to be honest with you is the best way to go in reestablishing trust, but it's not always easy or pleasant." Paula agrees: "As much as I don't like it, I understand that some amount of relapse is a normal part of recovery. The most important thing for me is whether my husband is being honest, is taking steps to not repeat the slip-up, and is getting better as time goes on."

How conscientiously you communicate as a couple during porn recovery can affect the success of healing your relationship. Many recovering couples employ a twenty-four-hour rule, meaning the recovering porn user has twenty-four hours in which to tell his partner about a relapse. A short wait can provide some time for reflection and input from others, so that the recovering porn user can be better able to discuss his relapse calmly and productively with his partner.

Brad changed how he handled discussing his relapses with his wife when he realized that the way he had been approaching conversations with her was unproductive. "I used to get all emotional when I confessed to my wife that I'd relapsed," he said. "It was like I 'threw up' on her, and used telling her as a way to lighten my burden. *I* felt better. *I* was being honest. But it absolutely destroyed Paula when I did it. All the drama made her feel just horrible. Now I talk about it with my counselor, my minister, and the men from my recovery group *before* I talk with her. It gives me a chance to examine what happened, be corrected, and 'put in my place.' They help me brainstorm ways to prevent relapse from happening again. Then I sit down with Paula and we have an intellectual conversation. I explain what I did and learned from the relapse. She still feels hurt, but at least the experience of my sharing doesn't devastate her. She hates it when I slip up, but says she's building respect for how I'm able to get help for myself, keep her informed, and improve over time."

Share the work. While rebuilding trust is up to the recovering porn user, the intimate partner needs to be involved in her own recovery process. Going to individual counseling and attending a twelve-step program, such as COSA or S-Anon, can be extremely helpful. As we discussed in chapter 5, many intimate partners respond to the discovery of a porn problem by trying to control and fix it themselves—monitoring behavior, violating privacy, and becoming a "porn cop." This behavior, while understandable, can create serious obstacles to rebuilding trust.

Both members of a couple always need to feel respected as adults. When an intimate partner spends her time snooping and spying and being overly controlling in order to make sure the porn use never happens again, mutual respect cannot thrive. An intimate partner needs to remember that she did not cause the porn problem, she can't control it, and that it's not up to her to cure it. Her focus must be on healing herself—communicating her feelings and needs, working together to set appropriate boundaries, taking care of herself, and resolving her anger— rather than trying to change the recovering porn user. "One of the first women I talked to after I discovered my husband Logan's porn use was a pastor at my church," Nancy explained. "She told me to stop playing porn detective, because it was self-destructive and wouldn't restore trust in Logan. I was trying to control something that's uncontrollable. She suggested I work on my own issues. It was hard for me to give up that role, and it actually took a lot of women telling me to quit trying to fix him. It helped to remind myself that Logan was working toward making a change for himself. It's been freeing to me to let go and get out of the way of his recovery."

If an intimate partner is seriously dissatisfied with the relationship, she needs to be prepared to take whatever actions are necessary, including separation, in order to honor her limits and to feel secure in her life. Debbie told us she only started to heal when she got out of what she called the "Mommy, Counselor, Cop, Confessional role" and made it clear that she would separate from her husband if he did not adhere to bottom-line conditions of recovery. "I told Roger: 'I don't want to take care of you in your recovery anymore. I am not going to be checking up on where you are, or whether or not you went to your meetings. I do expect you to be honest with me.' I was able to step back, because I knew he had other people to whom he was accountable in his recovery. Also, I made it clear that if he didn't live up to his commitment, I would divorce him." While this type of healing strategy may sound harsh, it's sometimes necessary in order to facilitate the restoration of trust and intimacy in the relationship.

With appropriate action, steadfast honesty, and a mutual commitment to recovery, a couple can restore trust and set in place the first building block for healing a relationship that has been torn apart by porn.

2. UNDERSTAND YOUR PARTNER'S EXPERIENCE

Once you have started to rebuild a foundation of trust, the next step in healing is to better understand what your partner has personally gone through as a result of the porn problem. This step involves the recovering porn user sharing important details about his involvement with porn as well as his recovery efforts, and the intimate partner revealing the various ways she has been affected by his porn use. When you share and try to understand each other's experience, you can develop deeper insight and empathy that will help you both heal. The more open and honest you are in sharing your experiences and patiently listening to what your partner has to say, the more you will be able to clearly comprehend how the porn problem has led to alienation and other difficulties in your relationship.

Reveal more about the porn problem. The moment when a porn problem is admitted or discovered is usually highly charged and stressful for both the porn user and his partner. Because the user often feels afraid and ashamed, he may hold back from revealing important information, especially if he thinks the revelation of particular details will get him in even more trouble. At the same time, his partner may be so shocked and distressed that she may not be in the right frame of mind to ask questions or listen objectively. As a result, the moment of discovery or disclosure is not the best time for an intimate partner to understand important aspects of the porn problem, such as: where it came from, what it has involved, and how troubling it has been for the porn user.

When you have started making progress in your recovery and your intimate partner has overcome her initial distress, in-depth sharing becomes more possible. Several months into his recovery, Logan sat down with his wife, Nancy, to describe his porn problem in greater detail. "I explained to Nancy how pornography had been a secret part of my life since I was eleven years old, how I had been masturbating to it since then mostly to relieve stress, and how I liked lesbian porn. She asked me questions and I answered them as best I could. I knew I could have lied my way through it like I'd done my whole life, but I also knew if we were going to have a chance at making it through this, I couldn't hold back and had to tell her the truth."

As difficult as it was for Nancy to hear Logan out, she said the experience helped her. "I liked that he was honest, straightforward, and didn't minimize what he had done throughout our marriage. If his attitude had been any different, say if he had tried to make excuses or blame me, for example, I don't think I would have stayed married to him. I had worried that he needed porn because he didn't find me sexually attractive. Logan reassured me that he finds me sexy and explained that his interest in porn wasn't about me—it was like a drug addiction."

Listening to Logan describe details about his problem helped Nancy realize that his porn use wasn't because there was something wrong with her. She was relieved to discover that his interest and reliance on porn started long before their intimate partnership began, and therefore it became less of a personal rejection. "I realized there was no way I could have competed with Logan's porn fantasies," Nancy said. "He'd been using them steadily for years before we ever met!"

Learning more about the porn problem can also ultimately help diminish an intimate partner's unresolved feelings of anger, contempt, and disgust toward the recovering porn user. While she may still see his porn behavior as unacceptable, knowing *why* he had become trapped in this unhealthy behavior can help her feel empathy and compassion.

However, sharing the history and details of a porn problem is not without stress or risk. Some partners can emotionally handle a lot of information, while others are disturbed by graphic details and overwhelmed when learning the full extent of past porn use. Nonetheless, research suggests that when disclosing sexually addictive behavior in a relationship, it's better to fully disclose everything, regardless of how initially difficult it may be, than to reveal additional information in a "drip and drag" manner over time. Partially disclosing a porn problem, while intentionally hiding or lying about the rest of it, can damage a relationship even further because this behavior can reignite a partner's suspicions and can easily intensify feelings of betrayal and distrust.

Most experts agree that an intimate partner has to know enough to make informed decisions about what she now needs from the relationship and be able to be realistic in her expectations of the recovery process. Due to differences in individual circumstances, we recommend that you and your partner discuss what degree of detail you both prefer *before* sharing specifics about the porn problem. The intimate partner may want to write down a list of questions ahead of time, spelling out the exact things she wants to know. Many couples find it beneficial to seek the assistance of a trained therapist familiar with helping heal relationships affected by porn problems when taking this step.

What matters most may not be what you say, but how you say it. Healing a relationship is more likely to occur when a recovering porn user is not only honest and forthcoming, but also accepts full responsibility for his actions and involvement with porn. At the same time, the intimate partner should try to recognize and respect the courage it takes for the recovering porn user to be open with her and to refrain from punishing him for what he has shared.

Find out more about the impact on the intimate partner. Just as the recovering porn user must be open and honest, it is also important for the intimate partner to share her feelings and concerns about the porn problem and recovery process, and be able to feel that her partner is compassionate and caring toward her and her feelings. Through verbal communication and/or letter writing, a partner can share how she feels about pornography in general and in her life; her personal history regarding pornographic material and sexual objectification; how emotionally hurt she feels due to the porn problem; and, her fears and concerns about the future of their relationship.

As we've discussed, many intimate partners are emotionally traumatized by the existence of the porn problem and suffer feelings of disbelief, rejection, disappointment, and fear for a long time. Being able to express the depth of her unhappiness and concerns, and see that her partner really understands and cares, can go a long way toward reducing an intimate partner's distress and feelings of alienation, and reassure her that she is important and loved.

The idea of revealing the full extent of her feelings and concerns about the porn problem may be frightening, however. Just like her partner, she may fear that "letting it all out" could cause even more problems in the relationship. But if she stays focused on stating *her* feelings and *her* experiences, while refraining from attacking and blaming the recovering porn user, chances for successful sharing are much greater. The recovering porn user can help the process by putting his focus on really trying to understand his partner's experience and what it would be like to be her in the relationship. This is not a time to defend past actions, justify behavior, make demands, or criticize in any way.

Given the anxieties that a couple may have about this kind of sharing, it is a good idea to approach this process with some form of structure in place. Special couples counseling sessions focused on learning more about the intimate partner's experience can be a good idea. In addition, some therapists suggest that the intimate partner use letter writing as a way to communicate how the porn problem has impacted her life.

Writing a letter to the recovering porn user allows the intimate partner time to think about what she wants to say and the way she wants to say it. If she is in counseling, she can work on and revise the letter with her therapist's help until she feels it is ready to be shared. Some intimate partners choose to read their letter aloud, while others prefer the recovering porn user to read it. The benefit of revealing the impact of the porn problem in letter form is that the recovering porn user can then refer to

the letter from time to time as a concrete reminder of the serious consequences of his behavior on his intimate partner and his continued need
to stay away from porn.

A couple's healing often takes a big leap forward when the recovering
porn user is fully committed to understanding his partner's perspective
and reasons for her emotional unhappiness. "I'd always known that my
wife, Iris, didn't like porn, but I never really understood why until that
evening we talked out on the back porch," George said. "When she was
growing up her father had lots of porn—calendars featuring half-naked
women, stacks of books and magazines by his bedside, and porn magazines he insisted on keeping out in full view on a coffee table in the living
room, in spite of how much she and her mom begged him to put them
away. Iris hated that her father would rate the women's bodies and make
degrading, sexual comments. The pictures of the women in porn made
her feel powerless, even physically sick at times. After hearing Iris describe her experiences of porn in her childhood, I can see why my being
into it just tore her up."

Ed had a similar empathic reaction when his wife shared her experiences. "I used to think that using porn was no big deal, that it was the
same as having private sexual fantasies. After reading the letter my wife
wrote about how my porn use made her feel, I now realize that it was
basically the same as if I had had a real-life affair, or if I'd been with a
prostitute, in terms of the damage it caused her and our marriage."

Drew found it challenging to listen when his wife, Emma, told him
how disappointed she was in him when she first learned of his porn
problem. "It was hard being reminded of what I had done, but it was
important," he said. "Up until she found out I was using porn, Emma
thought we had a great marriage—two kids, nice jobs, and a good sex
life. Finding out I had a secret life that went on for years destroyed this
image. I went from being this great husband and provider to being a
threat to the family. For a long time she lived in fear that if my porn problem ever became known, it would ruin the children's lives and get us run
out of town. I realized her concerns were totally understandable."

The ultimate goal of this type of in-depth sharing is not only to increase mutual understanding and empathy, but to start reconnecting as
a couple again. "When I first learned about Logan's porn addiction, I
had a hard time imagining how we were ever going to pull together in a

healthy way and make it as a couple," Nancy said. "But now I feel we're working as a team. We understand each other more. It's taken a long time, but I finally 'get it' that his interest in porn wasn't about me, and he finally 'gets it' why I was so hurt by what he did."

As you learn to see beyond your own initial emotional reactions and develop a deeper understanding of your partner's experience, you can move beyond feeling that one partner has been "bad" and the other "betrayed." You can begin to realize that porn hurt you both and that by working together you can help each other to heal.

3. MOVE FROM ANGER TO FORGIVENESS

Another important step in a couple's healing is to resolve angry feelings and create conditions for forgiveness. Many intimate partners feel extremely angry in the wake of a serious porn problem. Their anger not only reflects the degree of emotional pain and outrage they feel, it can be used as a hammer to punish the recovering porn user for having violated trust.

The manner in which an intimate partner's anger surfaces and is expressed differs for every couple. Debbie told us she stayed angry for well over a year after her husband, Roger, began serious recovery work. "I was just furious with him," she said. "At first I just needed time to be hurt and angry about what he had done. Finding out that he had lied to me and had used porn for years was like a death. I suffered the death of every dream and hope I ever had in our marriage. I hated and blamed him for this loss. I was also angry and blamed him for how much suffering I went through with the breakdown of our sex life and him losing his job. At first I just held in my anger. But after a while of living separately under the same roof I decided not to mask it anymore. I wasn't consciously being vindictive or wounding, but I think I used it to punish him. I started saying whatever I felt inside. It got ugly. Some days he would come in and I would say: 'Don't come near me. Today I cannot stand the sight of you.' And I'd leave the room."

While Debbie was aware of her anger and of her tendency to use it to punish Roger, for many partners, their anger only surfaces during emotionally charged interactions with their partner. Although she didn't feel angry all the time, Karen found that every time she and her husband, Johnny, fought, she felt seething resentment. "If we were having just a normal disagreement about something, and he thought I was being unfair, it was really easy for this ungraceful part of me to just rise up and say: 'After everything I've gone through and put up with, you have the gall to think *I'm* being unfair?' It wasn't a real productive reaction on my part and I didn't want to feel that way for the rest of our lives."

Some partners unconsciously push their anger down for a long period of time and when it finally surfaces, it can be difficult to handle. "For months I was emotionally numb," Emma said. "When my anger finally surfaced, it just erupted. It didn't matter that my husband, Drew, was in recovery. I started feeling the pain of all the years he'd been absent, all the lies I'd believed, how tired I was raising the kids by myself, and how alone I had felt in the relationship. For a long time, I just came at him with the force of my anger, condemning and blaming him, because that's the only way I knew how to express myself."

While understandable and legitimate, an intimate partner's anger— especially if it is expressed in hurtful ways or it lasts for a long time— can stymie progress in rebuilding the relationship. Unresolved anger can get in the way of an intimate partner's acknowledging and supporting the positive changes the recovering porn user has made. It is an obstacle to reestablishing trust and mutual understanding in the relationship. And it can keep both people feeling unloved and alienated from each other.

Working together to resolve anger. Both the intimate partner and the recovering porn user need to work together on resolving anger and moving toward forgiveness. An intimate partner can begin to resolve her feelings of anger by recognizing and admitting that she is angry, learning techniques for expressing her feelings in more productive ways, letting go of her preoccupation with the betrayal, creating opportunities for her partner to make amends, and supporting her partner in his overall recovery.

When Debbie realized her anger was preventing the rebuilding of intimacy in her marriage, she asked her husband to help. "I asked him to tell me when I seemed angry or unapproachable and encouraged him to suggest we sit down and talk about what I was feeling and deal with it in the moment. I wanted us to be friends again." And when Karen and her husband, Johnny, are having a normal disagreement, she now makes a special effort to leave his past porn use out of the discussion and "not hold it over his head."

When anger is prolonged it often disguises emotions such as disillusionment and sorrow that result when we suffer a major loss. The key to letting go of anger is learning how to get in touch with our more vulnerable feelings. Emma took this route in overcoming her anger. "I had to figure out what was underneath my anger, to dissect it and get to the other feelings that were there. I realized it was a cover for sadness, disappointment, and fear. In couples therapy I found ways to open up and tell Drew more directly and honestly how hurt I was. I hated revealing these other feelings at first, because I felt so vulnerable. Letting go of my anger meant letting down my guard, and showing him my weak side. The anger felt strong, and these other emotions didn't feel strong to me."

The new skills Emma developed to express herself had an immediate positive effect on her marriage. "When Emma used to get angry with me I'd withdraw, because it triggered all my shame and fear and that only made things worse," Drew said. "But once she started sharing how afraid and alone she was, it was easier for me to understand how she felt and be there for her. This was a huge change for us and felt so much better than any way we had treated each other before."

In addition to being rigorously honest and fully committed to the recovery process, recovering porn users can help their partners work through anger by understanding and acknowledging their own emotional pain and expressing genuine regret for hurting their partner. In order to be effective, this type of empathic response needs to be expressed not just once, but as often as it takes for an intimate partner to feel emotionally healed.

The recovering porn user can also use letter writing as a tool to communicate his feelings. In the letter, he can respond to specific concerns his partner has expressed—for example, putting the family's welfare at risk, directing sexual energy elsewhere, or lying throughout their relationship. Jon, a forty-five-year-old recovering porn addict, wrote the following letter to his wife, Kay, to let her know how genuinely sorry he was.

My Dearest Wife,

I am so sorry for betraying you with my porn use and my dishonesty. I realize that I lied to you for many years, not only about my sexual activities and use of porn, but also about my finances, alcohol use, and legal problems.

I doubt I will ever truly be able to understand the depth of the pain I have caused you. I know you love me and wanted so much for me to be the loving, honest, and faithful man you deserved. I know I shattered your belief that you matter to me, and I created enormous problems for you in trusting yourself and trusting your own judgment of reality. I wish I could erase the damage I caused to your self-esteem and confidence.

I recognize the shame you have felt because of my behavior, because you didn't end the relationship with me, and the shame you felt telling select friends what was going on with us only to have me repeatedly get caught in more lies about porn and masturbation and adult bookstores. I saw you withdrawing from supportive friends and becoming more and more isolated as my behavior continued.

I am sure there are things I am missing. I just wanted to put in writing my understanding of how I have hurt you. Since writing this letter I have nearly always kept it either on me or very close and it has been a constant reminder of the pain I have caused you. I hope and pray every day to stay sexually sober and honest with you. I believe we are ultimately very good for each other and that God does want us to be together. I want with all my heart to be the loving, honest, and faithful man you deserve. I will never be able to express my gratitude enough to you for sticking by me.

> *Your Loving Husband*

For his wife, Jon's letter served as a turning point in being able to let go of her anger and forgive her husband. In addition to its heartfelt sincerity, the reason Jon's letter helped Kay so much is because it told her what she needed to hear—that she matters more to him than porn, that he takes responsibility for his actions, and that he is committed to not hurting her again. Reading this enabled Kay to start opening her heart to Jon again.

As with trust, forgiveness cannot be demanded, expected, manufactured, or forced. It has to emerge naturally over time as a result of new understandings and healing activities. If you are an intimate partner, you forgive by overcoming your negative feelings and judgments toward the recovering porn user, not by releasing him from responsibility for the harmful things he did in the past, but by accepting his humanness, history, limitations, and imperfections. It can also be helpful to acknowledge the steps he has and is taking to rectify the hurt and damage he has caused. If you are a recovering porn user you become worthy of forgiveness by being consistently honest, taking responsibility for the harm you have caused, doing your recovery work, demonstrating empathy for your partner's pain, and expressing your genuine regret. When you do whatever is necessary to move toward forgiveness, you'll find that not only does your relationship start to heal, but you personally start to heal as well.

4. Improve Communication to Build Intimacy

The fourth step in healing as a couple is to learn to communicate with each other in ways that help you regain feelings of closeness and intimacy. Couples who have been successful in rebuilding their relationship while one partner recovers from a porn problem often attribute their progress to having established routines for sharing information and discussing their feelings and needs with each other.

As part of their recovery, Logan and Nancy read books on communication and attended couples therapy sessions in which they were frequently coached by their therapist on effective ways to express themselves. "We needed to learn how to recognize our innermost feelings and communicate them clearly without doing it in a hurtful way," Nancy said. "In addition to therapy, we developed a habit of spending time together after dinner as a way to check in with each other daily. We go on a walk or sit on the couch and just talk about what we feel, what we're dealing with, and any needs we want to address. I know what's going on with Logan every day—we're no longer living in separate worlds."

Logan agrees. "We used to avoid conflicts, but now we are actually able to have differences of opinion, get into some pretty good discussions, and work through them. Learning how to communicate with each other has given us a closeness and intimacy we didn't have before, and as a byproduct we both trust each other more."

Jon and Kay sit down together each Saturday at breakfast and fill each other in on how they are doing and any concerns they are having with recovery. This degree of openness has been a challenge for Jon who learned early in life to keep things inside. "I'm slowly getting a little better at sharing my inner thoughts and feelings," he said. "Hiding my true feelings has always come easy to me. Our talks are helping me deal with resentments as they come up rather than stew about them. It's critical to my recovery because holding on to my anger and feeling victimized in the relationship could set me up for a relapse." The fact that Jon is sharing more with Kay has helped her too. "I no longer feel dismissed," Kay said. "When Jon tells me how he's doing, I know I matter to him."

Establishing a regular habit of communicating with each other works best if the focus of each discussion is on better understanding and supporting each other—even when you disagree or feel disappointed by what your partner is telling you—and finding solutions to problems that stand in the way of regaining emotional closeness. Good topics for discussion may include:

- Current challenges in your life
- Your feelings and concerns
- New ideas and insights you have had about yourself
- Progress you have made
- Setbacks you have experienced
- The type of support you'd like from your partner
- Praise and appreciation for what your partner has done and is doing
- Positive changes you are making as a couple

Scheduling regular meetings can help both partners learn and practice more positive communication skills that can benefit the relationship overall. "Now I'm able to listen and not withdraw when Debbie shares her feelings," Roger said. "I can stay calm now even when she's emotional and we disagree about something. I tell her honestly when I'm struggling with thoughts of porn. Having this line of communication open is an immense help in my recovery. We've both learned so much about our emotional states and how to communicate our needs."

And Debbie said, "I'm able to be more direct with issues that concern me and what I really want to know. I can tell that Roger is seriously listening to my questions and not evading. He's even coached me on how I could be more effective in asking questions about his recovery so there is no way that he is tempted to get around it. Roger talks more and makes a lot of eye contact. When we share like this I'm confident that he's really changed."

By taking an active interest in what is going on in each other's lives and communicating in supportive and loving ways, you rebuild bonds that may have been missing in your relationship since porn became a problem. These connections can create a sense of feeling special and known and safe, which in turn enhances affection and a natural desire to become physically and emotionally closer with each other.

The four steps for healing a relationship during recovery—restoring trust, gaining understanding, resolving anger, and improving communication—all work together to help you make the journey back to each other. For the recovering user, consistent and reliable actions that let your partner know you are committed to quitting porn, committed to her, and committed to healing the damage you have done are vital. For the partner, understanding the reasons behind the porn behavior, letting go of anger, and working together to rebuild communication will help restore what had been lost or damaged because of porn.

Couples who work on these four steps often report many positive changes. "The biggest change for me is just this sense of hope," Karen said. "For a long time I honestly thought my options were divorce or being miserable the rest my life. To actually be having the kind of marriage Johnny and I both wanted from the very beginning is a real gift." Similarly, after five years of healing, Emma reflected, "My marriage with Drew is better now than it ever was before. We understand each other better and are able to work things out when we have a conflict. I don't doubt that we're going to make it as a couple. I'm more in love with Drew than I ever was before. We have a deep respect for each other and a shared sense of purpose."

And for Debbie and Roger, recovery has brought them a lot closer. "Roger and I are a team now," Debbie said. "When we deal with porn issues, it's the two of us against this common enemy, instead of it dividing us. Roger used to see me as a threat to his relationship with the porn. Now he sees porn as a threat to his relationship with me." And, Roger agrees. "After four years of healing we have such a different relationship. It's so much deeper and healthier now. With all the help we got and the work we've done, it's like we knocked out a faulty foundation in our marriage and rebuilt it with something that is so much stronger. I'm deeply grateful that Debbie stayed with me and we're still together."

When the Four Steps Are Not Enough

As effective as the four steps are for most couples, there are a few for whom trust, forgiveness, and deeper intimacy seem impossible to achieve due to the extent of past lies and deception. Wes and Marge are one such couple. At the recommendation of their therapist, they decided to use a lie detector—also called a polygraph test—as a therapeutic device to help them restore trust, move through the impasse, and save their marriage. Because it provides an intimate partner with a way to objectively and reliably confirm that the recovering porn user is telling the truth, this technique is gaining popularity with recovering porn addicts as an adjunct to couples counseling. When honesty is firmly established, a couple is then able to proceed with, and benefit from, all four of the healing steps previously discussed.

How Lie Detector Testing Can Save a Marriage: Wes and Marge's Story

Wes and Marge, both in their mid-fifties, held hands as they shared their difficult tale of healing their relationship after porn. The parents of three grown children, they had been together for twenty-five years. Wes used porn for most of their marriage and lied about it throughout the relationship. He'd tell Marge he'd stopped when he hadn't and lie about relapses. After discovering that he had never quit using porn as promised, Marge was devastated and lost all trust in him. She kicked him out of the house.

They each knew that with their youngest child leaving home for college, divorce was eminent.

WES: "We had been separated for two years. I thought Marge was so angry with me for having lied to her about porn throughout our marriage that getting back together was out of the question. One afternoon I woke from a nap and realized that what I really wanted was to be with Marge for the rest of my life. Pornography and other sexual acting out were no longer meaningful or important. They became things to give up to get Marge back. It's hard to explain that moment of awareness. It felt like an epiphany, just a sudden 'blip' and it was different. I felt ready to do whatever I could to win back her trust and affection."

MARGE: "Wes told me he had given porn up for good, and wondered if I'd consider getting back together with him. I knew he was basically a wonderful person with a lot of potential. I wasn't sure what to do. I had fallen for Wes's convincing lies for many, many years. Our breakup had been devastating. How could I justify ever trusting him again?"

WES: "Here I was, finally committed to staying away from porn, and with zero credibility. When my therapist suggested polygraph testing to prove my honesty to Marge, I thought, *Wow, that's a great idea!* I had already determined that I wasn't going to lie to her, and the lie detector test sounded like a great way to verify that, and it wouldn't take fifteen years to win back her trust."

MARGE: "I was impressed when Wes told me he wanted to do this. It reaffirmed that he meant what he said. When your partner has a porn problem and lies about it, you not only can't trust him, you can't trust what you think is true. You sense something is going on and you ask about it, but all you get back is a denial or an evasion. It was refreshing for me that now the burden of truth was on him. No longer was I expected to blindly trust him. He had decided to prove to me that he could be trusted."

WES: "It was kind of exhilarating to say I'm going to do this and then to go through with it. I had a little apprehension about false negatives, but those are rare so I didn't let it get in the way. My therapist recommended a polygraph examiner who was experienced administering the test as a marital trust-building aid for porn and sex addicts. The whole process took about three hours. First the examiner talked with Marge and me together, then he talked with Marge about what specific questions to ask and how to word them. Then he gave me the test, which took about half an hour. While I was taking it, Marge went for a walk."

MARGE: "The polygraph examiner made it really clear that he was my advocate. He told me: 'The only reason we are here is because you have been lied to and because you have been hurt. I want you to come up with questions that will answer what you need to know.' It was so validating, but also brought up an incredible surge of emotion. It's like, God, we're here because *I* have been lied to for fifteen years. We're doing this so that *I* can find out whether Wes can be an honest, reliable, sexual, and safe partner with me. It was really powerful."

WES: "When I was strapped in the chair with all the 'whiz bangs,' it was a little bit tense at first. All the gadgetry and the procedures had been explained to me, and I knew that the chances of it reporting I had lied when I hadn't were very rare, but still you can't help being worried your first time. I knew what the test questions were beforehand so I just relaxed. When the examiner got to the question, 'Have you viewed or possessed sexual imagery in the last six months for your sexual pleasure?' I simply told the truth and said, 'No.'"

MARGE: "When I came back from my walk, I felt really on edge. The examiner greeted me with this big grin on his face and said, 'Well, Wes really means business. He passed.' Since he is the expert in determining if someone is telling the truth, his reaction gave me the confidence to trust Wes. I felt this huge sense of relief. I was happy and overwhelmed."

WES: "I felt relieved too. Not just because I passed—I knew I was telling the truth—but because Marge was happy and able to believe me. We had a basis for a future together. We made arrangements to come back every six months for retesting and Marge has the option to request a test at any time. Following the test, I moved back into the house with her. It's been several years since that initial test and I've passed all my six-month follow-ups. It feels so good not having to conceal things, not having to watch what I say. When you lie about things you have to remember what you lied about. When you don't, all you have to do is remember what happened."

MARGE: "We have both felt freed up because of the testing. I don't feel a need to question him about what he might be doing or doubt what he tells me. Whether or not he's using porn has become a non-issue in our marriage. I really love and respect Wes for being committed to doing this. I don't think we would be together today if it weren't for the lie detector testing."

WES: "Knowing that I will be tested every six months has changed the way I think and respond in terms of pornography. It's like wearing a seat belt or having a security blanket. My mind just doesn't spend time on the possibility of looking at porn, because I know that I'm not even going to go there. Even if I'm tired or feeling tense, I am not going to sit back and start fantasizing about that stuff. If it enters my mind, it's gone in a second. I push it aside in a second. I just think the lie detector is great. I recommend it for anybody who wants his partner to know the truth."

Wes and Marge's story is a good example of how determined and courageous some people are in their quest to rid themselves and their relationship of the destructive influence of porn. It is also a testament to the power of love and commitment to prevail even in the most challenging of circumstances. As we've seen from all the stories in this chapter, when you work together and persevere, recovery from porn addiction can lead to renewed trust, improved communication, and increased caring and affection.

11

A New Approach to Sex

*The seriousness of my porn problem made me scared of sex and
left me wondering whether I could ever have sex again without
falling back into old bad habits. But I know that if I don't learn
new ways of sexual expression, my old destructive ways will have
all the power.*

—MARIE

Like Marie, many people who quit porn are apprehensive about
returning to sexual activity. They often question whether it will
ever be possible for them to have sex without being reminded
of porn or triggered into wanting to use it again. Single recovering porn
users may worry that they don't have the skills to develop a healthy and
satisfying sexual relationship from the ground up, and former users in
committed relationships wonder how they can reconnect sexually with
an intimate partner who has been hurt by their past porn use. But even in
the face of these concerns, most people who quit porn want to find ways
to have a rewarding sex life free from porn.

You too may have questions about how to channel and express your
sexuality in new ways. The good news is that by shifting your approach to
sex and developing some new skills, you can learn to create sexual experiences that are satisfying and exciting without porn. Justin, for example,
who had been addicted to porn for twenty-five years, is pleased with how
much better he feels as a sexual person since he's gotten porn out of his life.
"A year after I quit porn, I met a special woman," he told us. "We've been
together for the last four years. During that time our sexual relationship
has developed into something wonderful. My girlfriend says I've become
an incredible lover. I'm so glad because when I was married before and
into porn, my wife used to complain that I acted like a robot during sex

and that she felt used. Now, with my present partner I feel no guilt when we make love—just this incredible feeling of spiritual connection."

Sexual healing is one of the most rewarding steps you can take after you've left the porn trap. It often follows naturally once a person has reestablished his integrity and self-worth, developed a strong support system, and started rebuilding trust and honesty in existing relationships. By taking this next step of reclaiming your sexuality as a positive force in your life, you can continue to heal in a profound manner, feeling better about yourself and able to experience the joy and pleasure of sexual relating.

Many former porn users have to learn a new approach to sex in order to stay porn-free. We are all sexual beings and the basic desire for sex is a vital and undeniable part of our nature. When you can express your sexual drive and desire in ways that are aligned with your values, you are less likely to get pulled back into porn use again. Following several relapses, Ethan concluded: "My future happiness depends on my ability to find a satisfying alternative to porn. My sex drive isn't going to go away. I need something that can compete with porn so I won't get stuck in a pattern of over-control and out-of-control sexual behavior."

An Intimacy-Oriented Approach to Sex

What kind of sex is capable of competing with porn? In our work with people overcoming porn problems, we have found that whether you are currently in an intimate relationship or not, an approach that is powerful enough to compete with and prevail over porn is one that has the primary goal of being intimate with a real partner. Because porn sex is all about fantasy, the sheer authenticity of sexual intimacy with another person generates new and compelling experiences for most former porn users. Intimacy-oriented sex, as we call it, provides a way to integrate the positive feelings you have about yourself and a current (or future) partner with sexual desire, arousal, and orgasm. It makes it possible for you to focus on being present in a real human relationship and express genuine emotions. It honors conditions of healthy sexuality, such as responsibility, equality, respect, and caring. Nobody is exploited or gets hurt. The sex is shame-free because it is consistent with your overall beliefs, values, and goals in life.

Intimacy-oriented sex allows you to explore dimensions of sexual experience not possible with porn, such as whole-body sensuality, self-respect, trust, warmth, playfulness, laughter, nurturing touch, profound love, and spiritual connection. By taking the time to get to know and like a partner, the sexual experience comes from genuine feelings of affection and appreciation. Both partners become comfortable with each other and can candidly share desires, needs, limits, and feelings about sex. Sexual encounters are mutually satisfying—you feel the joy of loving and being loved back. And because you are being fulfilled on so many different levels, intimacy-oriented sex can help you reshape your erotic imagination, enabling you to feel more comfortable with your sexual thoughts.

In this chapter, you will find a number of ideas and exercises[1] that can help you learn important skills needed for developing an intimacy-oriented approach to sex. You can do some of the exercises by yourself, while others require the participation of a partner. If you are not in an intimate relationship, you can read about and practice the exercises in this chapter to lay a foundation for a future sexual relationship with a partner. If you are presently in a committed relationship, you can learn the skills with your partner to heal the damage to your sex life caused by porn and experience a more fulfilling sexual connection.

The success of an intimacy-oriented approach to sex depends on your being able to forge a new pathway for your sexual energy that doesn't involve stimulation from porn. To that end, the exercises provide you with different opportunities to break the connection between porn and sexual arousal. Over time, by practicing these exercises you'll discover a new way of experiencing sexual energy in your mind and in your body. Although most of the exercises build self-awareness and intimacy skills, and don't involve overt sexual activity, ultimately they establish a strong foundation for your being able to enjoy intensely gratifying sexual pleasure without porn.

We have identified seven skills that can help you succeed in accomplishing an intimacy-oriented approach to sex. They are:

---

1. Many of the exercises presented in this chapter are adaptations of exercises originally developed by Wendy Maltz and described in her book, *The Sexual Healing Journey: A Guide for Survivors of Sexual Abuse*. Sensitive demonstrations of the exercises are provided in Wendy's video, "Relearning Touch: Healing Techniques for Couples." For more information on the book and video, see the Resources section or visit our Web site at www.HealthySex.com.

1. Engage in Courtship
2. Talk with Your Partner About Sex
3. Expand Your Sensory Awareness
4. See Your Partner with New Eyes
5. Increase Your Touch Vocabulary
6. Explore the Realm of Sensual Pleasure
7. Involve Your Heart in Sex

These skills are arranged progressively from those that help you build a strong and healthy foundation for a sexual relationship to those that involve specific sensual and sexual activities. Each skill contributes an important element of intimacy in sex. Because some of the exercises involve genital touch and stimulation, we recommend that you only do those that feel safe and that are consistent with where you currently are in your porn recovery. For instance, if you have been sexually abstinent as part of your recovery plan, we suggest you consult with a counselor or therapist to help you determine the appropriate time to practice a particular skill and do a particular exercise.

Let's explore the seven skills in detail.

Skill #1: Engage in Courtship

Blue whales rub each other with their flippers, male baboons swagger back and forth, chimpanzees kiss and hold hands, and female possums turn toward their suitors, cock their jaws, and look them straight in the eyes. All mammals, as well as many reptile and bird species, have their own, unique ways of courting each other. Courting is like a dance, with a set sequence of movements and touch that attract a mate and eventually lead into sex. Although the idea of courtship may seem strange and outdated—especially if you think of sex in terms of what is portrayed by porn—all studies of human relating and mating show that courtship is vital in forging lasting intimate sexual bonds between people.

Human courtship usually includes the following behaviors: smiling at each other; flirting; conversation aimed at getting initially acquainted; going out on dates; dancing together; sharing meals; extended conversations; holding hands; gazing into each other's eyes; touching each other on the shoulder, the knee, and the waist; kissing; and hugging.

These behaviors prepare both partners to feel comfortable enough with each other to consider more intimate physical sharing. Touch to the highly sensitive and sexually arousing areas of the body, such as the breasts and genitals, are the final steps in the human mating courtship sequence.

Whether you are beginning or repairing a sexual relationship with a partner, it's important to engage in a sequence of courtship behaviors. Skipping over steps, or rushing through the courtship process, could thwart the development of genuine sexual intimacy in a relationship. As you engage in courtship, if you find that your partner particularly enjoys certain activities, you may want to linger on those and repeat them often.

The reason that courtship behaviors are so critical to establishing intimacy is that they enable you to gradually develop a sense of familiarity and trust with a partner on a physical and emotional level before you become overtly sexual. You become friends before you become sexual partners, thus laying a strong foundation of friendship that supports your entire intimate relationship.

Courtship gives you time to learn to accurately interpret each other's facial expressions, tone of voice, gestures, laughter, casual touch, and other forms of nonverbal communication. Your ability to determine what your partner is communicating with these cues will improve the quality of your sexual relating. It's very difficult for someone to be a good lover if he can't tell what his partner's facial expressions, sounds, and gestures truly indicate. One person's expression of erotic ecstasy may be another's grimace of pain.

Courtship activities help you become physically attuned to each other. Often without realizing it consciously, you begin to mimic each other's gestures, move in tandem at times, synchronize the way you look, smile, and talk to each other. Spending time together as you court also creates positive associations with the way each of you moves, feels, smells, and sounds. As you develop these powerful positive feelings, sexual interest and desire naturally arise. And as a result, when you do eventually relate sexually, your ability to be attuned to each other in multiple dimensions makes for more comfortable and fulfilling sex.

You can develop your courtship skills by getting to know each other in ways that are not focused on having sex. For example, you might spend time holding hands during a walk or massage your partner's back for a few minutes before dinner. During a conversation, you could smile gently and look into your partner's eyes. Or put on some music and dance together. Going slow in courtship enables you to truly connect with your partner before moving forward to the next step in intimate relating. Your top priority is developing a sense of trust and comfort with each other, both physically and emotionally.

The following "Intimate Mirroring" exercise gives you an opportunity to experience how coordinating your physical movements with a partner's can stimulate feelings of unity and connection, which are basic building blocks for sexual intimacy. Taking turns initiating and moving together can help both of you focus on each other and be more comfortable with a common way of relating.

Intimate Mirroring

Purpose: To strengthen emotional connection and jump-start the courtship process by synchronizing your physical movements with those of your partner.

Suggested Time: 5 to 10 minutes

Sit facing each other, close enough that you can comfortably press the palms of your hands together with those of your partner. Imagine that your partner is a mirror image of yourself. Hold your hands two to three inches apart and slowly move them in any pattern you choose, such as up, down, sideways, or in a circular motion. Your partner's objective is to follow your lead. Go slow enough so that your partner can track your movements. When you feel ready, switch roles. Now your partner leads and your goal is to track your partner's movements.

Variations:

1. Do the exercise with your hands pressed together.
2. Take turns mirroring each other's facial expressions and gestures.
3. Stand up and take turns mirroring each other's whole-body movements.

No sexual relationship ever outgrows the need for courtship. It's an ongoing process no matter how old you are or how long you have been involved with a partner. Courtship both develops and constantly renews intimacy. The more frequently you engage in a variety of courtship activities you and your partner both enjoy, the stronger the foundation you will have for a dynamic and vibrant sex life.

Skill #2: Talk with Your Partner About Sex

Good verbal communication is an important component of intimate sex. Talking openly about sex enables you and your partner to learn about each other's sexual likes and dislikes, effectively address differences in preferences and needs, explore new sexual activities, and resolve any problems that might arise. Communication is the most effective way to ensure sexual relating will be mutually enjoyable and not result in a negative consequence or hurt feelings. It's no wonder that couples who can talk comfortably about sex report the highest levels of satisfaction with their sexual lives.

But talking about sex isn't easy, especially when porn has provided the model for sexual relating. In porn, people don't communicate forthrightly about sex. No one in porn ever says, "Slow down, I need more time to get in the mood," or "That's uncomfortable. I'd like it better if you touch me in a different way." No one asks, "Do you have protection?" or "Would you be open to trying this?" And no one ever addresses significant sexual realities such as being sexually abused as a child. Porn can create the false impression that serious talking about sex isn't necessary.

Becoming comfortable communicating about sex takes conscious effort and practice. There are many resources that can help you learn more effective sexual communication skills, and we've listed some of our favorites in the Resources section at the back of this book. In general, you and your partner will benefit by creating a climate for sexual discussions in which you both feel respected, safe, and encouraged to talk about sexual needs and concerns.

There are many important sexual topics for intimate partners to discuss in order to create and maintain a mutually rewarding intimacy. The questions listed on the next page can get you started in your discussions.

Because it is best to discuss these issues thoroughly, we recommend choosing one or two questions to focus on at a time.

Topics for Creating Intimate Sex

- What do you enjoy most about sex? What feelings do you hope to experience when you are sexual? What do you identify as the purpose and meaning of sex in your life?
- How do you feel about yourself as a sexual person? How has porn influenced your sexuality?
- What past experiences may be affecting how you feel about sex now? For example: Have you ever had a sexually transmitted disease? Have you been troubled by chronic sexual functioning problems? Do you have a past history of sexual abuse?
- What are your preferences for when, where, and how you would most like to engage in sex?
- How do you like your partner to initiate sex? What things get you in the mood? How do you show that you are interested in having sex?
- What type of language do you prefer when discussing body parts and sexual activities? For example, are you comfortable with slang terms or do you prefer medical terminology, or something in between?
- How do you want to protect against unwanted pregnancy and sexually transmitted infections?
- What do you need to feel physically safe and comfortable when you relate sexually? For example: cleanliness, nail care, privacy, pillows, or lubricants.
- What do you like to do following a sexual experience in order to continue feeling positive and intimate?
- What are your expectations regarding confidentiality, fidelity, and the future of your sexual relationship?

Remember, when talking about sex with your partner, there are no right or wrong questions or answers. You both will probably have different needs and desires. Your goal as a couple is to *understand* each other better and *negotiate* differences you may have without compromising your values, safety, personal comfort, or self-esteem. Don't try to impose a particular sexual agenda on your partner. Realize that you may need to let go of certain porn-related sexual expectations that are unrealistic or potentially damaging to your partner and to your relationship. When sexual concerns and differences surface, figure out how to address them creatively as a team. Be attentive, respectful, and find ways of integrating your own needs and desires with those of your partner.

In addition to discussing important sexual topics, it's helpful to brainstorm specific guidelines for sexual relating. Agreeing ahead of time on what is acceptable and unacceptable behavior reduces unnecessary guesswork and sets the stage for positive sexual experiences. You may want to consider the following set of guidelines that many couples in recovery decide to honor:

- It's okay to ask for what we each want.
- Ridicule, even disguised as teasing, is not allowed.
- It's okay for either of us to say no to a particular kind of touch or sex at any time.
- It's okay to stop and take breaks in our sexual interaction at any time.
- Our needs for comfort and safety are a priority and will be addressed as needed.
- We equally value emotional closeness and physical pleasure.

Honest communication about sex can lead to wonderful surprises. Brad told us, "My wife and I finally know what we want most from sex. Our sex life has more variety than I ever dreamed it could have before I quit porn. Paula's willingness to try new things, to be more intimate, to branch out in various sexual activities has increased tenfold. I never knew she could be so open. She says talking with me about sex makes her feel emotionally close and has brought her out of her shell."

For Logan, being able to share his anxieties about his sexual performance with his wife has made him much more comfortable initiating sex with her. "I used to avoid sex because I was afraid I'd lose my erection and not be able to complete the experience," he said. "Now, when I feel like making love, I let Nancy know I desire sex, but also that I'm anxious about it. The talking calms my fears. We're having much better experiences when we do make love now, and it's empowering."

Skill #3: Expand Your Sensory Awareness

Your ability to be intimate in sex increases when you are able to be aware of and enjoy *all* of your senses—sight, sound, smell, taste, and touch. A full range of sensory experiences is a dynamic resource that you can use to enhance sexual pleasure. And, when you have the capacity to tune into any of your five senses at any time, you are able to be a more complete and emotionally available lover.

Porn trains people to rely primarily on their sense of sight for sexual stimulation. They look at visual images and respond with genital arousal. This is why many recovering porn users find it difficult to be present with a partner during sex—their mind automatically shifts to porn images because they find it hard to become stimulated without them. When your visual sense is preoccupied with images of porn, your ability to enjoy a wider variety of sensory experiences is compromised. Fortunately, this is a pattern that can be changed.

With conscious effort, you can develop skills that enable you to stimulate and awaken your visual sense and your other senses in new ways. The following "Sensory Exploration" exercise is a technique you can use to become more aware of each of your senses and the unique pleasures they have to offer. This exercise should be practiced in a nonsexual setting so that you are not distracted by sexual arousal. Without sex involved, you can slow down, pay more attention, and learn how to connect to and appreciate more fully each of your senses. The skills you develop will provide a basis for being able to generate, express, and receive sexual desire and arousal through each sense. This is an easy exercise you can do whether you are currently single or in an ongoing relationship.

Sensory Exploration

Purpose: To increase awareness of your senses, experiment with sensory stimulation, discover what kind of sensory experiences you like, and remain relaxed and present during sensory arousal.

Suggested Time: 10 to 20 minutes

Collect a variety of small, preferably natural objects, such as rocks, seashells, spices, fabric of different textures, pine cones, fresh flowers, and fruit. Choose objects that you find interesting or pleasurable to look at, touch, smell, listen to, or taste. Place the objects in a bowl or on a table near you.

Sit comfortably, relax and breathe slowly. Focus for a few minutes on your breathing. If your mind wanders, gently bring it back to the present and your breathing. When you are ready, reach for an object and spend a few minutes exploring it. Look at it closely first, noticing patterns, color, and texture. Then close your eyes and hold it up to your ear and rub it or shake it. What sound does it make? Is the sound pleasurable? Next, put the object under your nose and smell it. Is it musky or sweet, and does the smell evoke any memories? (Smell is highly connected to memory.) Now try rubbing it against the inside of your arm or on your cheek. Is it soft or hard, smooth or textured? Does the feel of it raise goose bumps or tickle? Then touch your tongue to the object, if you wish (as long as it is safe to do so), to discover if it has a taste. Have fun and don't judge your experience.

When you're done with the first object, explore the rest of the items, examining each one slowly and remaining relaxed and focused throughout the process. After you've explored each object, reflect on your experience. Which objects intrigued you? Which of your senses did you tend to rely on most? Which combination of object and sense provided a novel and enjoyable experience?

Variations:
1. Repeat this exercise with an entirely different set of objects, or as you encounter things throughout your day, such as a soft T-shirt, a leaf on a plant, or the food you eat.

2. Explore a part of your body, such as your hand or foot, in the same relaxed and curious way. Pay attention to the sensations you experience through your fingertips as well as the sensations you experience when you shift your consciousness to be inside the hand or foot you are touching, aware of what it feels like to receive touch. In contrast to touching objects, human touch offers two pathways to pleasure—the experience of touching as well as being touched.

The "Sensory Exploration" exercise helps develop an attitude of curiosity, appreciation, and enjoyment when interacting with something at a sensual level. This attitude can later be applied when relating with a lover, allowing you to more consciously explore and appreciate on multiple levels the joy and pleasure of sensually connecting with your partner. And, when lovers share a strong sensual connection they often feel closer to each other emotionally, sexually, and spiritually.

Skill #4: See Your Partner with New Eyes

The eyes have been called the initial organ of romance. Gazing at a lover can trigger a smile of interest and activate the courtship dance. Your visual sense also plays a key role in stimulating and maintaining sexual desire. Former porn users are often challenged in their ability to comfortably use these natural and positive functions of sight in an intimate relationship. Past porn use may have trained you to look at a person in ways that are alienating and cause a partner to retreat instead of wanting to open up and get closer to you. Reliance on porn for sexual stimulation may have also created an unrealistic standard for sexual desirability and attractiveness that may inhibit your ability to get or stay sexually turned on by your partner. As part of sexual healing, you may need to address these repercussions and begin "seeing" with your eyes in ways that will enhance sexual intimacy.

Look with love. How do you look at your partner's body? Do you stare and examine in the same way you scanned images of people in porn, or do you look in a sexual way that is also personal and conveys caring and respect? Unlike a porn image, a partner has a personal reaction to the way you look at her, either liking or disliking it. If your partner feels good about your gaze before, during, and after sex, she'll probably be more comfortable relating sexually with you.

It's not always easy to be consciously aware of how you are looking at a partner. In porn use, staring insensitively at someone for sexual arousal is standard practice. Porn's conditioning may run deep and be so automatic that you don't even realize the times when you are visually treating your partner like porn.

In order to begin using your eyes in ways that improve sexual intimacy, it's a good idea to find out how what you're doing now is received and perceived, and learn to pay more attention to what feelings you are communicating when you fix your eyes on your partner. Ask your partner how she feels when you look at her in different situations. Encourage your partner to speak up and request a change if she is feeling uncomfortable with how you are gazing at her. Keep in mind that—like your words and your touch—your eyes communicate different things to your partner as well.

"Looking with Love" is a simple technique that teaches you how to use your eyes to convey feelings of affection to your partner. It's a great skill to have because you can use it to shift out of ways of looking that were learned from porn and help your partner learn to feel more trusting and comfortable with your gaze. Looking with love can be interwoven with feelings of sexual desire, which can help your partner to not feel sexually objectified when you are in an amorous mood.

Looking with Love

Purpose: To practice communicating feelings of love through your eyes.

Suggested Time: Several minutes

Imagine that your eyes are windows to your heart. Look at your partner while focusing on your feelings of love and appreciation. Let those feelings move up from your heart and out through your eyes. Smile and make eye contact every now and then, letting your partner see the happiness in your eyes. Feel free to verbalize the feelings of caring and appreciation you are experiencing to your partner as you look. Repeat this exercise frequently in different circumstances and settings that you are in with your partner.

Expand what you find appealing. Partners who feel they are being seen as attractive are more open sexually. This can't happen in a relationship when a former porn user is still saddled with a narrow and limited range of what he finds sexually arousing and attractive. Many partners can sense when they are being compared to porn and, as a result, can end up having a negative emotional reaction that interferes with intimacy in the relationship. If you are a former porn user, learning to value and become more attracted to the natural and unique qualities of your partner can forge a stronger emotional bond and enhance sexual pleasure for both of you.

Since no one is 100 percent sexy—including you—you can begin to accept and appreciate your partner's sexual desirability by retraining your eyes to focus in on what appeals to you most about her presence. Consciously acknowledge to yourself the traits your partner has that you find most attractive. For instance, it might be the sparkle in her eyes, the breadth of her smile, the way her hair falls, or the curve of her neck. As you look, also be aware of other nonvisual aspects you appreciate, such as her voice, scent, movements, or the feel of her skin. By concentrating on what you're attracted to, the characteristics you have typically judged as sexual turn-offs will begin to fade into the background. You might tell your partner how much you enjoy and value her attributes.

Changing the way you look at your partner can translate to a sexual relationship that is more fun and adventurous. For example, Debbie told us: "Roger and I are a whole lot more spontaneous now. There's a lot more teasing. We do playful things now. Like, I'll just walk out naked and go, 'Have you seen my pajamas? I seem to have lost them.' He'll give me a wink and a smile and go, 'No, but I think you ought to wear that set. Those look real good.' I'm comfortable with him looking at me because I feel honored and respected by him in our everyday life."

When you and your partner feel secure that you are valued and accepted for who you are you will be more confident and expressive in your sexual interactions.

Skill #5: Increase Your Touch Vocabulary

Touch has been called the true language of sex. From the first gentle grazing of fingertips to sexual intercourse, touch is how we form an intimate bond with a partner and experience a wide variety of physical pleasures. Your ability to communicate different positive moods and messages with touch can greatly enhance your sexual experiences.

Just as it helps to improve your ability to talk about sex and the way you "see" your partner physically, it is also important to be proficient in the language of touch. The way you touch, where you touch, and when you touch communicates to your partner how you feel and what you desire.

Touch communications are not always easily understood. You may think you are saying one thing with your hands or fingers when your partner interprets it as something else. Unless you take the time to understand each other, it's easy to misunderstand what is being communicated and jump to a false conclusion about what your partner wants or is willing to do sexually. It's no wonder that many of the difficulties couples encounter with sex can be traced to problems caused by misunderstandings about touch and its intention.

The following touch exercise can help you expand your touch vocabulary and communicate more clearly with sensual and sexual touch.

What Type of Touch Is This?

Purpose: To improve your ability to communicate with touch and interpret what kind of touch you are receiving from your partner.
Materials: Two pencils and two sheets of paper
Suggested Time: 20 to 30 minutes

Sit facing your partner's back and write down in any order you choose the following four types of touch: "Playful," "Therapeutic," "Loving," and "Passionate." When you've completed your list, use one or both hands to touch your partner's back in a way that conveys the type of touch you wrote down first. For example, if you wrote "Playful" then you might skip your fingers over your partner's back in a light and tickling manner or pretend to be playing the piano or make funny drawings with your fingers. Sweep your hand across your partner's back when you are done. Ask your partner to try to silently guess what type of touch you were doing and then write it down on a piece of paper. Repeat the touch if your partner needs more time. Then communicate the next type of touch on your list. Keep going until your partner has had an opportunity to guess at and write down all four types of touch.

When you are done, sit facing each other so you can compare lists. If your partner guessed any types of touch incorrectly, ask to be shown ways you can touch differently to convey that particular kind of touch more accurately. Practice touching your partner's back using this new information. Then get feedback on whether you have successfully improved in your touch communication.

Next, switch places and let your partner touch your back to communicate the four types of touch in whatever order your partner selects. Remember, there is no right or wrong way of touching that corresponds with each type of touch. Your goal is to expand your touch vocabulary as a couple, better understand the meaning of each other's touch, and bridge any differences in your communication styles.

Variations:

1. Experiment with more types of touch such as, "Flirtatious," "Nurturing," "Sexy," and "Adventurous."
2. Touch other parts of the body, such as the head, face, hands, legs, feet, chest, abdomen, and genital area, with different types of touch.
3. Practice the exercise without clothing.

A richer touch vocabulary can come in handy any time you and your partner want to relate intimately and sensually, whether in or out of bed. And when you do make love, you can weave in types of touch that you both clearly understand and find pleasurable.

Skill #6: Explore the Realm of Sensual Pleasure

It is so important for every adult, especially those who have been involved with porn, to learn to give and receive sensual pleasure with a partner in a way that does not have genital arousal and orgasm as its immediate goal. Being sensual with a partner can heighten physical fulfillment, allow your partner to feel appreciated for being herself, and encourage both of you to be more curious and open to trying new ways of being together.

The "Sensual Pleasuring" exercise we describe in this section provides a step-by-step approach to finding and enjoying new pathways to pleasure with another person. By going slowly and not touching with the intention of initiating sexual interaction, you both have time to really tune into what you like and can learn more about each other than you've ever known.

Couples we have counseled like this exercise a lot. They get a chance to integrate intimacy skills they have already practiced, such as giving each other honest feedback and helpful direction, requesting changes in how they like to be touched, and looking at each other with love in a leisurely and relaxed manner. Because actual sexual interaction is not part of this exercise, you and your partner can follow your natural curiosities spontaneously, free from feeling you need to perform or behave a certain way. Sensual pleasuring helps you move away from rigid—and perhaps boring or porn-influenced—approaches to sex and find new ways to turn each other on.

While the skills you develop in "Sensual Pleasuring" can significantly inform and enhance your sexual activity, it is important, at least initially, to practice these skills separately from sex. You and your partner may want to start out with a clear agreement you'll both refrain from initiating sex during the exercise.

Sensual Pleasuring

Purpose: To sensitively explore each other's body, learn touch preferences, and broaden the range of pleasurable experiences.
Suggested Time: 30 minutes or longer

Wear whatever is comfortable, whether it is loose clothing, underwear, or no clothing at all. Being nude makes it easier to feel each other's touch, but if you are concerned about the possibility of unwanted sexual arousal, you may want to remain clothed. You may also want to increase comfort in other ways, such as bathing before the exercise, making sure the room is warm enough for you both, clipping your nails, applying lotion, and making sure you will not be interrupted.

Invite your partner to lie down on a comfortable surface on her back or stomach. Your goal is to lovingly touch your partner from head to toe. Begin by exploring parts of your partner's body that you do not automatically associate with sex. Exclude breasts and genitals for now. Touch in ways that feel pleasurable to you, taking time to become sensually aware of one area of your partner's body before moving on to another. Notice the different textures of your partner's body—hairy, smooth, hard, and soft. What places do you find most enjoyable to touch?

Touch your partner in ways that communicate different emotional feelings, such as playfulness, passion, and caring. Notice how your experience changes when you close your eyes compared to when you have them open. Focus on the sensations in your hands as you touch, and the stimulation coming into your other senses—what you hear, see, taste, or smell. Encourage your partner to tell you what she likes most and least. Ask for specific directions for how to make your touch more comfortable, then vary your touch pattern and pressure accordingly.

When you have finished, ask your partner to roll over so you can explore the other side of her body. When you and your partner are ready to stop, you may want to hold each other or sit and talk for a while, sharing what you both enjoyed and learned from the experience.

Switch roles so that your partner is the one exploring your body sensually. When you are being touched, find a breathing pattern that enables you to remain relaxed. You can deepen your breathing and sensual experience by consciously softening the muscles in your chest and abdomen. Stay present and aware of the different sensations you experience as different parts of your body are being touched. Put your consciousness in the part of your body that is being touched, noticing what types of touch you enjoy most. Speak up and give directions for how your partner can vary the touch to be more comfortable and enjoyable for you. Be aware of the different positive feelings that are being communicated by your partner through touch.

Receiving touch from a partner can be exhilarating because it is random and unpredictable. Enjoy the anticipation and sense of being surprised. If thoughts or fantasies of porn are triggered and intrude at any time during the exercise, let your partner know what you are experiencing. Then make any necessary adjustments to reduce the trigger potential, and resume participation in the exercise when you feel able to remain relaxed and tuned into the touching again.

Variations:

1. You and your partner may also want to explore sensually touching each other's bodies at the same time. You can start by hugging or lying next to each other. You may want to play a follow the leader kind of game in which one person touches the other's body in a certain place and way, and the other person touches back in the same place and way. Relax your breathing and pay attention to your partner's breathing as well. Gaze with affection into each other's eyes and smile. Attune your movements to those of your partner. This mutually satisfying and synchronized pleasuring is a way that you and your partner can deepen your sense of connection.

2. Include breasts and genitals in the sensual pleasuring. When you do this, make sure that you and your partner treat these more sexually associated body parts with the same goals in mind as you did the other "nonsexual" parts of the body. Again, stay relaxed, breathe slowly and deeply, and focus on the sensual pleasure of touching and being touched radiating throughout your body. When including areas of the body such as the breasts, nipples, genitals, and groin area, be aware that the skin tissues in these parts of the body are sensitive and may benefit from a more gentle touch.

Becoming sexually aroused during the exercise can happen naturally, but if that happens don't conclude that you must move into overt sexual activity. Reactions such as erections and other kinds of tissue engorgement are normal responses to intimate touch that you can learn to appreciate as part of the overall sensual experience.

Your ability to appreciate and become adept at leisurely, full-body sensual sharing takes time to develop. It can be a good idea to practice the "Sensual Pleasuring" exercise regularly for several weeks. The advanced touch and communication skills you develop through this exercise will ultimately enrich your sexual experiences. Exploring sensual touch with a partner teaches you to touch more creatively and personally. You learn to express more of yourself with your partner and enjoy the uniqueness and caring of your partner's touch.

When it fits with your recovery, these new skills can be used to awaken your sexual energy and enhance your sexual experience. You can use these sensual pleasuring techniques as part of foreplay and sex, enabling you to experience sexual activity with a present and relaxed mind. Justin has seen benefits in changing his approach to touch and sex. "When I was into porn, sex was mechanical. I never paid attention to what I was doing and how different things felt. Now I'm always exploring what sensations feel good and are pleasurable and which ones are not."

Skill #7: Involve Your Heart in Sex

Love can add a powerful dimension to sexual relating. When two people experience genuine feelings of affection for each other along with sexual desire and arousal they can reach unparalleled levels of sexual enjoyment and satisfaction. Unfortunately, old associations learned from porn can make it difficult for a former porn user to easily tune into feelings of love when his genitals are aroused. Porn use conditions a direct stimulus-response relationship between pornographic mental imagery (the stimulus) and genital sensation (the response) that leaves out the heart altogether. As one man shared, "Porn connects a penis with a peephole. Love has nothing to do with it."

Learning to connect your feelings of love and affection with the positive sensations you experience in your genitals is a two-step process. First you must establish a link between your experience of loving and your awareness of your genitals. Then you need to find a way to remind yourself of that link and feel it when you are with a partner.

The following exercise, "Hand on Heart Anchoring," can help you accomplish both of these steps. It is a relatively easy technique for forming and reinforcing a positive mental association between genuine feelings of affection (which we encourage you to imagine as residing in your heart) and the sensations in your genital area. You start by learning "Hand on Heart Anchoring" in a relaxed setting, either on your own or in the presence of a partner. Although there is some touch to the genital area, active sexual stimulation and orgasm are not involved. Later, you can use a variation of the "Hand on Heart Anchoring" technique when you are relating sexually with a partner to awaken and enhance feelings of love during sex.

Hand on Heart Anchoring

Purpose: To develop and experience a connection between loving feelings and sensation in your genital area.

Suggested Time: 5 to 10 minutes

Wear soft, loose-fitting clothing. Sit back or lie down in a private space, such as your bedroom. Place one hand over your heart. Breathe deeply, relax, and feel your hand rise and fall with each breath. Consciously soften the muscles in your chest and abdomen as you breathe fully. Smile into your heart with appreciation for its steady beat and life-giving energy. Open or close your eyes depending on what helps you feel present, relaxed, and more comfortable.

With your hand over your heart, focus on what you like and appreciate about yourself. Recall things you have done in the past that you feel good about and traits that you admire in yourself. If you are in an intimate relationship think about your partner—what you love and admire about her and your relationship.

Keeping one hand on your heart, place your other hand on or near your genital area in a position that feels comfortable to you. Continue to breathe and relax. Notice the link you are forming with your two hands between your heart and your genitals. Become aware of what it is like to touch both your heart and your genitals simultaneously, and feel sensations from both areas at the same time. Focus on the positive things your genitals have brought to your life. As you breathe, shift your consciousness back and forth between an awareness of your heart and genitals, and the energy connection your hands help them form. If your mind begins to wander gently bring it back to your relaxed breathing. Maintain this position for several minutes, or as long as it feels comfortable to you. When you feel ready to stop, remove both hands and breathe deeply for a few more minutes, reflecting on the experience.

Variations:
1. Practice the exercise without clothing.
2. If you are in a relationship and your partner is willing, practice the exercise at the same time in each other's presence. Include gazing and smiling at each other from time to time. When you both feel ready, switch the hand that was resting on your own genitals to rest gently over your partner's genital area. Continue to breathe and relax. Pat or rub with the hand that is over your heart as needed from time to time to stay connected to feelings of love toward yourself and your partner.
3. Practice this heart anchoring exercise prior to any kind of sexual experience.
4. When you are engaged in sexual activity, take a moment to touch your heart or your partner's heart to activate or stay connected to feelings of caring and love.

There are many ways of expressing loving feelings during sex. You might try using some of the following techniques that apply skills discussed earlier in this chapter, such as:

- Take time to smile and make loving eye contact with your partner.
- Temporarily shift your awareness from your genital arousal to the attributes you most admire and appreciate about your partner.
- Take time to verbally express your feelings of affection to your partner.
- Touch in loving and affectionate ways that you have learned will be valued and appreciated by your partner.

As important as it is to express your love in sex, remember that making love is a two-way exchange of positive feelings. You also need to receive the admiration, caring, and love that your partner expresses toward you. Pay attention to your partner's tender words, touch, movements, and facial expressions and imagine them traveling into your heart. Let yourself feel how satisfying it is to be with someone who loves you and truly enjoys being with you. You might even ask your partner to touch your heart at times during sex as a nonverbal way of expressing love and reminding you to receive it.

The time you spend with your partner after sex presents another valuable opportunity for intimate sharing. Once the sexual heat is off, it's a good idea to continue relating in loving ways, such as by holding each other, talking affectionately, taking turns listening to each other's heart beat, taking a shower together, or even falling asleep in each other's arms. Being actively intimate following sex through touching, talking, and spending quality time together can begin a new courtship cycle and prime the pump for the next sexual encounter.

You can also take time following sex to reflect and be grateful for the intimate encounter you experienced. By consciously thinking about the pleasure you have in intimacy with your partner, you can reprogram your erotic imagination. Memories and fantasies about real-life sex with your partner can replace porn imagery as your primary fuel for sexual desire and arousal.

Intimacy-oriented sex involves connecting to your partner with your body, your senses, your mind, and most of all, your heart. The seven skills we have described in this chapter work together to help you create a stronger, more lasting, and more fulfilling sexual relationship with a partner. This approach to sex can also result in profound healing not only for former porn users but also for their intimate partners. Karen, whose sexuality had been filled with sadness and disconnection because of her husband Johnny's porn use, felt a huge burden had been lifted when he not only stopped using porn, but changed from "making porn" to "making love." She told us, "Now that porn is out of the picture and we've been approaching sex differently, I trust Johnny and feel freer being sexual with him. I don't have to hold back as a protective measure. I'm open and expressive with him, and I naturally want to please him."

Relearning how to be a sexual being in a way that forms deep bonds with another person and is emotionally as well as physically rewarding, can provide you with deep feelings of satisfaction you may never have known before. George, whose porn habit started in his twenties, said it best: "My goal used to be hot, hot, hot sex. That basically is all that pornography is about. But I've found there is so much more in sex beyond that, such as being flirtatious, playful, loving, gentle, and caring. Here I am at fifty-six years old, and I'm having richer and more enjoyable sexual experiences than I've ever had before. I used to think that really intense sex would result in true intimacy with my partner. But I had that completely backward. Physical intensity doesn't guarantee emotional closeness. It's the other way around. The foundation for a really good sexual experience is a genuinely loving relationship."

12

True Freedom and Fulfillment

*Yes, I've been through a lot in my recovery. But I finally feel normal,
like a regular person. I feel like it's spring—it's spring and I've gone
outside and the air feels clean and good.*

—BILL

As tough as it may be to finally get there, life is good outside the
porn trap. Almost everyone we've spoken with who has severed
a relationship with pornography has been eager to share how
much better they now feel about themselves, their relationships, their
sexuality, and their future. Passion and optimism shine through their
stories of accomplishment as they told us of their newfound sense of
happiness and self-satisfaction.

Wherever you are on the spectrum of quitting porn—thinking about
quitting, taking the first steps, wrestling with relapse, or well on your way
to being porn free—we hope you find the stories of former porn users
in this chapter inspiring and helpful. You'll recognize many of the names
from other chapters—now you get to read about how these people have
moved beyond their struggle with porn and emerged into personal freedom and fulfillment.

You'll find that although everyone's path has been different, most
former porn users end up feeling more positive about life, relaxed, and
generally more emotionally balanced once they quit porn for good. They
are more comfortable being around other people now that they're able to
relate with mutual respect, concern, and consideration. This is especially
true in their intimate relationships, where reestablished communication
and trust lead to strengthening of the bonds that hold people together.

Clearly, whether physically, sexually, emotionally, or interpersonally, every part of life can improve once you've successfully climbed out of the porn trap.

Of course, in spite of the tangible, positive results gained from quitting porn, there are times former users may feel a little sad about what they've given up. That's understandable. Quitting porn involves saying good-bye to something that they relied on to feel good. But, while some of the former porn users we spoke to talked about feelings of loss, they were quick to emphasize that their lives are much better now without porn. Laura, for example, said that she missed porn's "friendship." She told us, "Before I quit, I had been involved with porn for more than thirty years. The fantasies were like a friend, offering me comfort in times of stress. But, those same porn fantasies also led me into dangerous sexual experiences that could have killed me. I don't have to worry about that now. That's a big relief!" Ethan said, "I miss porn like I miss the high of getting stoned on marijuana. But now I'm with a wonderful woman who is nurturing and honest. That's what I value. I never would have had that if I hadn't made the choice to stop using porn."

In this chapter we present stories that illustrate what you are likely to experience as a result of committing to the porn recovery process we have outlined in this book. You'll find out how, once you are out of the porn trap, you can take your life in new directions to build upon your successes and reach new heights in your recovery. This is the story of freedom and celebration. These former porn users made it. You can too.

RECOVERY GETS EASIER WITH TIME

One thing you can look forward to as you recover from porn is that the journey will eventually get easier. Bill told us that after several years of attending meetings and talking with a counselor, he is now more self-assured in his ability to stay away from pornography for good. "The first six months of my recovery were the most difficult. I had to face the fact that my thinking was all wrong. All the assumptions I made about porn—that it was no big deal, that no one was getting hurt, that it was actually just harmless fun—were wrong. Now that I know these things,

I am more relaxed in my recovery. It's not a constant struggle to keep away from porn."

Similarly, Marie, who has spent the last five years involved in recovery work, says, "I feel good about what I've accomplished so far. I've come a long ways from where I was that day the youth pastor found the porn on my computer. Group work and counseling have helped me face my issues and be able to deal with my emotions when I'm under stress. At this point in time, I'm confident in my ability to choose to remain porn free."

As time goes by, many former porn users develop an expertise in being able to keep porn out of their lives. When porn pops up unexpectedly, they stay conscious of their commitment to avoid it and take action steps to not use it. Porn no longer throws them off course, and they are able to remain true to their values and goals. Corey proudly told us he was recently able to smoothly and effectively handle a potential relapse situation. "I was on the Internet looking for a utility for an operating system I was working with, and it directed me to this Web site that ended up being an archive for some pornography newsgroups. A little thought ran through my head: *Hey, click of the mouse, it's right there*, but I didn't act on it. I just smiled and calmly clicked my way out of there. I have enough life experience now to know that regardless of porn's momentary allure, it doesn't offer satisfaction."

Recovery can also become easier with time as you gain new insights that reinforce the fact that porn is harmful to you and can no longer be considered an option. "I've recently accepted that pornography is something that is just not for me," Logan said. "Some people are casual drinkers. I don't know if a person can be a casual porn user. I do know that I cannot. Just like people say, 'Once an alcoholic, always an alcoholic,' I feel that way about being a porn addict. I am one. I can't go near porn if I want to stay healthy." When former porn users finally accept the fact that they must avoid porn for the rest of their lives, they experience a decrease in the frequency and intensity of cravings for porn. As Logan added, "I stopped compulsively thinking about using porn when I finally admitted to myself that using it again is simply out of the question."

Freedom Is About
Making Choices Every Day

As we've mentioned before, the world is filled with porn and porn-like images, and it's impossible to avoid them completely. So every former porn user will find him- or herself having to make frequent choices to reaffirm the commitment to stay away from porn. It's a lifelong process, but the feeling of accomplishment you can get from being able to keep porn out of your life can be an amazingly powerful experience. Randy feels stronger now that he's taken on the ongoing challenge of quitting porn for life. "I was duped by the porn industry and taken for a ride. Now that I know what real sexuality and real passion are I feel bad that I invested all that time and wasted so many years preoccupied with a product that did me no good and nearly got me addicted to it for life. But I've got my life back now and I'm in control. I make the choices, not porn. That makes me feel good. Porn is a powerful enemy and I'm beating it every day."

Alex also talked about making daily choices and how much pride he takes in being able to stay committed to staying away from porn. He told us, "When I was using porn I had this dirty little secret that I constantly had to keep hidden. I felt constant shame about it and held myself back from others. I was enslaved. Now every time I make a choice not to use porn, I feel a real sense of freedom and community. I get to make decisions and be open and upfront about them. Sure it can be hard having to turn down porn every time, but I love the feeling I get when I do."

The Personal Rewards Are Gratifying

Many areas of your life can improve when you make a lifelong commitment to stay away from porn. Hank told us, "For thirty years, from the time I began using porn compulsively until I hit bottom with it in my mid-forties, I was completely unsatisfied, undeveloped, and unhappy as a human being. Since I quit porn three years ago, my whole life has changed. Now I feel I'm finally an adult. My life is exciting, wonderful, and stimulating. I'm able to express my true self. This is really me."

The process of quitting porn develops and strengthens skills that can contribute to you feeling more responsible and more in charge of your life. Recovery teaches you to recognize feelings when they happen, tolerate emotional distress, and delay gratification. You come to know yourself better—know what is really important to you and why. Rather than succumbing to your impulses, you are able to cope with them through taking care of yourself in life-affirming ways. "Now I'm able to focus my time and energy and get things done that are important to me," Bill said. "I'm more alert and able to enjoy what I'm doing in the moment without being distracted by unwanted fantasies and old adolescent feelings of anger, fear, and defensiveness. Porn was a big diversion. I like being more productive."

One of the major rewards for giving up porn is improving relationships with other people. As we've discussed, porn use often results in a person becoming isolated, socially out of touch, and dishonest. By contrast, when you follow the steps in recovery you develop the ability to reach out for support, empathize with others, and be more responsive to the important people in your life, such as your intimate partner, family, friends, and coworkers. "I feel really good about who I am and how I relate with others now," George told us eagerly. "I can wholeheartedly look at a woman I know with caring and support, and appreciate her heart and her unique being. Because I'm no longer involved in pornography, I am becoming the trustworthy man I always wanted to be."

Even though it's taken him many years to make significant changes, Rob is grateful that he has stayed with his porn recovery process because it has allowed him to finally be honest with himself and with others. "My addiction to Internet porn got me arrested and cost me my marriage, kids, and job," he said. "As challenging as it's been, quitting porn has given me my life back. For the first time I'm truly connecting with other people. I'm no longer experiencing the pain of living a double life, living a lie. I'm now a more complete, whole person. Whatever I was trying to get from pornography doesn't even come close to the benefits and value of what I experience in my life today."

Developing honest relationships with other people has the additional advantage of increasing self-esteem and integrity. Mitch said, "I feel spiritually renewed. My life is no longer a contradiction. It is in line with my moral values and spiritual beliefs. I'm honest about who I really am. I tell people the truth now, whereas before I would measure the truth. My marriage is better now. Our physical relationship is rewarding and satisfying and has more depth than ever before. I'm living a principled life of integrity, and this reward for being free is much greater than the shallow world of porn."

Like many other former porn users, Nick described his sex life as much better now. "It's just me and my wife in bed now, instead of me and my wife and some pornographic fantasy figure that I was replacing her with. Our sexual relating is not a sham and there's no guilt about it. It's a long-term high that makes me feel good about myself twenty-four seven. For the first time in my life I feel complete and sexually healthy."

Hank summarized the many advantages of living porn free this way: "I'm more of a human being than I ever was when I was using pornography. I am present and much less detached from other people. I feel more a complete adult, because I am not sexually objectifying people and things anymore. I'm alive with my current partner in a way that I was never alive before when I was intimately involved with a woman. Now, free from porn, I feel like I've been given a wonderful gift, not just of my own consciousness, but of my own humanity."

UTILIZING YOUR SUCCESS TO HELP OTHERS

Becoming more aware of how significantly porn use harmed their lives—often from an early age—leads many former porn users to want to do something to help and protect others from experiencing the same problems with porn that they encountered. Once their own recovery feels secure, they often become involved in educating others about the dangers of pornography and in providing direct support to people who are in the early stages of their healing journeys.

After completing five years of his own healing work in Sex Addicts Anonymous, Victor began giving inspirational presentations to groups of men who are also in recovery. "I remember how helpful it was for me to work though the first step with my sponsor and identify very specifically how I was powerless over my addiction and how it rendered my life unmanageable. Now, it's rewarding to focus my active imagination and energy on projects that not only restore my spirit but also produce something that is worthwhile in the world and beneficial to other people's lives."

Although it's been more than seven years since Nick stopped using pornography and over six years since he had a relapse, he remains active in attending faith-based recovery group meetings through his church. He said, "I have compassion for the men in our group who are caught in the grip of porn. Now that I've become healthier, I'm able to offer them ideas and information on how to fight it. I help them by sharing my experiences—how I stand up against porn's temptations and how I'm no longer ashamed of my sexual behavior. Participating in this way gives me a feeling of being needed, useful, accepted, and complete."

Tom hasn't forgotten how alone and powerless he felt when he was trapped in a porn addiction. Now he makes a conscious effort to be alert to signs that someone else might be suffering in a similar way and reach out to him. "I'm not shy about talking with my friends about sexual issues in general," he said. "If a friend of mine is depressed or isolating, I'll ask him if he is struggling with pornography and compulsive masturbation. I go out of my way to try to break the cycle of sexual shame and addiction and give somebody the kind of help I needed when I was caught in it."

Some former porn users channel their desire to help others by getting actively involved in supporting organizations that provide services to people with sexual addictions and other pornography-related problems. They donate money or volunteer their time to help administer and run resources such as toll-free hotlines, informational Web sites, national treatment provider associations, faith-based services, and local twelve-step recovery programs (see "Organizations, Programs, and Web Sites" in the Resources section). Their behind-the-scenes contributions are building a critically important network of services for men and women seeking to overcome problems caused by pornography.

Another avenue that former porn users take to help others is through getting involved in work that helps to *prevent* pornography problems. They take seriously the old adage: "An ounce of prevention is worth a pound of cure." Corey, for instance, told us that he feels motivated to work with other people to get public service announcements in the media and on Web sites informing people about the dangers of pornography use. He explained, "Think about how helpful it would be if all porn sites, like cigarette packs and medicines, had to post warning labels about the possible negative side effects of using porn. The problem with pornography is not just an individual problem. It's a social and cultural problem. We need more awareness and open social discussion about its impact. We need to remove the shame and start talking about what's wrong with Internet pornography—how it can make a train wreck out of your life. In my whole life, I spent less than ten dollars on porn and ended up in jail. I want to spare others this kind of pain."

Ed speaks to local service groups and classrooms in his community about the hazards of becoming hooked on porn. "My involvement with porn was harmful to myself and others. I'm active in educating the public, because it helps overcome our society's denial and makes me feel good. Talking with others reminds me to continue in my commitment to abstain from porn, and it serves as a way for me to make amends to those I've hurt as a result of my porn use in the past."

Laura feels strongly motivated to break the silence that exists about the serious problems females are encountering with porn. "Now that I have found healing and help from the harm pornography has done in my life, I am reaching out and educating other women," she said. "My advice to young women who are getting involved with porn is a strong *DON'T DO IT!* Using porn is progressive. It's easy to become addicted. You can think you are only experimenting with it, and then suddenly find yourself sliding into behaviors that compromise your physical, spiritual, and emotional health."

An Interest in Protecting Children

Many former porn users are deeply concerned with wanting to protect children from getting involved with porn. They know how easy it is to be exposed to porn at an early age and develop a serious problem in the absence of appropriate information and guidance. It can be very healing to come out of the porn trap and then direct your energies to protecting children from having to experience the negative consequences of porn.

Laura is passionately concerned with keeping kids safe from porn. She told us, "It's very upsetting to think that at this very moment some innocent little boy or girl is being exposed to porn. I wish our culture would wake up to the fact that it's a contaminating influence that robs children of the opportunity to learn about sex in healthy ways and cultivate their own sexual imaginings. Unless we change something fast, today's kids won't stand a chance against it. We need to be protecting our children from porn. We need to teach them that the human body is beautiful and divine, that everybody deserves respect, and that wonderful sex is a product of deep intimacy. Kids need to know that like drugs, porn may seem exciting, but it's a dead end and doesn't lead to real sexual satisfaction."

Many former porn users are aware of how pervasive pornography is in our culture and, as a result, how vulnerable children are to getting involved with it. Jack believes it would be irresponsible for parents to ignore educating their children about the dangers of pornography. "It's tough for children today," Jack said. "They live in a society that both encourages and condemns porn use. When I have kids I plan to initiate a dialogue with them about pornography. It would be unrealistic to assume they won't be exposed to it. If my parents had at least gone over some of the problems with pornography—the way women are made to look, the misogyny, the misinformation—it would have been comforting to know that it was not real life, was not how sex works, and was not how to have an appropriate relationship with a significant other."

If you are a parent, one of the most important and empowering things you can do in conjunction with your own recovery is to protect your children from exposure to, and developing an involvement with, porn. In addition to doing what you can to limit their contact with porn, it's also wise to maintain an emotionally close and healthy relationship with your children, discuss the serious problems porn use can cause, and provide resources about healthy sexual behavior and intimate relationships. With a comprehensive approach, you can help make sure a problem with pornography doesn't get passed down from one generation to the next (see box on the following page).

How to Decrease the Likelihood Your Child Will Develop a Problem with Porn

The following list identifies things you can do to help protect your child from the negative impact of pornography. We suggest that you follow these recommendations throughout the course of your child's life, changing the sophistication of your approach and the level of detail to coincide with what is age appropriate for your child.

___ Maintain a porn-free home environment.

___ Develop an emotionally sensitive, attentive, and caring relationship with your child.

___ Have regular, supportive conversations about your child's concerns, challenges, and problems.

___ Promote healthy sexual attitudes and boundaries in the family.

___ Validate your child's curiosity and desire for information about sex.

___ Encourage your child to talk with you about sexually explicit materials he or she encounters.

___ Respond to your child's questions, concerns, and disclosures about sexual matters in a calm, productive, and non-shaming manner.

___ Educate your child about the inaccurate, misleading, and harmful messages in porn.

___ Educate your child about the reality of porn addiction and other negative repercussions of porn use.

___ Openly discuss sexual concerns that exist in our society, such as sexual abuse, sexual addiction, sexually transmitted infections, and unwanted pregnancy.

___ Help your child access community resources for sex education and counseling as needed.

If, by chance, your child is inadvertently exposed to porn or intentionally seeks it out, you can be instrumental in helping to prevent him or her from developing a problem with porn. One father told us about what he did when he discovered his teenage son up in the middle of the night looking at sexy pictures on the Internet. "I used it as a teachable moment when I could have just yelled at him and gone back to bed," he said. "I sat down and talked with my son about where porn comes from, who puts it up there, and why. I explained how porn is designed to turn people on, get people hooked, and get their money. I wanted him to understand and think critically about what he had seen so he can know the difference between fantasy and reality. At one point, I asked him how many people he knows look or act that way in real life. We discussed how being sexual with porn can be addictive, like taking drugs, and how it could end up lowering his self-esteem. I helped him to see how porn isn't going to help him tomorrow when he's talking to a girl at school. We talked about what skills he needs to actually have a relationship with a young woman—and, had a good laugh at how that's very different from moving a mouse around for a computer!"

As awkward and emotionally charged as discovering a child's porn use can be, it's important to find a way to respond with understanding and information. A parent's ability to promote healthy and responsible attitudes about sex can go a long way in helping his or her child safely navigate through today's porn-saturated world.

CELEBRATING TRUE FREEDOM
AND FULFILLMENT

Much of this book has been focused on the difficulties and pain that a life consumed with porn can create. What starts off for many as an exciting and highly sexually arousing habit can ultimately compromise everything—self-respect, sexuality, intimate relationships, family, friendships, livelihood, freedom. And the journey away from porn and out of the trap can be long and tumultuous, filled with denial, rationalizations, and relapses.

But as we've seen from the stories of former porn users who made it through the struggle, leaving porn behind leads to something far better than even the false promises of porn—Freedom. We don't mean freedom in the adolescent definition of being able to do whatever, whenever. True freedom is being able to make choices regarding your behavior that enable you to live your healthiest, happiest life. It is a freedom that only someone who has known what it is like to be completely under the control of a powerful substance like porn can fully understand.

True freedom allows you to be open and honest about the life you are living. It gives you the opportunity to live in a way that is consistent with your life goals, your mission, your values, and your dreams. It is the freedom to form meaningful relationships with others, to experience love, respect, and a sense of dignity. And it is the freedom to heal your sexuality and be needed, accepted, and affirmed as a sexual being.

Former porn user Brad understands true freedom. He told us, "Before I had no choice. I was a slave to my addiction. I was such a slave that I didn't even understand that freedom existed. Now because I'm able to say no to porn, I am free to choose the course of my life." Mitch also knows what both slavery and freedom feel like. "I feel a lot better about myself. Night and day. I'm so blessed. I'm so much better. When I was using porn I was in bondage. Now if I'm tempted by porn, I have free will to make a choice. I'm free and able to express who I am deep down in my soul."

Finding a way out of the porn trap is never easy. But we hope that by breaking the silence that has surrounded this huge problem so many men and women face today—either as porn users or their loved ones—you've begun to address vital issues and see that change is possible. We are confident that with the tools we've offered in this book, you can move forward into successfully healing your sexuality, your emotional wounds, your relationships, and your life. And that once you've traveled far enough down the road of recovery, you'll realize the rewards are immensely gratifying and truly worth the effort.

The journey out of the porn trap is one from ignorance to knowledge, from avoidance to taking action, from deception to honesty, from shame to integrity, and from self-centeredness to loving and being loved by others. As the people whose stories we've told throughout this book have shown us, if you've been harmed by porn, you can reclaim your life, heal from the wounds, and free yourself from porn's influence forever.

Resources

This section co ntains books, articles, videotapes, DVDs, audiotapes, and CDs that can help you in sexual recovery, relationship healing, and personal growth. In addition you will find a list of organizations, programs, and Web sites that are important resources for overcoming pornography-related problems.

BOOKS

SEX AND PORN ADDICTION RECOVERY

Black, Claudia. *Deceived: Facing Sexual Betrayal, Lies, and Secrets.* City Center, MN: Hazelden, 2009.

Carnes, Patrick. *Don't Call It Love: Recovery from Sexual Addiction.* New York: Bantam Books, 1992.

Carnes, Patrick. *Facing the Shadow: Starting Sexual and Relationship Recovery.* 2nd edition. Carefree, AZ: Gentle Path Press, 2005.

Carnes, Patrick. *Out of the Shadows: Understanding Sexual Addiction.* 3rd edition. Center City, MN: Hazelden, 2001.

Carnes, Patrick, et al. *In the Shadows of the Net: Breaking Free of Compulsive Online Sexual Behavior.* 2nd edition. Center City, MN: Hazelden, 2007.

Carnes, Stephanie. *Mending a Broken Heart: A Guide for Partners of Sex Addicts.* Carefree, AZ: Gentle Path Press, 2008.

Corley, M. Deborah, and Jennifer P. Schneider. *Disclosing Secrets: What, to Whom, and How Much to Reveal.* Carefree, AZ: Gentle Path Press, 2002.

Grundner, T. M. *The Skinner Box Effect: Sexual Addiction and Online Pornography.* Lincoln, NE: Writers Club Press, 2000.

Hunter, Mic. *Hope and Recovery: A Twelve-Step Guide for Healing from Compulsive Sexual Behavior.* Center City, MN: Hazelden, 1989.

Kasl, Charlotte Davis. *Women, Sex, and Addiction: A Search for Love and Power.* New York: HarperCollins, 1990.

Reid, Rory C., and Dan Gray. *Confronting Your Spouse's Pornography Problem*. Sandy, UT: Silverleaf Press, 2006.

Roberts, Ted. *Pure Desire: Helping People Break Free from Sexual Struggles*. Ventura, CA: Regal Books, 1999.

Sbraga, Tamara Penix, and William T. O'Donohue. *The Sex Addiction Workbook: Proven Strategies to Help You Regain Control of Your Life*. Oakland, CA: New Harbinger, 2003.

Schneider, Jennifer. *Back from Betrayal: Recovering from His Affairs*. 3rd edition. Tucson, AZ: Recovery Resources Press, 2005.

Schneider, Jennifer, and Burt Schneider. *Sex, Lies, and Forgiveness: Couples Speak on Healing from Sex Addiction*. 3rd edition. Tucson, AZ: Recovery Resources Press, 2004.

Weiss, Robert. *Cruise Control: Understanding Sexual Addiction in Gay Men*. Los Angeles: Alyson Books, 2005.

Weiss, Robert, and Jennifer Schneider. *Untangling the Web: Sex, Porn, and Fantasy Obsession in the Internet Age*. New York: Alyson Books, 2006.

SEXUAL EDUCATION AND ENRICHMENT

Anand, Margo. *The Art of Sexual Ecstasy: The Path of Sacred Sexuality for Western Lovers*. Los Angeles: Jeremy Tarcher, 1991.

Carnes, Patrick, with Joseph M. Moriarity. *Sexual Anorexia: Overcoming Sexual Self-Hatred*. Center City, MN: Hazelden, 1997.

Castleman, Michael. *Sexual Solutions: A Guide for Men and the Women Who Love Them*. Revised edition. New York: Simon & Schuster, 1989.

Chia, Mantak, et al. *The Multi-Orgasmic Couple: Sexual Secrets Every Couple Should Know*. San Francisco: HarperSanFrancisco, 2000.

Chia, Mantak, and Douglas Abrams Arava. *The Multi-Orgasmic Man: Sexual Secrets that Every Man Should Know*. San Francisco: HarperSanFrancisco, 1996.

Crooks, Robert, and Karla Baur. *Our Sexuality*. 10th edition. Pacific Grove, CA: Brooks/Cole, 2007.

Heiman, Julia, and Joseph LoPiccolo. *Becoming Orgasmic: A Sexual and Personal Growth Program for Women*. New York: Simon & Schuster, 1988.

Henderson, Julie. *The Lover Within: Opening to Energy in Sexual Practice*. Revised edition. Barrytown, NY: Barrytown Limited, 1999.

Kaplan, Helen Singer. *How to Overcome Premature Ejaculation*. Florence, KY: Taylor & Francis, 1989.

Kerner, Ian. *She Comes First: The Thinking Man's Guide to Pleasuring a Woman*. New York: HarperCollins, 2004.

Love, Patricia, and Jo Robinson. *Hot Monogamy: Essential Steps to More Passionate, Intimate Lovemaking*. New York: Plume, 1995.

Maltz, Wendy. *Intimate Kisses: The Poetry of Sexual Pleasure*. Novato, CA: New World Library, 2001.

Maltz, Wendy. *Passionate Hearts: The Poetry of Sexual Love*. 2nd edition. Novato, CA: New World Library, 2007.

Maltz, Wendy, and Suzie Boss. *Private Thoughts: Exploring the Power of Women's Sexual Fantasies*. Charleston, SC: BookSurge, 2008.

McCarthy, Barry, and Emily McCarthy. *Rekindling Desire: A Step by Step Program to Help Low-Sex and No-Sex Marriages*. New York: Brunner-Routledge, 2003.

McCarthy, Barry, and Emily McCarthy. *Sexual Awareness: Couple Sexuality for the*

Twenty-First Century. Revised edition. New York: Carroll & Graf, 2002.

Metz, Michael E., and Barry W. McCarthy. *Coping With Premature Ejaculation: Overcome PE, Please Your Partner & Have Great Sex*. Oakland, CA: New Harbinger, 2003.

Moore, Thomas. *The Soul of Sex: Cultivating Life as an Act of Love*. New York: HarperCollins, 1998.

Ogden, Gina. *The Heart & Soul of Sex: Making the ISIS Connection*. Boston: Trumpeter, 2006.

Ogden, Gina. *The Return of Desire: A Guide to Rediscovering Your Sexual Passion*. Boston: Shambhala, 2008.

Zilbergeld, Bernie. *The New Male Sexuality*. Revised edition. New York: Bantam Books, 1999.

INTIMACY AND COUPLES COMMUNICATION

Chapman, Gary. *The Five Love Languages: How to Express Heart-Felt Commitment to Your Mate (Men's Edition)*. Chicago: Northfield, 2004.

Doherty, William. *Take Back Your Marriage: Sticking Together in a World That Pulls Us Apart*. New York: Guilford Press, 2003.

Gorski, Terence T. *Getting Love Right: Learning the Choices of Healthy Intimacy*. New York: Fireside, 1993.

Gottman, John. M., and Nan Silver. *The Seven Principles for Making Marriage Work: A Practical Guide from the Country's Foremost Relationship Expert*. New York: Three Rivers Press, 2000.

Grayson, Henry. *Mindful Loving: 10 Practices for Creating Deeper Connections*. New York: Gotham Books, 2003.

Hendrix, Harville. *Getting the Love You Want: A Guide for Couples*. New York: Owl Books, 2001.

Markman, Howard, et al. Revised edition. *Fighting for Your Marriage: Positive Steps for Preventing Divorce and Preserving a Lasting Love*. San Francisco: Jossey-Bass, 2001.

Real, Terrence. *How Can I Get Through to You? Closing the Intimacy Gap Between Men and Women*. New York: Simon & Schuster, 2002.

Lerner, Harriet. *The Dance of Intimacy: A Woman's Guide to Courageous Acts of Change in Key Relationships*. New York: HarperCollins, 1990.

Schnarch, David. *Passionate Marriage: Keeping Love and Intimacy Alive in Committed Relationships*. New York: Owl Books, 1998.

SEXUAL ABUSE RECOVERY

Bass, Ellen, and Laura Davis. *Beginning to Heal: A First Book for Men and Women Who Were Sexually Abused as Children*. Revised edition. New York: Collins, 2003.

Bass, Ellen, and Laura Davis. *The Courage to Heal: A Guide for Women Survivors of Child Sexual Abuse*. 20th anniversary edition. New York: HarperCollins, 2008.

Davis, Laura. *Allies in Healing: When the Person You Love Was Sexually Abused as a Child*. New York: HarperCollins, 1991.

Dolan, Yvonne. *One Small Step: Moving Beyond Trauma and Therapy to a Life of Joy*. Lincoln, NE: Authors Choice Press, 2000.

Lew, Mike. *Victims No Longer: The Classic Guide for Men Recovering from Sexual Child Abuse*. 2nd edition. New York: HarperCollins, 2004.

Maltz, Wendy. *The Sexual Healing Journey: A Guide for Survivors of Sexual Abuse.* Revised edition. New York: HarperCollins, 2001.

GENERAL INTEREST

Beattie, Melody. *Codependent No More: How to Stop Controlling Others and Start Caring for Yourself.* 20th anniversary edition. Center City, MN: Hazelden, 2006.

Bradshaw, John. *Healing the Shame That Binds You.* Revised edition. Deerfield Beach, FL: Health Communications, 2005.

Brooks, Gary R. *The Centerfold Syndrome: How Men Can Overcome Objectification and Achieve Intimacy with Women.* San Francisco: Jossey-Bass, 1995.

Burns, David D. *The Feeling Good Handbook.* Revised edition. New York: Plume, 1999.

Carnes, Patrick. *The Betrayal Bond: Breaking Free of Exploitive Relationships.* Deerfield Beach, FL: Health Communications, 1997.

Davis, Martha, et al. *The Relaxation and Stress Reduction Workbook.* 5th edition. Oakland, CA: New Harbinger, 2000.

Fisher, Helen. *Why We Love: The Nature and Chemistry of Romantic Love.* New York: Owl Books, 2004.

Forward, Susan, and Donna Frazier. *When Your Lover Is a Liar: Healing the Wounds of Deception and Betrayal.* New York: HarperPerennial, 2000.

Jeffers, Susan. *Feel the Fear ... and Do It Anyway: Dynamic Techniques for Turning Fear, Indecision, and Anger into Power, Action, and Love.* 20th anniversary edition. New York: Ballantine Books, 2007.

Lerner, Harriet. *The Dance of Anger: A Woman's Guide to Changing the Patterns of Intimate Relationships.* 20th anniversary edition. New York: HarperCollins, 2005.

McKay, Matthew, and Patrick Fanning. *Self-Esteem: A Proven Program of Cognitive Techniques for Assessing, Improving and Maintaining Your Self-Esteem.* 3rd edition. Oakland, CA: New Harbinger, 2000.

Norwood, Robin. *Women Who Love Too Much: When You Keep Wishing and Hoping He'll Change.* New York: Pocket Books, 1990.

Paul, Pamela. *Pornified: How Pornography Is Transforming Our Lives, Our Relationships, and Our Families.* New York: Times Books, 2005.

Peck, M. Scott. *The Road Less Traveled, 25th Anniversary Edition: A New Psychology of Love, Traditional Values, and Spiritual Growth.* New York: Touchstone, 2003.

Potter-Efron, Ronald, and Patricia Potter-Efron. *Letting Go of Shame: Understanding How Shame Affects Your Life.* Center City, MN: Hazelden, 1989.

Real, Terrence. *I Don't Want to Talk About It: Overcoming the Secret Legacy of Male Depression.* New York: Fireside, 1998.

Schaeffer, Brenda. *Is It Love or Is It Addiction?* 2nd edition. Center City, MN: Hazelden, 1997.

Schiraldi, Glenn R., and Melissa Hallmark Kerr. *The Anger Management Sourcebook.* New York: McGraw Hill, 2002.

Spring, Janis Abraham. *After the Affair: Healing the Pain and Rebuilding Trust When a Partner Has Been Unfaithful.* New York: HarperPerennial, 1997.

PROFESSIONAL BOOKS AND ARTICLES

Bergner, Raymond M., and Ana J. Bridges. "The Significance of Heavy Pornography Involvement for Romantic Partners: Research and Clinical Implications." *Journal of Sex & Marital Therapy* 28 (2002): 193–206.

Bridges, Ana J., et al. "Romantic Partners' Use of Pornography: Its Significance for Women." *Journal of Sex & Marital Therapy* 29 (2003): 1–14.

Brosius, Hans-Bernd, et al. "Exploring the Social and Sexual 'Reality' of Contemporary Pornography." *The Journal of Sex Research* 30, no. 2 (May 1993): 161–170.

Carnes, Patrick, and Kenneth M. Adams, editors. *Clinical Management of Sex Addiction.* New York: Routledge, 2002.

Cooper, Al, and David Marcus. "Men Who Are Not in Control of Their Sexual Behavior." In Stephen B. Levine, editor, *Handbook of Clinical Sexuality for Mental Health Professionals.* New York: Routledge, 2003.

Cooper, Al, et al. "Online Sexual Compulsivity: Getting Tangled in the Net." *Sexual Addiction & Compulsivity* 6, no. 2 (1999): 79–104.

Cooper, Al, editor. *Sex and the Internet: A Guidebook for Clinicians.* New York: Routledge, 2002.

Corley, M. Deborah, and Jennifer P. Schneider. "Disclosing Secrets: Guidelines for Therapists Working with Sex Addicts and Co-addicts." *Sexual Addiction & Compulsivity* 9, no. 1 (2002): 43–67.

Doidge, Norman. *The Brain that Changes Itself: Stories of Personal Triumph from the Frontiers of Brain Science.* New York: Penguin, 2007.

Earle, Ralph, and Marcus Earle. *Sex Addiction: Case Studies and Management.* New York: Brunner/Mazel, 1995.

Ferree, Marnie C. "Sexual Addiction and Co-Addiction: Experiences Among Women of Faith." *Sexual Addiction & Compulsivity* 9, no. 4 (2002): 285–292.

Fisher, Helen. *Anatomy of Love: A Natural History of Mating, Marriage, and Why We Stray.* New York: Ballantine Books, 1994.

Goodman, Aviel. *Sexual Addiction: An Integrated Approach.* Madison, CT: International Universities Press, 1998.

Hamann, Stephan, et al. "Men and Women Differ in Amygdala Response to Visual Sexual Stimuli." *Nature Neuroscience* 7 no. 4 (April 2004): 411–416.

Heider, Don, and Dustin Harp. "New Hope or Old Power: Democracy, Pornography and the Internet." *The Howard Journal of Communications* 13 (2002): 285–299.

Jensen, Robert. "A Cruel Edge: The Painful Truth About Today's Pornography—And What Men Can Do About It." *Ms.* (Spring 2004): 54–58.

Jensen, Robert. *Getting Off: Pornography and the End of Masculinity.* Cambridge, MA: South End Press, 2007.

Kimmel, Michael S., editor. *Men Confront Pornography.* New York: Meridan, 1991.

Kort, Joe. "The Men in the Mirror: Understanding Gay Men and Their Porn." *In The Family* 8, no. 1 (Summer 2002): 8–12. Also available at Web site: www.joekort.com/news5.htm.

Maltz, Wendy. "The Maltz Hierarchy of Sexual Interaction." *Sexual Addiction & Compulsivity* 2, no. 1 (1995): 5–18. Also available at Web site: www.HealthySex.com.

Manning, Jill C. "The Impact of Internet Pornography on Marriage and the Family: A Review of the Research." *Sexual Addiction & Compulsivity* 13, no. 2 (2006): 131–165.

Mitchell, Kimberly J., et al. "The Exposure of Youth to Unwanted Sexual Material on the Internet: A National Survey of Risk, Impact, and Prevention." *Youth & Society* 34, no. 3 (March 2003): 330–358.

Morris, Desmond. *Intimate Behaviour: A Zoologist's Classic Study of Human Intimacy.* New York: Kodansha Globe, 1997.

Schneider, Jennifer P. "The Impact of Compulsive Cybersex Behaviours on the Family." *Sexual and Relationship Therapy* 18, no. 3 (August 2003): 330–354.

Slade, Joseph W. *Pornography and Sexual Representation: A Reference Guide (Volume I and Volume III).* Westport, CT: Greenwood Press, 2001.

Steffens, Barbara A., and Robyn L. Rennie. "The Traumatic Nature of Disclosure for Wives of Sexual Addicts." *Sexual Addiction & Compulsivity* 13 no. 2/3 (2006): 247–267.

Yoder, Vincent Cyrus, et al. "Internet Pornography and Loneliness: An Association?" *Sexual Addiction & Compulsivity* 12, no. 1 (2005): 19–44.

Zillmann, Dolf, and Jennings Bryant, editors. *Pornography: Research Advances and Policy Considerations.* Hillsdale, NJ: Lawrence Erlbaum Associates, 1989.

Zitzman, Spencer T. and Mark H. Butler. "Attachment, Addiction, and Recovery: Conjoint Marital Therapy for Recovery from a Sexual Addiction." *Sexual Addiction & Compulsivity* 12, no. 4 (2005): 311–337.

VIDEOTAPES, DVDs, AUDIOTAPES, AND CDs

Relearning Touch: Healing Techniques for Couples. Produced by Wendy Maltz, Steve Christiansen and Gerald Joffee. A forty-five minute videotape (also available in DVD) moderated by Wendy Maltz, sensitively demonstrates the relearning touch techniques originally developed for survivors of sexual abuse. Includes interviews with three couples that have used the techniques to improve communication, deepen emotional intimacy, and create positive sexual experiences. Distributed by InterVision Media, 261 E. 12th Avenue, Suite 100, Eugene, OR 97401, (541) 343-7993, www.intervisionmedia.com.

Contrary to Love: Helping the Sexual Addict. A twelve-part PBS video series in which noted addiction psychologist Dr. Patrick Carnes discusses the spectrum of compulsive/addictive behavior and recovery treatment. Available as a complete set or individually, in videotape or DVD. Distributed by Gentle Path Press, P.O. Box 3172, Carefree, AZ 85377, (800) 708-1796, www.gentlepath.com.

Relaxation/Affirmation Techniques and *Relax-Quick.* Produced by Nancy Hopps. These two helpful audiotapes (also available in CD) offer a variety of straight forward ways to facilitate relaxation and strengthen body/mind connection. Synergistic Systems, P.O. Box 5224, Eugene, OR 97405, (541) 683-9088, www. relaxintohealing.com.

Letting Go of Stress: Four Effective Techniques for Relaxation and Stress Reduction. Produced by Emmett E. Miller, M.D., and Steven Halpern, Ph.D. A popular classic. Available on audiotape and CD. Fulfillment Center, P.O. Box 6028, Auburn, CA 95604, (800) 52-TAPES, www.drmiller.com/products.

Enhancing Intimacy. Produced by Steven Halpern. Music, with subliminal messages, to help you become more open to touch and sensual pleasures. Available in audiotape and CD. Steven Halpern's Inner Peace Music, P.O. Box 2644, San Anselmo, CA 94979, (800) 909-0707, www.innerpeacemusic.com.

ORGANIZATIONS, PROGRAMS, AND WEB SITES

Many of the organizations listed here provide referral services for obtaining profes-sional and other supportive help in recovery. In considering a therapist, support group, or treatment program, you may want to consult physicians and mental health referral agencies for more information about the services in your area. Interview therapists and learn details about their program philosophy, expectations, and opera-tions before making your choice.

Inclusion in this list does not indicate a recommendation or endorsement by the authors. Use your own judgment when contacting any of these organizations or Web sites.

Advocates for Youth
www.advocatesforyouth.org. (202) 419-3420

Provides extensive information for young people to make informed and respon-sible decisions about their sexual health, as well as numerous articles on and guide-lines for parents to talk to their children about sexuality.

American Association for Marriage and Family Therapy (AAMFT)
www.aamft.org. (703) 838-9808

A good source of referrals for licensed marriage and family counselors in your community, and consumer information on important issues affecting marriages and families.

American Association of Sex Educators, Counselors, and Therapists (AASECT)
www.aasect.org. (804) 752-0026

A national organization that helps locate qualified sex therapists and counselors in your region, as well as providing links to resources on human sexuality and sexual health.

American Polygraph Association
www.polygraph.org/associations.cfm. (800) APA-8037

Provides referral links for polygraph examiners available in your community, as well as facts and data about polygraph testing.

Codependents of Sex Addicts (COSA)
www.cosa-recovery.org. (763) 537-6904

A twelve-step recovery program for men and women whose lives have been af-fected by another person's compulsive sexual behavior. Gives information on meet-ings and resources.

Dr. Carnes' Resources for Sex Addiction & Recovery
www.sexhelp.com.

This Web site contains information about sexual addiction, offers a Sexual Ad-diction Screening Test to help assess whether a person has a sexual addiction prob-lem, and has links to sexual addiction recovery resources.

Enough Is Enough

www.protectkids.com. (888) 744-0004

An organization dedicated to making the Internet safer for children and families by providing information on how to protect children and teens from exposure to Internet pornography.

GetNetWise

www.getnetwise.org.

A coalition of Internet industry corporations and public interest organizations that provides information on keeping children safe online, and how to block unwanted pornographic e-mail.

HealthySex.com

www.HealthySex.com.

Developed by Wendy Maltz, this site provides information on healthy sexuality. It includes articles, checklists, comparison charts, and resources to help individuals and couples understand and develop skills for healthy sexual intimacy. In addition, the site offers information on Wendy Maltz's books, videos, free posters, DVDs, workshops, and speaking presentations.

InternetFilterReview

www.internet-filter-review.toptenreviews.com.

This Web site helps evaluate Internet filter software programs available to purchase for your home or business computer. Also has information on Internet safety tips for children and extensive Internet pornography statistics.

MaleSurvivor

www.malesurvivor.org.

Information, resources, and support for men who were sexually victimized as children, adolescents, or adults.

Mental Help Net

www.mentalhelp.net.

A helpful, online mental health resource guide and directory. Includes articles, information, and links for a wide range of mental health issues and sexuality concerns.

National Coalition for the Protection of Children and Families

www.nationalcoalition.org. (800) 583-2964 (HelpLine)

This Christian organization provides assistance through their HelpLine to those harmed by pornography. They offer consultation to professionals and pastors regarding sexual compulsivity, as well as links to sites to help select Internet blocking or monitoring systems.

PornAddictHubby.com

www.pornaddicthubby.com.

Provides self-care and relationship advice for wives and girlfriends of Internet porn addicts.

Rape, Abuse & Incest National Network (RAINN)
www.rainn.org. (800) 656-HOPE (Hotline)

The nation's largest anti-sexual assault organization. Provides a twenty-four-hour National Sexual Assault Hotline, and carries out programs to prevent sexual abuse.

Recovering Couples Anonymous (RCA)
www.recovering-couples.org. (510) 663-2312

A twelve-step program where couples find support to recover from the impact of addiction—primarily sexual addiction—on their marriage. The site provides referral information on RCA meetings in your community, telephone meetings, and e-meetings, daily reflections for couples and other resources about twelve-step recovery for couples.

S-Anon
www.sanon.org. (800) 210-8141

A twelve-step fellowship for the relatives and friends of sexually addicted people who share their experiences in order to solve their common problems. Provides referrals to an established S-Anon group in your community.

SafeKids.com
www.safekids.com.

Offers tips and guidelines for parents to help their children be safe and responsible in their Internet use.

Sex Addicts Anonymous (SAA)
www.sexaa.org. (800) 477-8191

This group helps men and women overcome sexual addiction through a twelve-step fellowship. They provide extensive referral information for finding an SAA meeting in your area. Also provides SAA meetings via Internet chat and telephone conference calls.

Sex and Love Addicts Anonymous (S.L.A.A.)
www.slaafws.org. (210) 828-7900

A twelve-step program that helps participants to counter the destructive consequences of sex and love addiction. Also provides referrals to local meetings, as well as online meetings and regional teleconference calls.

Sexaholics Anonymous (SA)
www.sa.org. (866) 424-8777

This group helps men and women stay sexually sober through a twelve-step program. They also provide information on SA groups that are meeting in your community.

Sexual Compulsives Anonymous (SCA)
www.sca-recovery.org. (800) 977-HEAL

A twelve-step program whose members strive to obtain sobriety from sexual addiction and recover from sexual compulsion. Membership consists primarily, but not exclusively, of gay and bisexual men and women. Provides referral information to meetings in various communities and offers an online meeting.

Sexual Health Network

www.sexualhealth.com.

This site provides a wealth of information on sexual health topics and resources for men, women, and couples. Offers questions and answers on sexuality issues from their own network of experts.

Sexuality Information and Education Council of the United States (SIECUS)

www.siecus.com. (212) 819-9770

Extensive information on sexuality education, sexual health, and sexual rights. Provides numerous links to sexual health programs and organizations.

Smart Recovery

www.smartrecovery.org. (866) 951-5357

An alternative to twelve-step programs, provides referral to free face-to-face meetings around the world, as well as online mutual help groups for people recovering from all types of addictive behaviors, including sexual addiction.

Society for the Advancement of Sexual Health (SASH)

www.sash.net. (770) 541-9912

Provides a professional membership directory to find a therapist in your area who can help individuals and their families with pornography and sexual addiction problems. Also includes articles on sexual health and sexual addiction recovery.

Web Wise Kids

www.webwisekids.org. (866) WEB-WISE

Provides parents with tips for protecting their children from the dangers of the Internet, and guides teens in developing an Internet safety plan.

RESIDENTIAL AND OUTPATIENT TREATMENT CENTERS

Inpatient residential and intensive outpatient treatment programs that help people with serious pornography problems are located throughout the United States. The focus of these programs varies, but may include treatment for sexual addiction, sexual compulsivity, drug and alcohol problems, and past childhood trauma. Programs differ in approach, length of stay, and cost. Contact your local physician, counselor, clergy, or mental health center for information on existing programs in your area. The following are several nationally recognized centers.

Bethesda Workshops

Nashville, TN (866) 464-4325; www.BethesdaWorkshops.org.

A nondenominational Christian organization that provides residential workshops to help heal the spiritual, emotional, and relationship problems caused by pornography and other forms of sexual addiction. Separate workshops for women, men, spouses, and couples.

Center for Healthy Sexuality
Houston, TX (713) 785-7111; www.centerforhealthysexuality.com.
This outpatient treatment center offers ongoing individual and couples counseling as well as three- to four-day intensives for treating sexual addiction and relationship problems. Services also include comprehensive psychosexual assessments and evaluations.

Del Amo Hospital
Torrance, CA (800) 533-5266; www.delamotreatment.com.
Provides diagnosis and treatment for a wide range of behavioral health problems, including treatment for sexual addiction. Offers intensive, short-term, and partial hospitalization programs.

Faithful and True Ministries
Eden Prairie, MN (952) 746-3885; www.faithfulandtrueministries.com.
A Christian recovery ministry providing services for sexual addiction recovery, including men's counseling groups, men's recovery workshops, and couples intensives.

Keystone Center Extended Care Unit
Chester, PA (800) 733-6840; www.keystonecenterecu.net.
An inpatient program that offers a multidisciplinary approach to the treatment of sexual compulsivity and addiction. Treatment components address the cognitive, behavioral, spiritual, emotional, and psychological aspects of recovery.

Life Healing Center
Santa Fe, NM (866) 806-7214; www.life-healing.com.
A residential treatment program for post-traumatic stress, mood disorders, and addictions, including sexual addiction. Emphasizes that healing the wounds of trauma is a vital part of sexual recovery.

The Meadows
Wickenburg, AZ (800) MEADOWS; www.themeadows.org.
An inpatient facility specializing in the treatment of a broad range of addictions, including sexual addiction. Offers extended care for sexual recovery, addressing the deeper issues involved in addiction, including the impact of childhood and adult trauma.

Pine Grove Gentle Path Program
Hattiesburg, MS (888) 574-4673; www.pinegrovetreatment.com.
A comprehensive diagnostic assessment and residential treatment program for those suffering from sexual addiction, relationship addiction, sexual anorexia, and/or sexual trauma. Simultaneous treatment is available for mood disturbance, anxiety, or other addictions, such as chemical dependency.

Pride Institute
Eden Prairie, MN (800) 54-PRIDE; www.pride-institute.com
In-patient and out-patient mental health, sex addiction, and chemical dependency programs devoted exclusively to treating the needs of the gay, lesbian, bisexual, and transgender community. Offers services in several national locations.

Psychological Counseling Services (PCS)
Scottsdale, AZ (480) 947-5739; www.pcsearle.com.

Provides individualized outpatient therapy for individuals and couples wanting help to overcome sexual addictions, compulsions, unresolved past trauma, and intimacy problems. One- to five-week sexual addiction recovery intensive outpatient programs are available.

Sante Center for Healing
Argyle, TX (800) 258-4250; www.santecenter.com.

A residential treatment center that addresses addictive behaviors and associated conditions with an integrated treatment model, drawing from both traditional and innovative approaches.

Sexual Recovery Institute
Los Angeles, CA (310) 360-0130; www.sexualrecovery.com.

Offers a two-week intensive outpatient program to address recovery from sexual acting out behaviors. Provides a thorough process of evaluation and treatment, including intensive psycho-education and psychotherapy.

Sierra Tucson
Tucson, AZ (800) 842-4487; www.sierratucson.com.

A residential program for the treatment of addictions and behavioral disorders. Provides a sexual compulsive treatment program that includes individual and group therapy for individuals with issues of sexual addiction/compulsivity, co-sexual addiction, and sex and love addiction.

NOTES

Academic and statistical sources for *The Porn Trap* are available on-line at www. healthysex.com/books.php#porntrap.

Index

About the Authors

©Coleen Cahill

©Walter Grondona

Wendy Maltz, LCSW, DST, is an internationally recognized author, psychotherapist, and certified diplomate sex therapist. Her books include *The Sexual Healing Journey: A Guide for Survivors of Sexual Abuse, Private Thoughts: Exploring the Power of Women's Sexual Fantasies,* and two award-winning poetry anthologies on healthy sexual intimacy, *Intimate Kisses: The Poetry of Sexual Pleasure* and *Passionate Hearts: The Poetry of Sexual Love.* Wendy is the writer, narrator, and co-producer of *Relearning Touch: Healing Techniques for Couples,* a video on overcoming the intimate repercussions of sexual abuse. She is an experienced media guest, workshop presenter, and lecturer. Her Web site is www.HealthySex.com.

Larry Maltz, LCSW, is the executive director of Maltz Counseling Associates in Eugene, Oregon. A seasoned therapist and clinical supervisor, he has more than twenty-five years' experience providing individual, couples, and family counseling services. Larry specializes in recovery from pornography and other sexual addictions, marriage enrichment, couples communication, anger management, and men's issues, as well as in treating a wide variety of sexual intimacy and relationship concerns. He is a member of the Oregon Mental Health Associates and the Society for the Advancement of Sexual Health.

The Maltzes are married and live in Eugene, Oregon.